W9-AZA-500

PRAISE FOR *LIVING BRANDS*

"*Living Brands* signals the beginning of consumer empowerment, as Raymond Nadeau shows the way to a much-needed renaissance in advertising creativity (and perhaps a new golden age of marketing)."

—*George Lois,* legendary advertising pioneer

"*Living Brands* delivers a prescription for what is required to be successful in today's marketplace. It does so with grace, courage, and even humor. It's a wake-up call you won't want to miss."

—*Ivy Ross,* Executive Vice President of Design and Development for Old Navy, Gap Inc.

"Sweetface's success and the phenomenon of Tommy Hilfiger were built on a foundation of cultural collaboration. *Living Brands* just let the secret out of the bag."

—*Andy Hilfiger,* SVP of Music and Entertainment, Tommy Hilfiger Corporation, and founder of Music Entertainment Fashion, Inc.

"Discovery marketing has been the cornerstone of success for Ketel One. This book captures key insights that are valuable for any brand leader."

—*William L. Eldien,* President, Nolet Spirits U.S.A.

"Playboy's cultural connection with our consumer has continued to furnish the substance of a perennially vibrant, vital, living brand. The dreams may change—but the ability of Playboy to address those dreams, even if through other categories, remains constant."

—*Alex Vaickus,* Playboy Enterprises

"Chupa Chups was built on cultural collaboration, the concept behind Living Brands. Salvador Dali designed our logo and consumers designed our brand. *Living Brands* shares the surprisingly simple secrets of our success."

—*Marta Bernat,* board member, Chupa Chups

"*Living Brands* is a beautiful book about marketing. What next, a beautiful world?"

—*Tony Whitfield,* Chair, Product Design and Development, Parsons The New School For Design

"I have known and worked with Raymond for many years. He believes what's in this book. And he has proven over and over again that it works."

—*Jim Morrison,* former General Manager of Turner Media's Fashion & Beauty Network and CEO of Big Sexy Hair

"Much in line with Benedictine tradition, *Living Brands* demonstrates a renewed appreciation of brands as they relate to humanity, respecting both body and soul. The human person is seen as whole and shines with a new beauty. A vision from the past lays out a new vision for the future of both commerce and, more importantly, mankind."

—Abbot Primate, *Doctor Notker Wolf*, Highest Representative of the Benedictine Order

"*Living Brands* is about telling the truth. Try that on for size."

—*Nikki Sixx,* artist, rock legend, entrepreneur

"From fashion to celebrities to anthropology, technology, and economics—this book shares tomorrow's marketing insights today. It takes us all to an exciting, colorful place where brands and advertising bring us closer to our dreams."

—*Denise Sakuma Wertz,* Brand Director and Director of Global Licensing of Invista Apparel

"A fashionable marketing and advertising guide that crosses all categories. Raymond has never been a typical fashionista—he and this book use fashion merely as windows on the world, which is, after all, what fashion and great marketing are all about. *Living Brands* defines Democratic Style. It's the only book of its kind."

—*Massimo Redaelli,* Senior Vice President, IMG Fashion

"Nadeau's suggestion that brands are living, breathing (and ofttimes fragile) entities is spot on. This book forces us to see beyond convention and look twenty-first-century branding squarely in the eye."

—*Matt Eastwood,* former Chief Creative Officer, Y&R, current National Creative Director and Vice Chairman of DDB Australia

"There are those in all fields of marketing who struggle their entire careers, desperately attempting to reconcile what they do with what they believe. For those persons, *Living Brands* provides a road map to both professional success and personal redemption."

—*Dr. Peter Harf,* Chief Executive Officer of Joh. A. Benckiser GmbH, Deputy Chairman of the Board Rickett Benckiser plc., and Chairman of the Board Coty Inc

"*Living Brands,* a marketing and advertising guide written as romance novel. I love it."

—*Fabio,* living brand and entrepreneur

"*Living Brands* coupled with Living Media define marketing's new gold standard. We all knew it was coming. With the printing of this book, we now all know it's here."

—*Irene Gazis,* Client Communications Director, OMD

LIVING BRANDS

LIVING BRANDS

collaboration + innovation = customer fascination

Raymond A. Nadeau

McGraw-Hill

New York Chicago San Francisco Lisbon London Madrid
Mexico City Milan New Delhi San Juan Seoul Singapore
Sydney Toronto

The McGraw·Hill Companies

1 2 3 4 5 6 7 8 9 0 DOC/DOC 0 9 8 7 6

ISBN 13: 978-0-07-146614-1
ISBN 10: 0-07-146614-2

McGraw-Hill books are available at special quantity discounts to use as premiums and sales promotions, or for use in corporate training programs. For more information, please write to the Director of Special Sales, Professional Publishing, McGraw-Hill, Two Penn Plaza, New York, NY 10121-2298. Or contact your local bookstore.

Interior design by Charles Yuen.

Library of Congress Cataloging-in-Publication Data

Nadeau, Raymond.
Living brands / by Raymond Nadeau.
p. cm.
Includes index.
ISBN 0-07-146614-2 (alk. paper)
1. Brand name products. 2. Advertising—Brand name products. I. Title.
HD69.B7N33 2007
658.8'27—dc22

This book is dedicated to Danielle and her marvelous eyes.
Because of her I will always find courage.
Because of her
I will always see beauty.
I will always
see
love.

CONTENTS

FOREWORD

Just as business-to-business cobranding and licensing have accelerated in business, I can see how technology and the advent of the marketing-savvy consumer might create a new form of consumer cobranding. This cobranding even might go so far as to become the norm of future brand cocreation—a direct collaboration between consumers and every sort of business—exactly the sort of relationship Raymond projects in this book. For future and even existing brands, success will become increasingly dependent on the pinpoint accuracy with which we are able to decipher both real desire and real dreams rather than continually searching out new methods of creating artificial need. I agree with Raymond: The world already has too much need—why invent new need? Real money is made by satisfying a need better (with *better* being loosely defined) than your competition, not by creating more of it. I can only hope that if this sort of business evolution really occurs, the results will create increased satisfaction for consumers and business leaders (who are also consumers) and will bridge the credibility gap between the legitimate need for businesses to make money and our important obligation to create products and brand stories resulting from shifts in contemporary culture—brands created in a climate of mutual respect. Brands are good. Profit is good. Profitable brands that satisfy real needs and improve the human condition are absolutely best of all.

Living Brands brings together all that is good, enriching, and in the long run, most profitable in the process of brand creation within the context of a rapidly changing world. As Raymond puts it, it is essential that a workable marketing and advertising model exist to support the notion that even in this, the most complicated time in the history of brands, it is imperative that all of us do good in order to do well. Is it possible to do both good and well? As this book lays out, this is not a question anymore. It's a question of survival.

—Dr. Peter Harf
CEO—Joh. A. Benckiser GmbH
Deputy Chairman of the Board—Reckitt Benckiser plc.
Chairman—Coty Inc

SURVIVING CHANGE

The following original essay was provided courtesy of Creed O'Hanlon, one of the world's great brand provocateurs and highly acclaimed writer, artist, photographer, and outspoken activist in the area of mental health, as well as the future of brands. We begin our journey with one man's view of where brands and marketing are heading. From there, together we will refer to his roadmap as we evaluate the course and potential scenarios that lie ahead.

PUTTING A LITTLE AFRICA BACK INTO MARKETING: AN ESSAY BY CREED O'HANLON

Several years ago, I came across a wonderfully contentious quote in an interview with the ambient musician Brian Eno in *Wired* magazine: "The problem with computers," he said, "is that there is not enough Africa in them. . . . "

While the comment can be interpreted in a number of ways, one of them as a kind of inverted racism, I think what Eno was trying to get across was the idea of Africa as a metaphor for the fuzzy logic and intuitive rhythmic physicality that is entirely absent from a Western engagement with technology.

You could apply the same comment to marketing and communications today. They have become so hidebound by conventions and protocols, so inflexible, unimaginative, and lacking in real human engagement, that Eno's idea of putting "a little Africa" into our current ideas about them may be the only way to liberate our creative thinking—and rescue their diminishing effectiveness.

Which is to say, much of so-called smart thinking about marketing today is undone by a pervasive disregard for people's individual capacity for unpredictability. The fatal flaw of many "designed" environments, both physical and virtual—and for me, an "environment" can be anything from a Web page, TV ad, or a computer game to a living space, a shopping mall, or a household appliance—is that consideration for aesthetics and technology comes first, the expressive, improvisational nature of human functionality second. They lack not just basic utility but *soul.*

To put it yet another way, marketers and product managers too often think of their markets as somehow orderly, navigable, the result of a coherent architecture, rather like the cities of Brasilia in central Brazil and Canberra in southeastern Australia (both of which were purpose-built as their nations' capitals but suffer from a sterility that compels a degree of both individual isolation and collective dysfunction). In fact, most markets are like Lagos in Nigeria. If you have seen any recent photos of this city, you'll understand immediately what I mean: Freeways and main roads unfinished and blocked by cars for which they have become temporary parking lots, shanty towns, or makeshift bazaars; repurposed for social and commercial interaction, they're no longer useful as arteries for any kind of mechanized traffic, but they work in other ways.

Interestingly, in 1999 and 2000, the Dutch architect Rem Koolhaas and Harvard Design School's Project on the City studied Lagos, Nigeria, and the total breakdown of basic infrastructure and civil order there that defies all conventional wisdom on how cities develop. Koolhaas wrote: "We resist the notion that Lagos represents an African city en route to becoming modern. . . . Rather, we think it possible to argue that it represents an extreme and paradigmatic study of a city at the forefront of globalizing modernity. . . . That is to say, Lagos is not catching up with us. Rather, we may be catching up with Lagos."

If marketing is to evolve, if it is to continue to be effective, it has to acknowledge the increasing incoherence and lack of control inherent in today's fragmented, individualized audience/consumer base. It has to become chaos-compliant rather than operate on the artificial construct of demographic or social order.

It has to respond to the human and the natural disorder that defines it.

—Creed O'Hanlon, writer; former CEO of Australia's most successful Web development company, Spike Networks; and former "creative spark" for Mazda

ACKNOWLEDGMENTS

Nobody has ever measured, even poets, how much a heart can hold.

—Zelda Fitzgerald

This book has been a collaborative effort. I believe that there is no place for "marketing gurus" anymore, just enlightened human beings who market. In fact, I would go so far as to say that in the very near future there will no longer be brands, merely reflections of consumers' lives and value sets made manifest through marketing style and corporate infrastructure. In his latest book, *Marketers Are Liars,* Seth Godin, author and much-touted "marketing guru," alludes to the notion that fantasy ultimately will triumph over reality. He may be absolutely right. He will be right if and only if consumers themselves decide to create stories in the image of the world he projects. It will not happen because he or any one of us marketing professionals wills it.

Like many of us, Seth Godin squirms around the notions of fibs versus fraud and pleasure versus self-indulgence. He seems to propose that ethics and authenticity somehow are separable or measurable in degrees. What marketing and advertising forge from now on will be a collaborative effort with *uber*-informed consumers leading the way. We'll quite simply follow their lead, not the other way around. Their ethics and their stories (real or real fantasies) will become the words in brand stories. In a sense, marketing will never write an original word again, yet through enabling technologies and culturally sensitive marketing strategies, brands and brand stories will become more alive, more fantastic, more vibrant, and more vivid than ever before.

This book, like every future brand, is indeed a story. However, the story has not been mine alone; it has been the output, the manifestation, the collaboration of an interactive virtual salon of highly informed cultural intelligence consumers and providers. They are both the scribes and the pages on which a map of today's cultural landscape has been drawn. Each in his or her own way is a prime example of the consumer-as-creator approach to future marketing that is, fundamentally, my single contribution. I thank each of those persons who directly contributed case studies, opinions, visuals, and sweat during the course of this book, this brand's creation. I, quite literally, could not have done this without them. In particular, I would like to thank and congratulate all the cultural intelligence agencies who miraculously agreed to assemble together "under one roof." Their gesture is a sign of things to come; it is emblematic of the fact that the world and its consumers are vast and complex enough that no single entity can lay claim to completely comprehensive insight or pinpoint cultural prediction.

In addition, I would like to thank Donya Dickerson, this book's editor, who saw past my obvious agenda of bridging commerce and culture, profit and good, by understanding that beyond that agenda was the foundation of a methodology that marketing and advertising actually can use. And use it marketing people will; many already are. Many of us already realize that the worst thing that we can do is try too hard. Marketing in all its aspects has projected complexity where there was none. We have seen our own reflections of reflections instead of truly seeing the consumers staring us straight in our faces. We have resisted seeing eye to eye. We have chosen shadow over light. The answer was here all the time.

As important as eyes and light are, one can never discount the value of hands, hearts, and minds. Alisa Clark Ackerman, a brand provocateur, writer, and expert in her own right, has been vital in inciting some of this book's message and has eloquently contributed some of her own unique opinions—opinions I have valued given their respected and beloved source. I also thank Carolyn Shields, the voice of reason, the cheerleader, the referee, and the real "producer" of this show. Carolyn, on so many levels, I can never thank you enough. With so many disparate elements, jewels of information, literally threatening to drown me, I could have capsized easily; Carolyn kept me afloat. Rufus Lighty also was very important because he was in charge of special effects; that is, he saw me through a crashed computer hard drive, a broken-down modem, and a computer theft—all the while simultaneously holding my hand as various contributions arrived in formats known only on Mars. He was my enabler as I addressed the technology that I both adore and despise. For anyone needing a computer savior, contact him at lighty@gmail.com.

X'Ania Saldana, a brilliant young intern, came out of nowhere last summer and became my portal into a younger generation, captivating me with her commonsense wisdom. Bernd Beetz, CEO of Coty Inc; Steve Mormoris, senior vice president of global marketing for Coty Beauty, and his talented team; and Marie-Sabine LeClerque, formerly of Coty and now at LVMH, all have been sources of enormous inspiration. Their moral support, unconditional respect, and genuine courtesy, combined with an infectious spirit of collaborative creativity, gave me the strength both to write this book and to maintain a challenging day job. Although I am now involved in multiple new ventures, I spent almost seven years at Coty Inc (both Coty Beauty and Coty Prestige), including stints as vice president of new ideas as well as global creative director.

I would like to thank the following individuals for the contribution of photos used throughout the section in Secret #6 on Parsons The New School For Design: Mimi Chan, Hiroko Hayashi, Deborah Kirschner, Lucas Knipscher, Michael Lisnet, Dave Marin, Gary Robbins, Grace Song, Sara Stadtmiller, Tony Whitfield, and Ronald Wright.

And, of course, I must thank all those persons who not only have loved and supported me throughout the writing of this book but also have, each in his or her own way, enabled me to become the person, and perhaps, dare I say it, the living brand I am today.

Professionally, there have been so many persons in this category that I could never possibly list them all; however, I must acknowledge Ally Tomi, Francine Stessel, Brian Kelly, Theodora (Teddy) Borsen, and Julia Ledyard, my former (and in some instances occasionally current) creative partners and colleagues, who have all taught me that beauty is not negotiable—because beauty is truth, regardless of its face, and truth is inevitable unless we step in its way. I thank Frank Maddocks, Celine Dion, Kimora Lee Simmons, Russell Simmons,

Andy Hilfiger, Nikki Sixx, and Ivy Ross, who taught me that business can be kind and filled with joy. I thank Dr. Peter Harf, who taught me that giant corporations indeed can be human and even demonstrate a collective soul. I thank Jean Runel, Norm Cecere, Lee Vaughan, Bill Eldien, Matt Bousquette, Paula Meehan, Jim Mooney, and Anne Mincey for these same reasons. I thank Douglas Toews and Marc Krigsman, trailblazers in their own right, for bringing out the unexpected or, as they might call it, "the surprising" in me, challenging me to evolve professionally beyond my comfort zone. I can't ever thank them enough for that. Squirming is good for the soul.

And, of course, I also must especially thank Joanne DeLuca, Janine Lopiano, Mary McGuinness, and Lisa Weidner, along with everyone at Sputnik, Inc., who have broadened my understanding of culture in ways I can't begin to ever fully express. I also must thank Kate Ancketill from GDR (Global Design Resources) Creative Intelligence, who paints the impossible with ultimate ease, and Karim Rashid for his creative courage, wrapped beautifully in a cloak of functional, democratic beauty. I also thank the many other designers, educators, marketers, and artists with whom I have worked (particularly Parsons The New School For Design's Anthony Whitfield). And, of course, I can never give enough thanks to Jim Morrison, Kerry Kinney, George Lois, Madonna Badger, Jim Feldman, Elie Papiernik, Dennie Passion, Rick Kinsel, Bruno Lacoste, and Heinke Martens. They taught me to truly respect and value my unique point of view, style, and talent, such as it is. In their own ways, they each contributed to my courage. As my French friends might say, *Gardez votre courage*. You too will need it.

Most personally, I also must thank my late, utterly insane parents, Raymond J. and Marianne Nadeau, as well as my very living siblings, Roswitha DeToma, Charles Nadeau, and Viktor Nadeau, and their spouses and maniac offspring. This pedigree, as it were, accounts for my love for diversity and ability to see majesty (yes majesty), dignity, humor, beauty, and compassion in every face, every scene, every object, every catastrophe I see each day. Beauty is everywhere—even at work. Work, in fact, should be beautiful. Your work, in order to succeed, must be beautiful in some way to some one.

Hence it goes without saying that I also must thank my life partner, Jim Barritt, and his family, particularly Jim M. and Dorothy Barritt, who, for 22 years, have lovingly allowed me to be as weird as I wanna be—no questions asked. In some ways, this is what this book is about. In some ways, this is the greatest gift of all, which is why I am a proponent of sharing it with you.

As it turned out, the love and support of my friends, family, and colleagues have transformed me into an immortal idea, albeit only a single one. You too are each ideas. Like brands, it will be in memories and hearts that you and I will live forever, eternally fused within the very fabric of individual, living realities. This explains why I needed and wanted so many other ideas and a variety of collaborators for this book. In order to live in legacy, a story must be told a thousand times. My hope is that you can avoid that process and will really need to read this collection of contributions, this gift of collaborative wisdom, only once.

Ultimately, it will be you who will choose or not choose to join today's new marketing *operas,* or *soap operas,* depending on your point of view and preference. There is no denying it. We are on the verge of dramatic change, perhaps even a social revolution, led, interestingly enough, by commerce and the consumer. Prepare yourselves for *symphonies* of chaos. *Crescendos* of cultural collaboration. Brand *music* meant for human beings. Music meant for many. New, complex harmonies composed entirely for one.

The decision will be yours, and regardless of what it is, I respect your decision and thank you for at least attending this one recital.

With that said, I do invite you to join the following chorus or at least to lift your voice in tomorrow's next marketing song—perhaps a song only you can write. The process will not be nearly as difficult as you might think, given what you may currently consider the overwhelming complexity of our time. It will only take three things: (1) collaboration, (2) innovation, and (3) your commitment to fascination and your hunger to be fascinated. It will require your being fully alive. Living brands for loving people. This is what this book is about!

Love,

Raymond Nadeau

YOU WON'T FIND THE ANSWERS. THEY'LL FIND YOU.

(BRANDING MYTHS EXPOSED)

Chaos often breeds life, when order breeds habit.

—*Henry Adams,* The Education of Henry Adams

This whole creation is essentially subjective, and the dream is the theater where the dreamer is at once scene, actor, prompter, stage manager, author, audience and critic.

—*From "General Aspects of Dream Psychology,"* Psychological Reactions: A Jung Anthology

MARKETING HERESY: LET GO

So here goes. Here is the remarkable revelation: None of us should be deliberately creating demand anymore. There is so much need (both physical and emotional, both imaginary and real) in the world already, why should we invest our time, money, and energy to artificially create more? Apart from the fact that emotional manipulation is not a nice thing to do, it just won't work as well as it did before. Sigmund Freud and the neo-Freudian marketing he inspired have both been dead for a long time, and frankly, both are beginning to stink. The era of consumer as creator has begun. The revolution slipped by us, and the consumer won.

Whether you agree with me or not, the fact is that technology will enable the empowered consumer to dictate and spontaneously generate new brands and/or newly evolved versions of old ones. This will not happen in the indirect ways that may come to mind immediately—meaning through traditional focus groups or the reduction of human beings into demographic statistics, but rather in overt, deliberate, sometimes chaotic ways that at times may put us ill at ease given our previously comfortable, albeit fictional, belief in marketing cause and effect.

Marketing never was a science. No investment could ever truly be measured in direct proportion to its contribution to brand equity. Success and failure always have eluded explanation for most of us, with some notable exceptions, such as legendary adman George Lois, who has personally shared his timeless insight in this book.

YOU ARE AMONG FRIENDS: THE EXPERT VOICES IN THIS BOOK

Don't despair, my friends. I will provide you with a range of insights derived from the actual experience of a wide variety of marketing, advertising, and public relations persons; technology experts; and business and creative geniuses from all walks of life. These insights and the wide-reaching tools they provide us with will help you, by the time you finish this book, to understand precisely the type of "accidental" marketing that ultimately will lead to the creation of future consumer-generated brand biospheres designed and inhabited by satisfied human beings.

You may be asking yourselves, Who are these friends? I won't list them all here, but I will whet your appetite. First of all, for the first time in history, five of the world's leading cultural oracles will reveal their takes on where our cultural reality is heading and the impact this path will have on marketing. Sputnik, Inc., Genius Insight, GDR Creative Intelligence, Trend Union (under the guidance of famed Li Edelkoort), and Mirror Mirror's Jeanine Recckio all have lent their voices to this book. With their input, the first chapter alone is worth a thousand times more than the price of this book.

We will explore cutting-edge brand-development concepts drawing on my own experience working on brands ranging from Baby Phat to my friendship with Nikki Sixx of Mötley Crüe fame. You'll learn about what I refer to as *culture casting,* a new model of consumer segmentation. The metaphor between consumption and performance will be made clear—establishing once and for all that the object of tomorrow's marketing will be the enablement of what I term the consumer's *performance of self.*

And there's more. You will hear directly from the world's leading experts in the field of commercial technology application. These are the pioneers who at this very moment are creating and refining the communication and experiential infrastructures necessary for you to truly become part of twenty-first-century marketing, collaborating directly with consumers and, together with them, building *brand* new worlds. Les Neumann, director of the Globian Institute, Victor Chu, CEO of MIL. Digital Labeling, and David Polinchock, CEO of Brand Experience Lab, will shock you with the range of technologies that only five years ago would have been considered science fiction. Like the World Community Grid, the organization that allows anyone to "donate" the virtual memory power of their computers to collectively combine into a massive community think tank in order to tackle major catastrophic issues facing humankind, such as finding cures for diseases like AIDS (www.worldcommunitygrid.org), you will gain access to other existing technologies that will evolve marketing, transforming its very premise beyond anything known before.

You also will hear directly from cultural marketing geniuses such as Brian Feit, "chief buzz officer" of BMF Media Group, explaining how brands such as Jeep and Valentino are already building worlds of delight. Jim Morrison, general manager of the Turner Network's Fashion and Beauty Channel and former president of L'Oréal, will comment further on lifestyle geography and the growing tendency toward consumers considering themselves as the most compelling content and purveyors of lifestyle. We will explore increasingly crucial issues of branding ethics through direct case studies and exclusive interviews with persons such as Mark Baiada, CEO of Bayada Nurses; Gloria Steinem; Alex Vaickus, president of global licensing for Playboy Enterprises; and Matt Eastwood, national creative director and vice chairman of DDB Australia and former chief creative officer of Y&R North America.

We'll explore and expand the meaning of commercial ethics and cultural relevance to include, of all things, the changing, authentic notion of beauty. Karim Rashid, perhaps the world's leading designer and one of the hosts of television's *Made in America* reality show, will lend his voice to the voices of tomorrow, the design students of Parsons The New School For Design as they fuse the notions of commerce, culture, and social responsibility into a single idea. Theodora (Teddy) Borsen, creative director and partner of DFJ World, a division of Della Femina Rothschild Jeary and Partners, will speak to a broader definition of beauty and, through the lens of famed fashion photographer Richard Phibbs, help to define its future and confirm the notion of spontaneously created consumer-generated brands.

Bernd Beetz, CEO of Coty Inc, will share his global perspective on marketing vision. Ivy Ross, executive vice president of design and development for Old Navy, The Gap Inc., will share how she and David Kuehler, director of the Clay Project at Procter & Gamble, transformed the vision of toy giant Mattel through the groundbreaking initiative known as Project Platypus. Mukara Meredith of MATRIXWORKS and a leading advocate of the application of Hakomi Collaborative techniques to business will join Ivy in an exclusive interview to reveal how marketing has the potential to change for the better the lives of both consumers and those marketing to consumers.

To conclude, you'll be touched by the wisdom of Abbot Primate Dr. Notker Wolf, the highest representative of the Benedictine Order, learning just why the world's oldest brand is still going strong and why, even to this day, its potential for brand stretch has just been barely tapped. You'll also hear from Executive Vice President and Creative Director Jeff Danzer, the creator of PL>Y™ by Intimo, the first iPod-enabling underwear, which is a brand capable of application across a range of other categories.

And, finally, you will witness the birth of a culturally created brand, Rock Scene™ Brands LLC, the first clothing line ever to draw not only on the actual content of a magazine but also on living, breathing human beings as well as celebrity designers whose values it reflects—persons and groups such as Blondie and the Ramones. Famed rock photographer Mark Weiss; fashion expert and entrepreneur Andy Hilfiger; and partner and president of Global Beauty Brands, as well as Rock Scene partner, Tara Barrett will each lend their unique rock-and-roll visions of fashion marketing in an increasingly rock-and-roll, topsy-turvy world to be further addressed by my "comrade in arms," the famously notorious creative spark Creed O'Hanlon, acclaimed writer, photographer, and marketing catalyst.

CONSIDER ME A PARTNER: My Role on Your Collaboration Team

Having created and propelled successful brands across multiple categories and in a variety of marketing roles, I have learned to listen to everyone I meet and constantly marvel at the sounds and sights that I consider my personal sensory playground. I have created world-class, stellar brands in the numerous creative, promotional, licensing, and marketing-management positions I have held across a variety of consumer product categories in more than 20 countries around the world. My experience has been broad, having worked in categories from liquor and food to giftware at Fortune 500 corporations such as

Redken 5th Avenue NYC, Heinz Pet Products (later acquired by Del Monte), Teleflora, Coty Inc, Hunt-Wesson, and Heublein/UDV.

I also have loved working on the agency side, where I've been proud to be a part of several organizations, culminating in my last agency position as vice president and managing director of the New York office of Maddocks & Company. I still work as a freelance writer and, in some instances, active creative director for a number of prominent New York advertising agencies such as Badger and Partners and DFJ World Advertising, as well as Kinney + Kinsella and Brune, a Paris-based agency, and centdegrés, a premier design and branding firm also based in Paris and whose U.S. operations I coordinate. And most recently, I have added media to the mix, working as executive creative consultant and "keeper of the keys" for the Turner Media Group, as well as consulting for The Kind Group, an entirely new type of organization committed to brand incubation.

At the risk of being repetitive, my experience has taught me that creating demand is a lie. Marketing and great brands satisfy real needs (whether actual or imagined, physical or emotional) on a truly personal level. Creating demand for a dream that is not your own or someone else's is like dancing with a shadow; the experience and the brand die before they really begin because there simply is no music. The following two very brief excerpts from chapters in my professional life laid the foundation of my revelation.

Jose Cuervo Tequila shooter parties taught me half of what I know about marketing. Yes, that's right. I began my career in bars. And when I wasn't in bars, I was traveling the streets of Los Angeles searching out men and women looking to buy what I had to sell. And they wanted it bad; believe me they did. One of my very first jobs was working for Heublein/UDV (a division of international food and drink giant Diageo plc), hosting on-premise promotions at bars and restaurants, as well as working with a real genius, the late Lee Vaughan, who pioneered such things as sponsorship of Black Velvet Canadian Whiskey beauty contests and rodeos as well as Smirnoff Vodka jazz festivals. He also saw that beach volleyball was an amateur sport attended by buff men and women who loved to party. Therefore, for miniscule budgets (by today's standards), he and others from other brands began sponsoring Jose Cuervo beach volleyball tournaments. He observed a lifestyle, matched it with a need, and applied a brand to it. Today, Jose Cuervo is a brand that initially captured the lion's share of the market and remains a hugely successful iconic brand. Today, beach volleyball has become an Olympic sport. End of story. So that's why my earliest insights into marketing happened in bars and on the beach.

As an outgoing but inwardly shy young man, I often found myself smack dab in the middle of a room filled with living consumers, not in front of a desk with a mission statement and promotional plan to guide me. My job really did become a party of sorts, and with nowhere to hide, and because I was in their midst, I saw true lives and true needs. The needs I saw were simple. They included the desire to connect, to laugh, to flirt, to feel happy. I went where a certain set of consumers lived, lived where they lived, played with them, loved them, gave them what I could—including both a brand and an experience—to build on the world they were themselves building brick by brick, shot by shot. As an aside, I, along with many others, helped to create from the ground up the mystique surrounding one of the world's great beverage brands.

Fast forward to the second half of my basic training and the second driver of this book. While working for Redken, a leading manufacturer of professionally distributed hair care products, now part of L'Oréal, I was introduced to the idea of "consumer as creator," a subject to be explained in depth throughout this book. I was international marketing director and led a full-scale European reimaging and advertising campaign. I helped to enable European expansion into 18 countries and developed and facilitated the launch of multiple leading salon brands, including Solargenics, as well as one of the first in-salon hair analysis computers, HairProbe. At Redken, I found myself in an organization that actually loved its consumers—both professional and lay. At first, I thought everyone at Redken was insane—refugees from some sort of California-concocted, hair-fixated, self-actualization program run amuck. I soon learned better.

Paula Kent Meehan, founder and former owner of Redken, began as an actress, perhaps best known as the receptionist on the hit television show *77 Sunset Strip*. With money she earned from a commercial, she and her partner, Jerrie Redding, developed a shampoo in her bathtub to address Paula's sensitive scalp and minimize the negative effects of harsh shampoos for other men and women with similar problems. The rest is history. Today, Paula is still helping the profession she loves, and the company she founded is still going strong. The part of all this that shaped my thinking most was the degree to which both stylists and their clients were respected at Redken. I can't remember a single product or advertising campaign in which both stylists and consumers were not intimately involved. They told us when a product was good or bad. They told us what they wanted to see developed. Their love of red hair influenced many a photo shoot. Stylists and consumers told us things to our faces. We responded. Redken answered their needs and built an immortal brand in the process.

Redken staff created opportunities to actually interact directly with professional stylists, gaining both insight into product performance and first-hand knowledge of consumer desire. Redken sponsored thousands of professional educational workshops, teaching both technical and business techniques while listening for new opportunities and gaining practical professional guidance. And once a year, Redken sponsored an international symposium where thousands of stylists from around the world met, shared experiences, and attended seminars addressing issues such as best business practices, practical product usage techniques, fashion trends, and what may be considered by some to be the equivalent of interactive support groups. Redken "spontaneously" had built a collaborative brand model that literally was decades ahead of its time. And now, with the aid of advanced direct consumer-to-brand and brand-to-consumer communicative technologies (to be explored throughout this book and especially in Secret #3), the rest of us can now catch up.

From Redken, I went back to the agency side, eventually joining Maddocks & Company, the internationally renowned integrated strategic design and branding firm. Maddocks & Company developed initial concepts, brand platforms, and advertising campaigns for such successful brands as Limited Too, Bath and Body Works, Walt Disney, Johnson & Johnson, Warner Bros., Ketel One Vodka, KMS, Rexall Showcase International, Kanebo, St. John, Outlook Sports, and Satalife, a nonprofit organization dedicated to disseminating vital medical information around the globe.

After Maddocks, I later went on to become vice president of new ideas and global creative director for Coty Inc, Coty Beauty, and the Lancaster Group (now known as Coty Prestige), where I developed advertising, created product concepts, often spearheading licensing and acquisition opportunities, built corporate identity, propelled media strategies, applied proprietary technologies, maintained consumer connections, conducted corporate think tanks, and influenced aesthetic decisions for some of the world's leading fragrance, personal care, and cosmetics brands, some with names that are perhaps better know than Coty itself, brands such as adidas, Cutex, Vivienne Westwood, Jil Sander, Wolfgang Joop, Jetta Joop, Marc Jacobs, Kenneth Cole, Davidoff (best known within the Coty Prestige portfolio for Davidoff Cool Water), Isabella Rossellini, the healing garden, Calgon, Mary-Kate and Ashley Olsen, Rimmel London Cosmetics and Fragrances, Lancaster Skin Care and Cosmetics, Astor Cosmetics and Skin Care, Stetson, Jovan, Pierre Cardin, Chupa Chups, Shania Twain, Baby Phat by Kimora Lee Simmons, David and Victoria Beckham, Sarah Jessica Parker, Nautica, Miss Sixty, Calvin Klein, Lagerfeld, Jennifer Lopez, Celine Dion, Vera Wang, and most recently, a fragrance inspired by the hit television program *Desperate Housewives.*

One of the first things I did at Coty was to advocate an "entertainment credo" and suggest that Coty redefine itself as an entertainment provider. Since then, this philosophy has been copied by many other companies. Because of its early adoption of this credo in its category, Coty preempted many of its competitors, resulting in some of the most successful fragrance launches in history, such as the tremendously popular celebrity-inspired Celine Dion and Jennifer Lopez fragrances. Its entertaining media philosophy and willingness to go beyond category convention also resulted in fragrance and beauty licensing for nontraditional category-oriented brands such as Chupa Chups—not to mention a collaborative branding effort with LYCRA®, designated as one of the world's superbrands, resulting in one of the most successful coventures and licensing projects ever seen in cosmetics.

I also played a key role in creating Coty's groundbreaking Living Brands Living Media® strategy, which has been embraced companywide and has been profiled in media such as *Brandweek* and CNN. Proving that sometimes the best media can be free, I also spearheaded an initiative at Coty to seek out and develop product-concept applications around the most cutting-edge new technologies, even resulting in the negotiation of an official, governmentally sanctioned Space Act Agreement with NASA.

I also was part of the team responsible for the futuristic fragrance concept 001Coty, resurrecting what I considered to be a variation of the historically significant Coty Award through a program at Parsons The New School For Design, where tomorrow's talent was cultivated via Coty's donation of a scholarship award. 001Coty is now in the permanent collection of the Cooper Hewitt Museum, as well as the Munich Museum of Modern Art and the Royal Danish Museum.

Like any living brand, this book is a composite, and you should know in advance that it could not have been created alone. It is a collaborative effort, much like the collaborative brands of the future it portends. In it you will hear voices never before assembled together to express one common idea. And, as a reader, you will gain access to this exciting dialogue.

Through actual interviews and first-hand case studies, you will explore the views of some of the most influential thinkers not only of our profession but also of our time. Most important, you will be exposed to mechanisms and techniques to help you navigate what may seem at times to be an entirely new world of marketing—a world where the tables have turned and cause and effect are less predictable than ever before. The aim of this book is to provide us all with a compass of sorts for a voyage bound to encounter the turbulent yet extremely exciting waters that lie ahead.

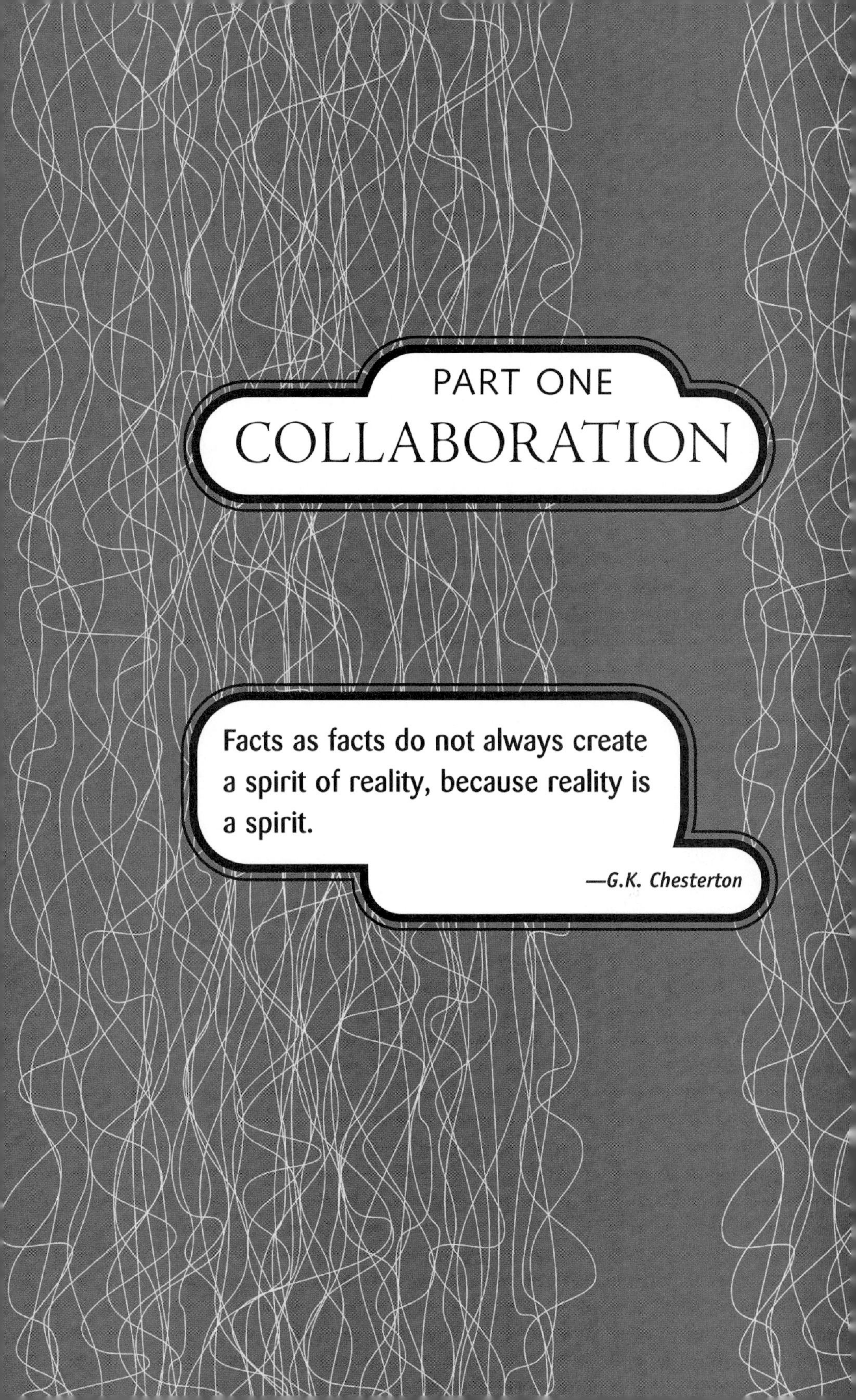

PART ONE
COLLABORATION

Facts as facts do not always create a spirit of reality, because reality is a spirit.

—G.K. Chesterton

SECRET #1

BE THERE

SEE THE NEED, REVEAL THE DREAM

> The sky is not less blue because the blind man does not see it.
>
> —*Danish Proverb*

INTRODUCTION:

Culture Is the Mother of Great Brands

It's not news that brands have evolved from being products with purely functional benefits into highly emotionalized personalities that represent an entire intimate lifestyle to consumers. This "revelation" is already "last century." However, there is renewed interest in the word *lifestyle,* which has resurrected itself once again as the marketing *mot du jour.* That's fine. Recycling is not a crime—particularly when the recycled concept improves on the original. But be warned: Any originality or modernity associated with the evolved "lifestyle" marketing concept has to do with the realization that lifestyles are just stylized adjectives describing real, ever-changing lives. This book is about marketing. And this marketing lifestyle story always begins and ends with the integration of real lives and the role and successful establishment of brands within those real lives. Lives first, lifestyles second—got it? Let's begin.

Becoming a legitimate part of people's lives is the new minimum price of brand entry and is the only method for a brand's sustained longevity. The challenge inherent in this new requirement is that it requires a far greater understanding of and genuine sensitivity to the human condition, psychology, and cultural influences. Like lifestyle, *culture* as a word has both expanded as a concept and contracted in terms of the number of people who fall easily into any one cultural group. There are both fewer and more cultures depending on how one defines the word. Demographics are misleading. Psychographics are speculative. Marketing has become more complex than ever before. We must connect with more people in more languages, addressing needs and experiences we often don't understand—all within the context of cultures and cultural values we may not fully grasp. Still, we push forward, and we wonder why many of our strategic initiatives fail. It's more of a surprise that some of them actually work.

As brands play a more emotionalized role in people's lives, any brand's intrinsic value will be linked to the degree to which it is value-based. I am not referring to brand values. I am referring to *human* values. Brands have value; consumers have values. What you will discover is that brand value declines the more disconnected it becomes from the authentic values of prevailing culture and, more important, the real lives and needs of human beings.

The fact is that consumers now demand far more personal contact from highly emotionalized, living brands. This means that marketers need to develop increasingly intelligent ways to provide some level of personal intimacy between their brands and their customers. How can they do this? By creating customized, authentic brands with multifaceted projected personalities instead of homogenized global brands with monolithic, marketing-created value sets. It is my strong belief that culture creates the best brands—but in order to allow this to happen, we need to understand the collective dreams and true needs on which culture and/or cultures are built.

As marketing departments shrink and new brands and media channels proliferate, you may feel overwhelmed by the notion of becoming "one with your consumer." Rest easy, you are not going to have to become one with your consumer. However, you will need to understand the difference between his or her real needs versus the commercial and competitive landscape that best suits the reality of your brand. As marketers, our job is to focus, above all, on creating great products that are inspired by the consumer's actual versus perceived lifestyle patterns by tapping directly into people's unexpressed and/or unfulfilled desires as opposed to trying to "create artificial demand."

Discovering an intelligent way to respond to consumers' realities is always the most successful approach and is the only real way to build stellar brands that will stand the test of time. But remember, real does not mean better; it just means real. Fantasy is also a "real" human need. If you simply fix your sights on a real perspective (real or real fantasy), with any luck, you will observe the obvious. In actuality, it's not all that difficult to immerse one's self in consumers' lives. It often simply requires that we open our eyes.

Think about the huge phenomenon of reality television, which is a great example of the participatory era we are moving toward. It is now quite clear that this shift toward a participatory versus a voyeuristic culture is here to stay. What should we have seen earlier to suggest the advent of reality television and consumer-created everything? Apart from the many experts, books, and technology theorists that have explored this theme for the past 15 years, there also was early evidence in popular culture. Karaoke and to some extent performance and installation art were early signals that consumers were ready, even 20 years ago, to take center stage themselves.

The popularity of reality television literally has changed the rules of marketing, and now, advances in technology and marketing visionaries are accelerating this shift—moving us toward an imminent seamless integration of consumer need and marketing strategy, all based on direct consumer interaction. As we will see in Secret #3, consumer-to-brand interactive technologies are advancing more rapidly than even the most visionary among us truly appreciates. In that chapter we will explore some of the cutting-edge technologies already available to marketers that enable us to respond strategically to genuine consumer desire in ways that were unimaginable previously.

But first, in this chapter we will focus on how to recognize—and make intelligent use of—some of the most powerful collective waves of contemporary culture and unearth the most profound and relevant dreams and practical needs of today's consumer. This always should be the first step, and from there we can begin to build and rebuild culturally relevant brands.

If at any point along the way you become confused or dubious, just remember what's at stake. Remember karaoke. Remember that all anyone would have had to do was observe the karaoke phenomenon as evidence of people's desire to "be seen" by others and experience the fantasy of being a star (as well as people's desire to witness and participate in the public success or failure of others)—and that insight, coupled with an appreciation of the continuously growing desire for individual expression, would have signaled a gargantuan business opportunity surpassing the mere phenomenon of karaoke.

The fact is that marketing, product development, advertising, and public relations people had their eyes closed. Preventing future similar mistakes and the lost opportunities along the way is my objective. And lest you feel that the premise is too obvious to explore, you should realize that even *American Idol*—the classic poster child for interactive reality TV shows where "average Joes" get the chance to be stars—almost didn't happen. The contestants themselves created a buzz for a show that was going to be canceled. They fought to have it aired and eventually won. The rest, as they say, is history.

The four megatrends explored in this chapter (and throughout this book) are an attempt to synthesize today's most important cultural movements—those megatrends that will be the central driving forces behind the way we live our lives over the next several decades. Since one person's opinion does not a trend forecast make, I have joined forces with some of the world's most renowned "cultural sensitives," who have long established their credibility in this area and now provide us with insight into the social and psychological factors that have, and will continue to have, a profound influence on the ways we live and consume. Of course, these insights are only guesses—educated guesses but nonetheless extrapolations of behavior, technology, and scenarios to predict future behavior—the message being that I have culled the best of the best in terms of social forecasting. But the funny thing about culture is that it changes without warning. While I begin this first chapter with a snapshot of "now" in the hopes that each succeeding chapter will remain rooted in consumer reality, that reality may change. So read quickly. Start now. For now is all we have, and the notion of now, by its very definition, will never come again.

THE FOUR MAJOR MEGATRENDS ESSENTIAL FOR LIVING BRANDS

1. Mood and experience enhancement—reality versus synthetic reality—reclaimed sexuality versus sex

2. **Humanized technology/the quest for physical and psychological perfection/techno-organic balance**
3. **Everyman empowerment, self-creation, and personal expression**
4. **The luxury of ethics—humanity, ecology, righteous indignation**

I conceptualized these four megatrends based on material culled and cross-referenced from my collaborations with the following top cultural/consumer-sensitive organizations: Sputnik, Inc., Genius Insight, GDR (Global Design Resources) Creative Intelligence, Trend Union, led by Li Edelkoort, and Mirror Mirror Imagination Group. Each of these agencies views culture in its totality but tends to provide information that naturally gravitates toward various specific aspects of marketing, advertising, and design. Each, however, is committed to providing commercial, entertainment, and nonprofit clients with culturally relevant insight geared to help brands and organizations better connect with consumers.

This entire book is infused with collaborative intelligence from these top followers of culture, combined with even newer notions and insights (many of which are not new at all—merely forgotten and now newly recalled wisdom). You will be the ones to benefit from this amazing plethora of business and cultural voices—combined in a single collaborative format, perhaps a format seen for the very first time. The fact that "competitors" of this caliber have agreed to coexist in one book is a model of the future. Collaboration on every level—business-to-consumer, business-to-business, and consumer-to-business—is the hallmark of this new marketing era. True to their futuristic orientation, the agencies contributing to this book offer us a supreme example of collaborative spirit. Each of these agencies has its own specialties:

- *Sputnik, Inc.* A cultural intelligence agency that provides business forecasting solutions. The cultural analysis that Sputnik, Inc., does is based on Mindtrends®, its proprietary mapping methodology that interconnects and interprets the ideas of leading contemporary thinkers within the arts, sciences, and technology (www.sputnikentertainment.com).

- *Genius Insight.* Consumer patterns and entertainment/celebrity trends. Genius Insight is a New York–based marketing strategy and research firm. It publishes the *Genius Insight, StarPower,* and *Genius Insight BrandPower* reports, as well as a range of other publications, including *Genius Insight StarPower Europe* and *Genius Insight BrandPower Europe* (www.geniusinsight.com).
- *GDR Creative Intelligence.* Analysis of design innovation in retail, hospitality, and leisure. GDR is a London-based research company known for its visually spectacular presentations that take clients through inspirational case studies in global retail and leisure innovation. Retained by clients to provide strategic insight into the latest consumer and creative trends, many of the concepts shown in GDR's highly visual reports are so new that they won't have been published anywhere else. GDR compiles its research into quarterly reports that show the latest innovations at all consumer touch points: in hotels, bars, restaurants, stores in all sectors, packaging, point of sale, service, and technology. GDR also uses its vast knowledge of design talent to select creative agencies for clients, acting as a global conduit between design buyers and design agencies/architects. Services include publication of quarterly reports on subscription, tailored sector-specific reports, seminar and conference presentations, workshops, and agency selection (www.gdruk.com).
- *Trend Union—Li Edelkoort.* Materials and aesthetic trends. Trend Union provides trend analysis and consulting services to international brands in a wide range of sectors from cosmetics to cars, telephones to public transportation, fashion, food, and flowers to bricks and paper. Since 1986, forecaster Li Edelkoort's trend books and magazines have been seasonal style bibles for the creative industries worldwide. Studying the links between art, fashion, design, and consumer culture, Edelkoort and her team ana-

lyze and advance the concepts, colors, and materials that will be important two or more years hence because "there is no creation without advance knowledge, and without design, a product cannot exist" (www.edelkoort.com).

- *Mirror Mirror Imagination Group.* Luxury and beauty futurism. Mirror Mirror fuses cultural and technological future scenarios with projections regarding their impact on consumption and consumer lifestyles. Although particularly well known for her work in the beauty and fashion categories, founder and owner Jeanine Recckio has worked with multiple Fortune 500 companies in a variety of segments (www.beautyfuturologist.com).

MEGATREND 1: MOOD AND EXPERIENCE ENHANCEMENT

MOOD AND EXPERIENCE ENHANCEMENT: THE TREND

The fusion of entertainment and adrenaline addiction to real life has driven the growing importance of intensified experiences. The advent of *experiential marketing* has exploded across many areas of everyday life, and we are now moving more toward the realm of experience addiction. This phenomenon explains why the entertainment industry, in its broadest sense, has become the most profitable industry, with seemingly never-ending potential for continued expansion into the twenty-first century.

I'll give an example of what I mean. Almost seven years ago, as the vice president of new ideas, which led to my eventually becoming the vice president of new ideas, global creative director, in one of my first presentations to Coty's then-CEO Peter Harf and our senior management team, I recommended that the company redefine itself as an entertainment company. And, to some extent, this has led Coty to some of the most rapid expansion in its hundred-year history. To the outside world, Coty's success simply has seemed to be the result of resurrecting the then-out-of-fashion notion of licensing entertainment properties, which resulted in its now-legendary success of brands created in conjunction with such entertainment icons as Jennifer Lopez and Celine Dion.

The notion of entertainment was applied in a far broader philosophical context, including the adoption of "living media" programs that focused on bringing to life for the consumer via nontraditional, fully experiential promotional efforts across a broad spectrum of brands based on cultural and lifestyle fashion icons such as Marc Jacobs, Chupa Chups, David Beckham, Chopard, and Vivienne Westwood. We'll look at a few of the most innovative of these programs in various parts of this book.

The cultural affinity for entertainment-modeled branding today is evident everywhere. It is evidenced by the boom in every facet of the portable electronics industry, from phones that play videos to the phenomenon of the iPod—people want to be "plugged in" everywhere they go. It also explains why "larger than life" one-stop entertainment complexes are popping up everywhere—including consumers' homes. In the search for intense experiences, the world has become our playground—from theme parks to cruise ships, people are avidly searching for the penultimate in experience consumption. This is why, of course, the entertainment mecca Las Vegas is the fastest-growing city in the United States and, on a size-equivalent basis, the fastest-growing economy in the world.

This trend will continue to be fed by advances in technology that allow for the intensification of experiences on a multisensorial level. Technology increasingly not only is delivering new ways to touch the senses but also is providing a deeper understanding of the physiologic and psychological human responses associated with those experiences. Through technology, marketers will be able to develop a truly holistic perspective on the consumer and his or her moods, desires, and expectations. As Sputnik, Inc., shows us in the following section on the cultural quest to "experience more," this ability to understand the consumer holistically will expand far beyond our traditional concepts of the physical and sensory world to the new frontier of what Sputnik, Inc., calls "hypersensing."

EXCLUSIVE TREND AGENCY REPORT

by Sputnik, Inc.

METASENSE: THE CULTURAL QUEST TO "EXPERIENCE MORE"

As the world becomes more virtual, ultimately we will use the organic—our bodies—to create the "ultraphysical." Why? Because culture's desire is to get back into the body, to feel a psychological and physiologic response, to feel like a "more human" human. This desire for the "real" will turn the tables on what we are experiencing in both our digital and physical products and services. *Organic* eventually will have a broader cultural meaning to encompass how we feel and experience our emotions and tastes.

The development of products that satisfy the consumer's sensations in many ways has just begun because recent scientific advances suggest that humans have more than five senses—actually, as suggested by Karen Olsen in her work *Synergy: Transforming America's High Schools Through Thematic Instruction,*[1] there are more than 20 recorded "senses" that define the human experience.

As companies come to develop new technologies, environments, experiences, and products based on the fact that we have more than five senses, the consumer will engage in a whole new range of extrasensorial experiences. Besides pure medical benefits, one of the exciting developments coming out of the Human Genome Project will be the genetic mapping of what we find "pleasing"—basically through taste and smell. One potential outcome of this is that there will be a vast library of trademarked simulacra, meaning naturally simulated scents and flavors, which eventually will become the new nostalgia. As we discover that we have more than five senses and

begin to awaken to multiple sensations, the experiences that products will be able to offer will expand to meet ever-growing consumer sensorial expectations. The future of branding is to move beyond the five senses and understand the emotional intelligence of the consumer. To engage the consumer mentally, physically, and sensorially. To evoke a full-body (mind-body-soul) response—a eureka sensation—because every part of the body thinks.

MOOD AND EXPERIENCE ENHANCEMENT: WHAT IT MEANS FOR BRANDS

The continuation of this trend means that the line separating entertainment and brands will diminish until marketing and entertainment almost completely converge. Consumers increasingly will crave and expect brands to provide them with fully evolved, entertaining experiences imbued with meaning. Make note of the word *meaning*. You will hear it repeated throughout this book. Consumers also will look for simulated alternative realities, especially those that provide instant gratification on some level and that place them in active versus passive roles. In order to respond to this trend, brands need to develop a holistic understanding of consumers that approaches their lives in a multilayered, multifaceted manner. Brands will have to stay relevant by integrating into the everyday lives of people in every way possible and by becoming a part of this entertainment-focused culture.

More and more brands will develop brand theme parks and experiential museums, stores, and events surrounding their brands to give consumers a more sensorial, evolved brand experience. But brands also will need to develop further the sensory aspect of their personalities using design and technology to the utmost in order to reach the consumer in new, physical, visceral, and more powerful ways. For example, Coty Inc patented a natural "happiness" compound scientifically proven to increase human serotonin levels. Coty Inc has used this special complex in the creation of fragrance and skin care products in brands such as Chupa Chups's I Love Me fragrance in order to enhance the user experience. Another similar example is Guerlain's Happyology skin care line, which is infused with mood-enhancing endorphins.

Smart brands will use this type of technology to create previously unimaginable experiential brand worlds or what I call *brand biospheres*. The question remains, though, of how to evolve conceptually beyond the basic "theme park" model to something people will find more interesting, meaningful, and satisfying with or without the addition of incredible new technology. See how GDR believes that this trend will move us even further toward what it refers to as "narrative and sensory retail environments" in the following section.

EXCLUSIVE TREND AGENCY REPORT

by GDR Creative Intelligence

NARRATIVE AND SENSORY RETAIL ENVIRONMENTS

Above-the-line spending on advertising is reaping ever-diminishing returns as the number of cable and satellite channels proliferates and consumers make use of ad-blocking technology such as TiVo. The trend is toward the three-dimensional (3D) environment as a sensory brand platform that allows for more impact and experiential storytelling. GDR has tracked the influence of museum exhibitions and theater scenography in recent leading-edge retail concepts. We're not talking about themed environments as conceived in the 1980s; new retail evolution is more culturally complex and an often abstract phenomenon, at times playing with performance art, unconventional spatial perception, metamorphosis, and transformation. Contemporary installation art will continue to make its presence felt in future retail developments. The creation of intense experiences that stimulate questions and challenge the preconceptions of the participant is set to continue. Let's look at some stunning examples.

Little Red Riding Hood (www.littleredridinghood.de)

German design consultancy Corneille Uedingslohmann Architekten created this Berlin flagship store for the fashion label LRRH. The vast majority of this store is underground, in a dreamlike space punctuated with books, accessories, sound, and moving images that reference Little Red Riding Hood and other fairy tales. To cross the threshold is to be transported to another world (see Figure 1-1).

FIGURE 1-1 ■ A modern retake on a classic tale, this store takes shoppers on an adventure through their childhoods.

Men's Superbrands (www.krd-uk.com)

London-based Ab Rogers Design (formerly KRD) has a track record of incorporating kinetic movement in its retail interiors—fixtures that dance, fittings that move mechanically to catch the eye, often creating surprising and entertaining environments using the simplest of mechanical devices. Men's Superbrands at Selfridges in London is a continuously changing landscape where movement and change are the only constant. Inspired by the color and space of a football field, the clothes represent the crowds, suspended from telescopic fixtures that expand, contract, and rotate to create a jungle of merchandise (see Figure 1-2).

FIGURE 1-2 ■ This in-store experience brings fashion to life with moving displays.

Peroni Beer (www.thebank.co.uk)

Italian brewery Birra Peroni has rebranded and relaunched its blond bottled beer Peroni Nastro Azzurro. To promote its exclusive and fashion-oriented positioning, the beer was taken off the shelf and placed in its own designer boutique in one of London's smartest shopping streets for one month only. Visitors couldn't buy the beer or even enter the store because the door was guarded by the quintessential Italian "bottle guard." The minimalist white space simply featured a single bottle of beer displayed on an uplit pedestal beside a classic Peroni-branded refrigerator. It was no coincidence that this pop-up store was located near other stylish Italian brands such as Giorgio Armani, Versace, and Alberta Ferretti (see Figure 1-3).

FIGURE 1-3 ■ Peroni takes lessons from high art to brand its high-end beer.

Bordello Chic—Fad or Trend?

Another example of this explosion of narrative and sensory environments is the advent of something referred to as *bordello chic.* GDR cites bordello chic as evidenced by the movement in the United Kingdom's market toward trendy and very innovative upscale sex retailers. Sex has hit mainstream retail in a big way in the United Kingdom. Sex shops run by women for women, such as Coco de Mer and Shh!, are increasingly popular. Humor and a sense of fun are key elements here. Star designers such as Tom Dixon and Marc Newson (surprisingly, both men) have created a successful range of expensive designer sex toys that are sold in upmarket department stores and outlets such as Agent Provocateur. The success of ventures such as Tabooboo (www.tabooboo.com), originally an online sex toy company with a cute logo and hilarious Web site, is due to this trend. This is a sector where we anticipate not just growth but significant investment in tactile 3D sensory branding.

While GDR's examples certainly indicate a shift in commercial tolerance of sexuality—reinforced in the United States by the success of brands such as Victoria's Secret—I believe that these manifestations are symbolic of a longer-term trend. Having survived decades of denial of male versus female differences, it makes sense that the backlash would be an acknowledgment of those differences, with both products and messages geared specifically toward women and men, both heterosexual and homosexual. This also applies to products designed to address real physiologic, cultural/racial, and age differences. Although brands such as Harmony Cereal for women and Maxim hair color for men and Grecian Formula hair colorings have specifically addressed sexual differences, I believe that you will see acceleration in this method of satisfying legitimate, existing though highly differentiated, specific demand that is driven by actual versus projected consumer need (see Figure 1-4).

FIGURE 1-4 ■ **Inspired by the building blocks of sexual connection, the concept and packaging behind Gaultier² cleverly acknowledges gender differences without necessarily defining them. The bottles inside reinforce the notion of invisible attraction through the use of clever magnets—causing the bottles themselves to draw near to each other when placed close together.**

MEGATREND 2:

Humanized Technology—The Quest for Physical and Psychological Perfection

HUMANIZED TECHNOLOGY: THE TREND

This second trend is about technology empowering and serving people, drawing on biological models for inspiration. One cannot remove the human from the science. The focus of this trend is the use of technology to help people live better lives by discovering new ways of reconnecting with their true power and value as human beings. As our understanding of biology has changed as a result of such things as the unraveling of recombinant DNA, gene splicing, the Human Genome Project, and other scientific breakthroughs, so has our perception of what it means to be "natural." Certain technological advances, such as learning how to use ultraviolet light and electromagnetic waves to stimulate an emotional sense of well-being, are already empowering people to live better lives. Take a look at some of the other areas of human perception being researched in order to create a more complete, more satisfied human being. Each and every one has both practical and business implications; in fact, some even may suggest entirely new industries or categories of brands. The following are just a very few of the 20 senses referenced by Sputnik, Inc., that some sources theorize may influence human perception and that have only begun to be addressed by marketers.

- *Infrared.* Long electromagnetic waves can be used to stimulate/balance metabolism.
- *Vomernasal.* Pheromone or sexually specific olfaction is being studied for its function as one's "scent of self," which is the basis of sexual attraction.

Eidetic imagery. Neuroelectrical image retention (memory) is a potential method of improving brand message retention in long-term versus short-term memory.

- *Magnetic-ferromagnetic orientation.* This is our sense of our place in space. Imagine the application to sporting equipment and automobiles.

We are currently entering a brave new world where a new kind of "wellness empowerment" will be available through advances in nanotechnology (despite some of the new controversy regarding it), in probiotic awareness, and in stem cell research—and this empowerment will not be relegated to medicine. The business implications are staggering because they represent opportunities to address need on a level never thought possible. In this new world, many drugs, such as Prozac and Zoloft, are no longer stigmatized but are hailed increasingly for creating solutions and contributing to people's well-being. Viagra has prompted the reclamation of sexuality for the "over 50 crowd." For Sputnik's very interesting take on this veritable smorgasbord of seemingly science-fictive solutions for every possible human need, see the following section entitled "The Beauty of Reality."

EXCLUSIVE TREND AGENCY REPORT

by Sputnik, Inc.

THE BEAUTY OF REALITY

The fountain of youth may no longer be a myth. We have reached a point in time where the worlds of science and science fiction have blurred. What was once seen as magic is now science future—and it has just begun. Today we have "cosmeceuticals," Botox, and human growth hormone injections. We have the convergence of beauty and food, beauty and pharmaceuticals, and tomorrow we enter the biotech age.

What we will be witnessing is the shift from treatments to "solutions." And, as a result, the consumer's expectations of brand promises will be challenged. This consumer will be looking for "products that work," both physiologically and psychologically. These days, the explosive demand for a "perfect" exterior is being joined with the consumer's desire for a "perfect" interior and is moving toward intellectual enhancement or "mental fitness." The new demand will be for "on-demand"—to perform better, to be smarter, to evolve as a species. We are moving beyond a fascination with artificial intelligence (AI) into a drive for *intelligence amplification* (IA). What happens then is that the brain becomes real estate. In our near future, products (i.e., drugs, computers, games, and cosmetics) will be geared toward putting more memory, more brainpower into ourselves.

We will not only have the means to "upgrade" our intellectual prowess, but slowly and steadily as science progresses, we will be given the option to reverse destiny itself. For example, in the future biotech age, cellular therapy, cellular replacement, and nanomedical techniques—cellular-scale robotic surgical devices able to sense and repair tissue with molecular precision—may keep us looking young forever.

Beyond the advancements in beauty and health, nutritional genomics will be the second wave of personalized medicine to come out of the Human Genome Project. Its basic premise: Eat according to your genes. "Nutrigenomics" won't be ready for mass consumption for years, but the potential is great. For one thing, it will usher in truly personalized foods tailored to our individual health and well-being, perhaps replacing our propensity for disease and old age. Could death become old-fashioned? Perhaps it already is.

Capitalizing on the trend just discussed, Herbalife, an international nutritional wellness product company, created energy-drink tablets called Lift Off to maximize performance (see Figure 1-5).

FIGURE 1-5 ■ **Fuel good on demand.**

A trend currently being explored by Genius Insight also fits right along with the concept of humanized technology—the quest for physical perfection. They call this trend "extreme self-determination," and as you read the next section, you will see that it also is very closely related to megatrend 3, everyman empowerment, because it is just as much about the psychology behind the science (i.e., "I have the right and the power to transform myself and my world as I wish") as it is about the enormous capability that science is and will be bringing for self-transformation.

EXCLUSIVE TREND AGENCY REPORT

by Genius Insight

EXTREME SELF-DETERMINATION

Extreme self-determination is the idea that everything about ourselves—how we look and even how we feel—is within our power to change. Within this concept, the individual becomes a product of his or her own deliberate (and ever-changing) choices. It's basically a form of wish fulfillment. This is realized through what we call *transformational tools,* which come in two forms: internal/chemical and external/physical. These tools are characterized by the willful control they provide the individual and their ease of use. These tools enable us to be the people we'd like to be: attractive and free of anxiety, insomnia, depression, and/or sexual dysfunction. Examples of internal/chemical "transformational tools" are marked by the move from disease treatment to "lifestyle" drugs, for example, "nutraceuticals" in everyday products (e.g., waters, meats, vegetables, etc.). This trend is growing because there is no longer a stigma associated to being "medicated." As a result, the old marketing axiom "better living through chemistry" is truer now than ever before. We can see this clearly in two categories of drugs:

- *Mood enhancement.* Depression, anxiety, sleep, exhaustion, hormone replacement
- *Performance enhancement.* Athletic, work/concentration, sexual, incontinence

Science, coupled with cultural acceptance, has driven the demand for transformational tools that focus on external/physical change. Examples include fragrances and cosmetics, of course, but also products and procedures that go further and make more lasting changes, such as Botox, collagen, Retin A, liposuction, and other cosmetic surgeries.

Cosmetic surgery in particular illustrates this trend. It has become part of the mainstream. Our society places a high value on looking young and fit. Today, people of all ages are requesting plastic surgery for cosmetic reasons. This trend is moving to increasingly younger patients and includes more men than ever. It's so much a part of the popular culture that there are successful reality and drama TV shows centered on cosmetic surgery. Increasingly, people are looking for a quick fix, and these tools give us fast answers to profound concerns; they address real needs. The lesson for marketers is that transformation is the name of the game. Marketers need to find ways to enable their customers' desires for fantasy and experimentation. They can provide the means to realize fantasy and enable people to "play" with their self-image, as evidenced by the recent advertising for Rosiblu diamonds created by Badger and Partners (see Figure 1-6).

FIGURE 1-6 ■ According to Madonna Badger of Badger and Partners, "When a woman wears a Rosiblu diamond, she reveals the true, rare beauty that lies within." The campaign featured the provenance line "The Soul of a Diamond" and the tagline "Diamonds Transform You."

HUMANIZED TECHNOLOGY: WHAT IT MEANS FOR BRANDS

Humanistic branding means giving people what they want—if the scent of armpits is soothing to babies, which some research suggests it is (most likely because of the armpit's proximity to mother's milk), then we should create comforting products for them that respond to this natural desire. Brands need to be vigilant about keeping in touch with recent cutting-edge transformational technologies that will help people to reconnect with their essential nature by allowing consumers to experiment with individual "performances of self." For example, advances in color/laser technology to stimulate sensations of well-being and relaxation have found their way into spas. Now this concept of "color therapy" is moving into a variety of mainstream products, such as an innovative new home decor/fashion brand based on esoteric color coding called *Colorstrology* that will be profiled in Secret #4.

Advances in communications technology also will continue to allow brands to customize their offerings and experiences to individual consumers' needs. Overall, technological advances will offer unparalleled opportunities for brands to create more personal and fulfilling brand experiences, fostering stronger emotional consumer bonds. Already in the beauty and fashion industries the enormous progress in microencapsulation technologies has produced many opportunities to create brands that better respond to consumers' customized needs. For example, adidas fragrance and toiletries, licensed by Coty, have, among other things, created concepts for the brand using a now trademarked and patented microencapsulation technology called *Smart Molecule Technology*®, where active ingredients in products can be engaged in response to specific physiologic consumer cues, such as enzymatic shifts, variations in wetness, or temperature shifts. Translation: The more a person perspires, the more active odor-reducing ingredients are released—achieving what was previously considered unachievable, a true, commercially successful manifestation of mass customization.

MEGATREND 3:
EVERYMAN EMPOWERMENT, SELF-CREATION, AND PERSONAL EXPRESSION

EVERYMAN EMPOWERMENT: THE TREND

The everyman empowerment trend is about the heightened desire for individual fulfillment (including sexual fulfillment) and a growing sense of entitlement for personal expression within a social context. The unstoppable phenomenon of reality TV is a great window into this trend because it provides a means for "everyday" people to live fantastic adventures, attain dreams, and explore, test, and develop themselves in every way imaginable. In the public consciousness, there exists a new possibility for the average person to play a heroic role on a mass level and reach celebrity status. This trend follows on the heels of the self-actualization movement through its emphasis on each person's unique potential for self-creation. It is also a new reflection of the celebrity mania phenomenon in our society because celebrities provide a heightened vision for an ultimate level of empowerment, self-creation, and unbridled personal expression.

But even as we continue to adore our chosen celebrities, this trend also means that the definition of celebrity is evolving to include a renewed and strengthened vision of the "everyday hero"—also evidenced by the reverence for the heroism of soldiers, firefighters, and police officers in a post-9/11 world. The advent of celebrity designers and certain brands being viewed as celebrities in their own right is also evidence of this trend. Overall, the trend reflects a deep psychological human need to find manifestations of the archetypal hero of mythic proportions both in oneself and in society at large. This hero not only must represent an archetype but also must add value to a brand given the various drivers of consumption so often unique among varying categories.

Interestingly, while many people credit the exaggerated melodrama of the reality television show *The Apprentice* with its success, the fact is that much of the public is just as fascinated by the mechanics of how products and brands are produced as they are by the "gladiator tone" of such shows. Consumer as creator is a frightening notion to some but may become an influence that marketing will either acknowledge or face the consequences of denying. For example, Gloria Steinem revealed to me in a recent discussion that during the early days of *Ms. Magazine*, when it was still accepting some commercial ads, the magazine featured a letter from one of its readers who recommended that women mix sunscreen products with moisturizing products, since sunscreen was still uncommon, but the danger of skin cancer was becoming clear. This public cry for a need-based product versus an imposed fabricated demand brand predated commercial introduction of products based on the identical benefit. If only the persons marketing skin care products to women at the time had been reading *Ms. Magazine* and actually listening to women's needs and respected their understanding of their own desires/needs, perhaps businesses could have profitably launched products women really wanted and simultaneously accelerated a new category and padded their own financial bottom lines.

A very important contributor to this book and the provider of the art for its jacket is Karim Rashid, arguably one of today's most acclaimed product designers and host of the television show *Made in America*. Not just another reality show, this program literally requires contestants to create products that address a variety of needs. It may supply ready-made, consumer-provided solutions to product and brand questions that our predecessors, the predecessors who didn't read *Ms. Magazine*, overlooked.

In the following section, Sputnik, Inc., shows us how the everyman empowerment trend is leading each one of us to become an "artist, image-maker, storyteller, director, and creator" through a plethora of new media that are seamlessly interwoven into our everyday lives more and more.

EXCLUSIVE TREND AGENCY REPORT

by Sputnik, Inc.

CONSUMER *IS* CREATOR, USER *IS* CONTENT

The nature of capitalism is changing. What we are moving into is the knowledge economy—from an economy driven by the production of tangible things to one driven by intangible ideas. Economists say that commercial products are best treated as though they were services. It's not what you sell your customers; it's what you do for them. It's not what something is; it's what is connected to what it does. One common example of this idea is the notion of *open source,* meaning that messages, stories, and narratives are never-ending and structurally Mobius. What started with Linux and Red Hat and revolutionized the music industry with MP3 file sharing is swiftly sweeping the world. And now of late we see the push of corporate giants such as IBM to boldly declare, "The Future is Open."

The *metagame,* an actual game being continuously created as we speak, is a metaphor for the creative influence shaping future brands and advertising. It is open-ended and open-source "play," the game of the game, a game in which the player extends the life of the game indefinitely, introducing subtexts and evolved variations resulting from the interaction of its virtual connection of consumer "brand owners." It satisfies our desire to feel connected, to participate, to create. Living among digital networks, the metagame usually is based on a continuing collaborative narrative—the metastory or metanarrative. A *metanarrative* refers to an all-encompassing story or philosophy that may be accepted as a universal truth, if only by a specific group. These tales generally have one thing in common: They all hold out what is believed to be a truth—with the same stories being told over and over but in different words—based on the context and individual lives of the persons telling the stories. Examples of this phenomenon can be found in everything from Marxism to Christianity. And interestingly enough, as *truth* becomes an increasingly important word within the lexicon of brand vocabulary, truth also takes on additional meaning.

Once run by government, religion, and big business, the metanarratives are now made by the individual within a community. A trend in the worlds of fiction, performance art, and independent films, the metanarrative is more than a subtext—it is a story that doesn't end. Like the campfires of our ancestors, the Internet and wireless networks are the arena in which we now gather.

Open source can be viewed as the precursor of the metagame, the game of the game. Beyond connection, information, and socialization, the Internet (and most of our digital devices) has provided consumers, the users, with the power to create the tools to play. Products provide the "toys," but it is the consumer who, in playing with them, is creating the experience. Mass culture has become the producer, the "story," the "program." The digital wireless networks are becoming a global "theater." The consumer is now the creator; the user is the content. Think about the telephone. When it was invented, the telephone was the talk of the town. Very quickly, however, it became the consumers' conversations with one another that replaced the novelty of the device. The telephone merely transmits the messages the consumer wants to transmit and hear.

Author's Note: Today's audience isn't listening at all—it is participating. In fact, *audience* is as antique a marketing term as *record* or *LP.* Why? Life is media. With every minute of our life immersed in some form of media, culture today wants to be engaged, not assaulted. The words *viewer* and *user* also will become antiquated. Instead, each new "user" within a network will be an artist, image-maker, storyteller, director, and creator. One example of this is the success of podcasts.

E-mediated entertainment of every nature will become the center not only of commerce but also of most brand communications, including marketing and advertising. As David Yakir of Yakir Group Communications and former senior executive at Young & Rubicam

advises: "The future is not about entertaining branding, pure sponsorship, or product placement. Consumers and brands will forge something new, something more appropriately labeled branded entertainment."

THE EVERYMAN EMPOWERMENT TREND: WHAT IT MEANS FOR BRANDS

Instead of being seen as static, controlled "intellectual property" belonging to corporations, brands will need to be viewed as cultural property that belongs fully to consumers. Brands will need to become more malleable so that they can respond to consumers' growing appetites for personal expression. In short, this means brands must practice collaborative branding. *Collaborative branding* is already a term that is beginning to surface in marketing. Unfortunately, for the most part, it still refers only to methods of gaining more accurate consumer insight in order to better further commercial goals, not what I refer to as a consumer performance of self.

Real collaborative branding, as I define it, is a partnership of equals where the consumer plays an active role in brand creation. Ultimately, technology and an empowered consumer will make this form of collaborative branding an everyday reality. To begin to practice collaborative branding, brands must create mechanisms by which the consumer plays a very powerful role in brand and product creation and messages, and the brand simply responds to the consumer's desires as style and pleasure "provider." This includes providing ways to make the actual physical reality of the product more malleable to the consumer and intimately customizable.

Two interesting examples of this are Jurgen Mayer's Heat Seat and the Avo phone. The high-tech Heat Seat is a sofa designed with material that is heat sensitive and takes on the imprint of the sitter's body so that the actual look and "branded design" of the product are created by the consumer himself or herself. The Avo phone, designed by Fuseproject, is an avocado-shaped phone that has a soft elastometric outer coating that actually conforms to the shape of the user's hand and, in time, adapts to it.

In what follows, you will see several more unique examples of the concept of performance of self.

EXCLUSIVE TREND AGENCY REPORT

by GDR Creative Intelligence

PERFORMANCE OF SELF

Current thinking holds that brand marketing of the future will be characterized largely by customization of product, experience, and environment. GDR sees a parallel here with what Martin Lindstrom calls the "Me Branding Proposition" in his book *Brand Sense.*[2] From Nike's online shoe design to Jones Soda Cola's personalized labels on fizzy drinks (www.jonessoda.com), everyone wants individualized products designed to his or her own specs. In the same vein, brands increasingly will help customers to avoid choice overload by offering "designer selections." GDR predicts that the technology-driven dressing rooms of the future (which in various forms already exist) will show you only clothes that suit your body shape and coloring. Take, for example, the "innovative communication experience."

The Innovative Communication Experience (ICE) (www.store-age.nl, www.f-w-d.com)

Amsterdam-based design firm Storeage has set up a joint venture with other forward-thinking agencies LUST and T.A.P.E. to "push the grand experience forward through the development, creation, and execution of new media retail solutions designed to empower the user."

One of the venture's collaborative projects allows users to try clothes on virtually and learn about the features and benefits of products. Visitors stand in front of a projection screen and view

themselves in a mirror beyond. Using the full-motion interactive system, they can bring up products, resize and reposition them, see other items in the range, or change the background to show themselves in various surroundings. The interface is integrated with a physical clothing rack, which stocks one of each item. Handling the item triggers the system to display that item on the screen (see Figure 1-7).

FIGURE 1-7 ■ The future of shopping is here. This technology scans customers' images and both selects products appropriate for their physiques and depicts their images in those products so that the customers see themselves as others do.

Another very interesting phenomenon related to the everyman empowerment megatrend is the movement toward "ethnic ambiguity," discussed in the following section by Genius Insight. This trend gives evidence for a growing acceptance of all races—truly an empowerment of "every man" in the literal sense and a further demonstration of the increasing consumer demand for choice in every aspect of life.

EXCLUSIVE TREND AGENCY REPORT

by Genius Insight

EMBRACING ETHNIC AMBIGUITY

Increasingly, the world embraces ethnic ambiguity and the adoption of cross-racial, cross-cultural attitudes. Prompted in part by the desire for self-transformation and in part by the reality of an increase in multiracial families, individuals of mixed or ambiguous heritage are celebrated and highly visible today. According to the U.S. Census, the number of people self-defining as "other race" or "more than one race" is the fastest-growing "ethnic" group among people age 35 and under. Mostly this increase is due to a larger number of interracial marriages and relationships resulting in children of mixed ethnicity since the 1970s. Regardless of how they classify themselves for census purposes, many young people de facto transcend race, at least when it comes to music and fashion, where racial lines no longer rigorously define tastes.

For celebrities, transcending traditional ethnic roles and stereotypes allows them to increase their "hip factor" by taking on music, language, fashion, hair, or makeup typically associated with a different racial group. In some cases it makes them more accessible and perhaps even less threatening. Of course, this also allows the stars to cast a wider net for potential fans.

Here are just a few of the icons who successfully ride this wave of ambiguity:

- *Gwen Stefani.* A white musical artist with alternative/rock roots, she is savvy in adopting elements of hip-hop and African-American culture in her clothing, fashion, and makeup.
- *Halle Berry.* An actress of mixed (black and white) parents, she identifies as African American but clearly has benefited from her crossover appeal.

- *Jennifer Lopez.* New York–born and Puerto Rican, she has leveraged her versatile looks to draw a large and diverse fan base.
- *Johnny Depp.* The actor often refers to his Cherokee ancestry, which he has said he welcomes, as adding another twist to an already somewhat mysterious image.
- *Tiger Woods.* Aggressively claiming a mixed ethnic heritage (black, European, and Filipino), the golfer alienated many African Americans but gained points with middle-class white golf fans and sponsors.

Another phenomenon associated with the lessening importance of race is the popularity of nonwhite celebrities. While this is nothing new for athletes or music artists, it is a recent trend for actors. Data from Genius Insight shows that in 2005, seven black actors (Will Smith, Bill Cosby, Denzel Washington, Eddie Murphy, Halle Berry, Samuel L. Jackson, and Chris Rock) were in the top 20 most popular celebrities for whites aged 13 to 49 years—and this trend is even more marked among teens.

Most people would argue that despite the tragic, often racially and religiously related conflicts we face, in general, a shift toward greater tolerance and, indeed, cross-cultural and cross-racial appreciation is happening. The world is not all doom and gloom. And this brings me to our next trend.

MEGATREND 4: The Luxury of Ethics

THE LUXURY OF ETHICS: THE TREND

This trend is about the increased importance of ethical ideals and how a sense of well-being on a spiritual and moral level has become the ultimate luxury in our society—more valued than any achievement on a material or practical level. This growing sense that ethics and opulence are not mutually exclusive ideas is truly the future of luxury. When the ultimate luxury is focused on spiritual well-being, then we have reached the pinnacle of Maslow's famed hierarchy of human needs. The pyramid, beginning at the wide base or bottom, shows how when once a person's basic material needs are met, he or she moves farther and farther up the pyramid, turning his or her attention increasingly to higher aspirations and the search for meaning on a spiritual level.

The idea is that given the fact that many elements of our postindustrial society are now reaching a solid level of material achievement, people in affluent countries are seeking greater fulfillment through an exploration of their own spiritual potential and through doing good for others. Developing one's spiritual potential means being fully human, which, ultimately, is tomorrow's measure of a luxury brand.

Among other things, this trend is evidenced by the current obsession with sustainability and environmental issues, the insistence on organic everything (and now the move to "biodynamism," a sustainable system of farming described as "beyond organic"), and a focus on "guilt-free indulgence" evidenced by consumers' demand for increased levels of corporate social and ethical responsibility. Beyond the politics, though, it has become just plain trendy to be ethical. A recent article in *Modern Brides,* for example, discusses how people no longer want gifts at their weddings. The ultimate status symbol is to create a "charity registry" and have people donate to a cause in the couple's name. This new practice has trickled down from celebrity weddings to the average person's nuptials.

This touches on a major part of this trend—the advent of what has been described by Sputnik, Inc., and others as the "glamorous green" phenomenon. Ecofriendly products have pervaded every aspect of life—and have become *de rigueur* for trendsetters—especially among the younger generations, who are clearly asking for "green" brands whether it be in their fashions, cars, or cell phones. Relevant brands—either new or existing—must demonstrate sustainability and, above all, be guilt-free. Who of us wants to pay good money to acquire a product, brand, or service saddled with guilt? Guilt you can get for free. From the red-carpet mind-set of hybrid luxury automobiles to the explosion of hemp-based clothing, sustainable, recyclable products are not just a fashion but a cultural marker, a symbol of an evolved, modern lifestyle. For more on this, check out the following section.

EXCLUSIVE TREND AGENCY REPORT

by Sputnik, Inc.

GLAMOROUS GREEN: MORE AESTHETICS, MORE ETHICS

The glamorous green movement began with the trend toward well-being. Unlike the 1970s or the early 1990s, organic food, holistic healing, and even herbal supplements now are considered the desire of the elite. Well-being has become both an industry and a mind-set. It marks a paradigm shift as culture has altered its perception of what it means to be "alive"—and how to live. As a result, health and wellness are now a consumer industry, as mainstream culture has turned its energy toward self-preservation. Case in point: The market for "natural" and "organic" skin care, hair care, and cosmetics products is expected to grow 50 percent, reaching $5.8 billion by 2008, according to the U.S. Market for Natural Personal Care Products. A key insight to understand is that the need for well-being coexists with the age-old desire for indulgence and luxury—guilt-free indulgence. The glamorous green movement has given birth to the ecocentric consumer who sees glamorous green products as a sign of status, a badge of intelligence, and a symbol of an "evolved" personality. The ecocentric consumer demands luxury products that are expensive but not pretentious, luxurious but

wholesome, products and experiences that are "light," sustainable, and guilt-free. Businesses with a green directive are attracting seed money from venture capitalists.

One example is the new startup company Revolution, the latest gig of Stephen M. Case, the Internet icon who built America Online. Believing that wellness will move from the elite to the mainstream in the next two decades, Case founded Revolution as a private holding company that will invest in health care, wellness, and hospitality. From the music phenomenon Cows With Guns, MTV's *Trippin,* green celebrities (i.e., Cameron Diaz, Leonardo DiCaprio, and Brad Pitt), yoga on JetBlue airline flights to red-carpet hybrid cars showcased during the past Academy Awards shows, glamorous green already has gone mass media. With the downfall of Enron and the advent of open-source economies, there is a demand for more aesthetics and ethics, a global movement to spend on brands that promote a feeling of "lightness" (guilt-free consumption). The cultural desire is to feel weightless, to achieve a "lightness" of being. Unlike the activist "ethics only" movement of the 1960s, this new demand will expect brands to deliver a high level of artistic, creative content, as well as an ethical message to the marketplace.

Industry is already taking note. Once known as British Petroleum for its U.S. expansion, the company rebranded itself as BP, or "beyond petroleum," with a bright sunflower logo. Another example is the "ecoimagination" advertising campaign by General Electric. While GE is credited with producing the first fuel-cell-based electrical power system for NASA in the 1960s, it has been importing auto brands that have been paving the way for a hydrogen economy, beginning with the introduction of the hybrid engine (first brought to the U.S. market in 1997 by Toyota in the Prius model). Lexus, Porsche, and Honda have since introduced luxury hybrid models. Beyond proliferation of the new energy economy, there are other natural and elegant technologies that not only will fuel our buildings and light our cities but also will restore and rebuild our bodies. The use of natural light and sunlight is becoming a new form of complementary therapy; sound frequencies and water are other energy sources that are being used for medicinal and healing purposes. The understanding of "more aesthetics, more ethics" is becoming inherent in many industries today. Besides the use of lighter materials, fabrics, and colors, the idea is to be sustainable, either in the development of elegant technology or in the life cycle of your product and service. Products with a life cycle have neither a beginning nor an end. The life cycle has been predetermined before manufacturing. The materials not only are typically lightweight but also are biodegradable. Biodegradable products are the key to the future of light design. These products emulate the smooth, non-wasteful processes of nature: Nothing lost, nothing wasted. One example is Motorola's cellular phone casing made of a biodegradable polymer, which comes with an embedded sunflower seed. Developed with researchers from the University of Warwick and PVAXX Research & Development, Ltd., the casing degrades in the compost and releases the seed from its viewable capsule. John Deere has developed a line of tractor trailers that are made of biodegradable soy-resin material that can be buried in the ground once the engine is removed.

Another example is nanotechnology. In one quick swoop, nanotechnology will flip the entire understanding of manufacturing upside down. Nanotechnology is the ability to construct products atom by atom very quickly through billions of simultaneous actions with no waste at all. Nanotechnology is an elegant technology that is sustainable and light. It is used to build widespread commercial products and is estimated to be common by 2020. The possibilities of nanotechnology are endless; entirely new classes of incredibly strong, extremely light, and environmentally benign materials could be constructed.

For now, the key in branding is to understand the "seventh generation" mind-set—an altruistic long view emerging from today's eco-centric baby boomer consumers who desire to invest in companies that are mindful of future generations and the future of the planet.

THE LUXURY OF ETHICS: WHAT IT MEANS FOR BRANDS

This trend signals completion of the shift from an emphasis on tangible benefits to a focus on intangible benefits. There is truly no place for cookie-cutter demographic profiling in the marketing of the new millennium; it is all about psychographics and now perhaps something entirely new—soul-supportive branding.

Brands legitimately can step into this new emotional territory and become people's partners in their search for meaning as long as they are rooted in the real desires and dreams of consumers. And I use the word *partner* deliberately—because it may include partnering with consumers in their spiritual quests, not to be confused with trying to lead them anywhere or trying to supplant the quest by becoming some kind of pseudoreligious icon. A brand should never become a graven image. If it does, it has gone too far.

People want most of all to star in their own dramas, their own journeys. Under the most evolved conditions, brands can become badges of honor that reflect an entire way of life and a humanistic philosophy that embraces people in a holistic manner. Brands have the capability of providing direct access to creating a better, albeit branded, world.

Of course, along with the increased importance of the role brands can and will play in people's lives comes an enormous increase in the necessity for corporate responsibility. This is a perspective that supports the notion that, as Henry Ford put it, "A company that produces nothing but profits is not a success." It is crucial (and even more profitable in the long run) to become a useful part of the community and contribute something positive to people's lives. The concepts of doing well and doing good are no longer mutually exclusive. Brands should take advantage of being on the cutting edge of the green trend or any other obvious cultural shift and move now. Later, it will just be a "bandwagon" move—which has the potential of being perceived as disingenuous and forced.

This phenomenon is evidenced in many current branding and advertising campaigns. Look at the automobile industry. From hybrid cars to hydrogen fuel cells, we are seeing a sweeping movement toward greener alternatives. Hybrids, although still a fraction of auto production, are expected to double in sales in 2005 from 2004, and Thousand Oaks, a California-based consultancy technology research group, estimates that by 2010, the hybrid market will be as strong as the minivan market.[3]

This trend also is evidenced in the growing reaction against economic/commercial imperialism and the success of certain brands in creating an "antibrand" stance, such as American Apparel, the "sweatshop-free, brand-free" fashion company. The luxury of the ethics movement also has been the powerful force behind galvanizing celebrities to participate in commercial endeavors on a level previously unheard of on the condition that the brands involved are associated with charitable causes. Nicole Kidman was one of the first to take this step in the Mercedes-Benz breast cancer campaign she endorsed—and the list just keeps getting longer.

Today, shopping for a cause has become one of America's favorite new pastimes. There are pop-up stores, such as Target's temporary store in Times Square to benefit breast cancer (with all-pink merchandise), and a plethora of high-end charity shopping events, such as the "Shop in the Name of Love" event, an exclusive four-day shopping extravaganza featuring fashion, home, and spa products generously donated by top designers and manufacturers in fashion, home design, and beauty, with honorees such as Jessica Lange, Sean Combs, and Nicole Miller. In the end, it is perhaps our deepening desire for wellness and reconnection with our essential nature seen in megatrend 2 that lays the foundation for ethical brand collaboration.

In the next section, GDR takes us on an interesting tour of manifestations of what it calls "balanced commerce," featuring some very smart responses to the desire of consumers for both ethical and exciting, fascinating brands.

EXCLUSIVE TREND AGENCY REPORT

by GDR Creative Intelligence

BALANCED COMMERCE

Balance seems to be what's missing in many Western consumers' lives. Many are preoccupied with the work-life balance, calorific input versus output, materiality versus spirituality, and the dreaded environmental consequences of failure to live in balance with nature. Guilt needs to be assuaged, and retailers that make an effort to right some of the imbalances most people feel powerless to affect will win serious consumer brownie points. Here are some examples:

Casa Camper (www.casacamper.com)

Camper is an environmentally aware shoe retailer. Its success worldwide has led to two brand extensions: FoodBall Café, which sells rice balls in biodegradable wrappers, and Casa Camper Hotel, in Barcelona, Spain. The brand profile is "Useful Shoes, Healthy Food, Friendly Shelter." The hotel blends harmoniously into the city, announcing itself with microsignage. Bikes are available for rent from the lobby, water is recycled and heated by solar energy, and prices are kept low (under 100 euros) despite the availability of free hot and cold snacks and the unusual provision of two rooms separated by a corridor for each guest, one for sleeping and one for lounging (see Figure 1-8).

FIGURE 1-8 ■ The Casa Camper hotel adds new dimensions to the word *hospitality* with its eco- and consumer-friendly attitude.

Progreso (www.gravenimages.co.uk)

Oxfam and the United Kingdom's largest independent coffee roaster, Matthew Algie, recently launched a chain of fair-trade coffee shops in the United Kingdom designed by British design consultancy Graven Images. Coffee grower cooperatives will own 25 percent of the shares in the venture, Oxfam will own 50 percent, and 25 percent will be held in trust for projects in the wider coffee grower community. The strap line for the cafés is "Without Coffee, There Is No Tomorrow," which can be taken more or less literally depending on which side of the economic divide you're on. In the United Kingdom, the sale of fairly traded products from People Tree clothing (www.ptree.co.uk) to fair-trade food grew by a staggering 52 percent in 2004. There is no question that green and fair-trade credentials soon will be the minimum requirement for brands to have credibility with a large proportion of consumers (see Figure 1-9).

FIGURE 1-9 ■ Progreso wakes up consumers to a more socially responsible world.

Emarat Reverse-Vending Unit (www.circle-design.co.uk)

The United Arab Emirates (UAE) generates the highest levels of consumption and per-capita waste in the world. The Emarat Oil Company, owned by the UAE government, takes its commitment to the environment seriously, and the company has worked with London-based consultancy Circle Design to develop the reverse vending concept. The unit sits on gas station forecourts, and users deposit plastic, glass, and aluminum cans. The machines automatically identify and sort the waste and print a voucher with an appropriate redemption, from drink and meal coupons to tickets for T-shirts, caps, bags, and pens, to be redeemed in the gas station's convenience store. The machines are in air-conditioned booths so that customers can be comfortable as they do their bit for the environment, and the ad space on the exterior of the unit makes a profit for Emarat (see Figure 1-10). Win-win certainly is possible.

FIGURE 1-10 ■ This recycling center gives users immediate gratification by instantly giving them credit for recycling.

OPPOSITES ATTRACT:

TREND FLIPPING FOR A NEW POINT OF VIEW

Letting culture lead in brand creation does not mean that, as marketers, we must become slaves to trends. This is not at all what I mean by my premise that in the consumer-empowered future we will become "style providers." Style providing merely refers to our providing alternative "styles" to consumers, allowing them to choose which style best reflects their own. The terms *style provider* and *style enabler,* for me, imply the very same thing. It's an academic point, and what matters is the result.

As style providers or style enablers, we must have a point of view about what is happening in our culture. We need to provide, as a part of brand style, a creative interpretation of what the world is telling us. And this means understanding as deeply as possible what's going on in culture and creating our own unique embodiment/reflection of it within the context of our specific fields.

It also means that we need to have the vision and courage to go beyond the trends we see and provide alternative interpretations of the trends. Remember, for every cultural movement, there is an opposing cultural opportunity. The green trend doesn't speak to Hummer lovers. And Red Bull and Jolt are expressions of countertrends to the wellness craze.

For an example of this creed of contradiction, as viewed from an aesthetic/conceptual perspective, take a look at two current opposing aesthetic and lifestyle trends, "sharp" and "warm," outlined by Li Edelkoort in the following section.

EXCLUSIVE TREND AGENCY REPORT

by Li Edelkoort

WARM AND SHARP

Warm. Seeking out a natural, organic harmony and development, we dream about tropical materials, dark wood, and basket work; of exuberant colors, tropical birds, and butterflies; and of an abundance of fruit and opulent blooms.

Motifs are bright and exotic, whereas the creative consumer is honored and adored, inspiring embroidered fashions, do-it-yourself projects, hand-painted ceramics, and pattern on pattern on pattern! Our meals are concocted using ingredients from all four corners of the globe, which we mix, stir-fry, blend, or grind. Bathing takes on a ritualistic notion, with sensual interiors and botanical fragrances in this quest for paradise.

We see makeup that helps us to imitate insects and animals, inspired also by the flesh elements of foods and the passion of succulent flowers.

Sharp. After the comfort of the lounge movement, we seek a more daring kind of assertiveness in order to reestablish a grip on the various facets of life. We are looking for rules within a continuously changing world, taking life into our own hands and searching for control.

This sharp perspective inspires new forms, such as the cut surfaces of diamonds, the perfect triangles of pyramids, and the angular plating of armor. We are in search of the perfect garment, from crisp shirts to flawless suiting and accessories, pinpointing design with select choices in the luxury end of the market. Makeup and fragrance take on a power status, assertively applied like a weapon. We also find a passion for the extreme not only through strong

alcoholic drinks such as vodkas and liqueurs but also, for example, in bitter chocolate.

MULTIPLE DIMENSIONS OF REALITY: WHERE WE'RE HEADED FROM HERE

One last overarching concept to consider is the ongoing influence of what I call *multiple dimensions of reality.* This is the idea that there is no one set reality. Reality today is fluid. Reality is not only transformable, according to our own individual wishes, but it is also openly "manufactured" through amazing new technologies that allow us to play with our notions of reality. We see the growing power of the media (rightly or wrongly) to manufacture trends and events. And as the consumer-as-creator phenomenon grows and people become increasingly technologically enabled and empowered, manufactured reality not only will be accepted but also will be embraced.

For example, some people have decided to experience the "reality" of a cultural fantasy that never was real to begin with—as in the case of the reality show *Return to Gilligan's Island,* a television show where people live out the premise of the fictional show in real life, suggesting that at times the divide between people will be felt more keenly than ever before. Different generations and different social groups will have, in effect, different realities based on their individual fantasies and personal histories/life experiences.

But don't dismay. You need only respond to one trend or one antitrend and one reality at a time. The final chapter of this book will demonstrate how easy reacting to this seemingly overwhelming, almost chaotic consumer anarchy can be and how it may signal renewed opportunity versus the death of brands. I look at the preceding trends whenever I make a decision regarding strategy or creative execution and have created my own rating system, checking off the number of cultural bull's eyes I may have hit. The more I connect with real lives, the more confident I am in the decisions I make. You can do this too. I will show you how.

SECRET #2

BE REAL

DANCE TO A COLLABORATIVE RHYTHM

> **Rhythm is one of the principal translators between dream and reality. Rhythm might be described as, to the world of sound, what light is to the world of sight. It shapes and gives new meaning.**
>
> *—Edith Sitwell, "The Canticle of the Rose"*

INTRODUCTION:

Rediscovering the Joy of Marketing

I often use the metaphor of dance to describe marketing. Dance is so intimate and revealing. It is a shared reaction to rhythm, which transforms movement into art. If the cultural shifts described in Secret #1 define the rhythms of today's consumers, then we as marketers must allow those rhythms to lead us and, when necessary, tell us when to dip and where to grind. In this new environment where consumer-based culture leads, brands inherently will need to assume a humanistic vision and become based on collaborative, need-based marketing strategies—strategies grounded in consumer respect.

One of the best examples of a brand created through real understanding and respect for the consumer is the label created by the legendary Arnold Scaasi, a veritable pioneer in the area of consumer-centric customized fashion. His love of women and his genuine interest in who they are and who they want to be drove and continue to drive his brand. He creates reflections of women as they, themselves, would be seen. He has enabled some of the most famous women in recent history to define themselves, dressing everyone from Joan Crawford, Mamie Eisenhower, Elizabeth Taylor, Barbra Streisand, and Aretha Franklin to Hillary Rodham Clinton, to name but a few.

The "Scaasi method," which has been applied to some of the most famous and infamous women of recent history, begins with a genuine, kind, objective appraisal of the woman's existing beauty. Scaasi's resulting overlay of style is completely consumer-centric, meaning that he creates for the specific woman. The woman does not exist to flatter his creations. When first working with Joan Crawford, Scaasi asked her to undress so that a complete set of measurements could be taken. He discovered that she had unusually broad shoulders, and rather than "correct" this flaw, he and other designers recognized it as an asset. Shoulder pads were born—influencing the fashion of an entire era.

This type of approach remains a part of his unique style—predating the alleged Dove "discovery" of feminine diversity and nontraditional beauty. Scaasi and brilliant designers of all types create designs to glorify consumers—not to disguise or remind them of their imperfections. The notion was clearly communicated in a series of ads running through much of the 1980s, the now-classic "Me and my Scaasi" campaign, where Scaasi was depicted admiring the center-stage beauty of a famous woman wearing one of his creations. The woman, not the brand, commands the focus. "Me and my Scaasi" presaged a brilliant formula that, in the advertising business—a business notorious for continually recycling formulas—unfortunately has not been copied nearly enough (see Figure 2-1).

FIGURE 2-1 ■ Me and my Scaasi: Diahann Carroll, the epitome of glamour, takes center stage during a time, not so very long ago, when glamour was still part of a "whites only" world. Ms. Carroll and Arnold Scaasi challenged that notion.

As we move forward, consumers—through technology and their purchasing power—will drive the creation and evolution of brands—and enable breakthroughs of their own. If a brand or celebrity does not satisfy a consumer's needs or enable his or her chosen values and lifestyle, the consumer will spontaneously invent new brands that do and will mercilessly obliterate culturally irrelevant ones. Of course, this means that as traditions of good taste, bad taste, humor, and entertainment evolve, so too, if need be, will brand communication be "forced" into submission. If you're feeling somewhat threatened, take heart. This emerging dynamic will make your role more important than ever before. You will become the keeper of dreams and the instrument enabling the realization of hope, of the satisfaction of desire. You will do more than merely market. You will be part of consumers' reinvention of the world.

The convergence of media and the rapid merging of entertainment with every element of our daily lives, along with major leaps in direct brand-to-consumer connective technology, now allow even the faintest voices to be heard. If you are wise, you will listen to those voices. For example, just look at the commercialization of all things organic. As the "tree hugger" green wave began to swell, many marketers took credit for inventing or evolving products and brands to address the once pejoratively labeled "nuts and twigs" consumer. This same consumer has been whispering his or her desire softly for decades—with the voice most often falling on deaf ears.

The fact is that these new tree-hugger-friendly brands or existing-brand evolutions rightly should be attributed directly to those patient consumers who made their demands known. In fact, the Four Seasons Hotels' ecofriendly practices are no longer a mark of differentiation but a sign of intelligence. The well-heeled Four Seasons clientele takes for granted that a premium hotel naturally would behave in an environmentally friendly, sustainable way. Frankly, from toothpaste (think Tom's of Maine) to designer tank tops, the same consumer's demand soon not only will be desired but also will be completely expected.

Because a collaborative branding approach is based on working with the consumer as an active participant early in the process and requires continually obtaining permission at each consumer contact point, it is noninvasive, humanistic, and even loving (not just brand loving but people loving). It is also highly effective because it is dynamic and intimately responsive to people's desires. In the end, I think that it has the potential to bring the joy back to marketing.

Regardless of what you do in marketing and its related fields, this new challenge will be one of cultural accountability, and it will require some stretch and effort. How will we address the cultural challenge? Certainly not by merely remixing variations of the old. But it may not be as difficult or mysterious as you think. We will need finally to break free of the focus-group hoax and collectively build a better cultural barometer that is tolerant of chaos and the terrifying notion of nonlinear strategy. While many of us already admit it, the focus group, as we have come to know it, is something akin to the emperor's unacknowledged nakedness in the children's tale *The Emperor's New Clothes*. Focus groups are not, nor have they ever been, real measures of culture. Now is the time in marketing when we all, at every level, finally must grow up. Maturity often involves allowing ourselves to become vulnerable and to some extent to abdicate what we thought was power, what we thought could be measured.

In this chapter we will discuss how to boldly leap beyond the focus group and get closer to seeing what's really happening in people's day-to-day lives. We will look at case studies including some of the newest and most exciting alternative methods of connecting with consumers, such as virtual salons. But most of all, this chapter will explore inspirational examples of how some brands are rediscovering the path back to marketing joy—joy for consumers as well as joy for those behind the creation of brands. We will look at some of the interesting and often very simple ways that brands have achieved an authentic reflection of their consumers' lives, exploring some of the most creative and successful product-development concepts/approaches, as well as some of the latest and most innovative examples of how to involve/reflect consumers.

Using examples from my experiences at Coty (without turning this book into my expanded résumé), I will show you how the infusion of an "entertainment-expanded" self-definition and philosophy has yielded some very impressive results and has led to the hugely successful fragrance franchises associated with such stars as Celine Dion, Sarah Jessica Parker, Jennifer Lopez, David Beckham, Kimora Lee and Russell Simmons's Baby Phat and Phat Farm, Shania Twain, and many others. Of course, harnessing a celebrity name is not the only or even the best way to make a brand part of the "entertainment economy." Celebrity association is not a panacea for instant brand awareness—or even the most expedient or legitimate inspiration for modern brand creation. The method of integrating entertainment methods and icons is only one tool, and like any other marketing tool, it only works within the context of cultural and category relevance.

I will discuss exactly how to assess and, most important, achieve greater levels of cultural relevance through a methodology I call *culture casting*—where cues are extrapolated from culture for brand enrichment. One recent example of culture casting and collaborative branding can be seen in how Madonna, a true master of intelligent marketing as evidenced by her success in adapting to culture and even reinventing herself in the wake (actually prewake) of cultural shifts, is testing her product, her music, with consumers in a natural environment before she produces the final cut. She recently arranged to have 20 or so of her songs—music only, no lyrics—played in the hottest nightclubs in Paris, London, and Ibiza, and she videotaped the response. She then chose the 10 songs that drew the largest and most enthusiastic crowd of dancers to the floor for her next CD. This is how many of tomorrow's most meaningful brands will be born. They will be created either in the image of or directly by the consumer as precise reflections of what the consumer loves most.

BRAND INVASION! BUT WHERE IS THE WAR?

Brands today are truly everywhere—but what kinds of connections are they really making with people? We know that consumers are now bombarded with choices. They are advertising veterans, inundated with up to 1,500 pitches a day! "Consumers are like roaches," said Jonathan Bond and Richard Kirschenbaum in their 1998 book, *Under the Radar: Talking to Today's Cynical Consumer.*[1] "We spray them with marketing, and for a time it works. . . . Then, inevitably, they develop immunity, a resistance."

Spraying poison is not the answer. First, because it's unethical. Second, because it is clearly no longer working. (Partially, I suspect, because human beings neither are nor ever have been roaches! The comparison itself is obscene.) Rather than bombarding consumers with ads or conducting "stealth attacks," we should be engaging and supporting consumers in multifaceted ways that touch every aspect of their lives. Nowhere is this more apparent than with the young. Nearly half of all American college students today have taken marketing courses, and they "know the enemy" extremely well.

But herein lies a great opportunity. I believe that although there is cynicism among young consumers, there is also a growing fascination with brands and marketing. This is a large part of why television shows such as *The Apprentice* and *Made in America* have met with success. People love the behind-the-scenes look at brand creation. This growing awareness and curiosity can be a real advantage to marketers if they can find interesting ways to invite consumers to actually become part of the creative process. This is what a collaborative branding approach is all about.

The difference between collaborative branding and traditional marketing is that it does not have an "us versus them" mentality. A truly collaborative branding strategy does not target, which sounds more like a big-game-hunting term; rather, it provides satisfaction to human needs. Collaborative branding discovers, delights, and satisfies.

Let's face it, the war is over! The consumer won. It's time to move on to reconstruction.

THOSE WHO EMPOWER CUSTOMERS:

WELCOMING A NEW GENERATION OF "BRAND CURATORS"

"Viral marketing" has the potential to be powerful because it can create the kind of excitement that results from a truly "shared cultural event." However, instead of attempting to virally "infect consumers with a disease," the collaborative branding approach is about offering exciting ideas to empowered consumers with free will. This can result in something I call *spontaneous marketing,* which is based on a "nonpredatory lifestyle or value affinity." This means that brands become embedded into people's activities and natural lifestyle affinity clusters. No matter how seemingly mundane, these clusters express the consumers' values and chosen ways of life. This eventually can allow for osmotic, organic cocreation of brands or revitalization of existing ones.

Take, for example, the new restaurant opened in New York by previous employees of Windows on the World, the restaurant formerly on top of one of the towers of the World Trade Center. United in their unwillingness to be crushed, these new owner/operators have collaborated to create an employee-owned restaurant called Colors. Each employee/owner is contributing one recipe from his or her family/culture, and these recipes will make up the menu. This is an example of "consumer as creator" *par excellence.*

We see this kind of lifestyle affinity in the passionate "brand clubs" formed around some brands, such as the much-talked-about Harley-Davidson aficionados or Oprah's book club. These brands are readily adopted by consumers as beloved expressions of their beliefs and aspirations.

What I find most interesting is that viral marketing actually has become a natural, expected part of our society and culture—sometimes with consumer collaboration, sometimes like the flu. Most persons have, at some point, participated in a grassroots promotion of some type via e-mail and have had a first-hand, positive experience with a grassroots or guerrilla marketing event—despite the manipulative, contrived format of some of these efforts.

To this day, I still run into people who attended those Jose Cuervo Tequila promotions I helped to organize in the 1980s. These promotions, which first brought tequila into the limelight (so to speak) as a drink and made the brand an icon, became iconic in and of themselves. As mentioned in the Introduction, Jose Cuervo Tequila was one of the first brands to think of sponsoring volleyball matches on the beach in southern California, even though beach volleyball had been part of the laid-back body-beautiful culture of southern California for decades. We created an opportunity for a direct consumer interaction in a fun environment, and our sponsored matches became a veritable cultural institution. Today, beach volleyball is an officially sanctioned Olympic sport, and Jose Cuervo Tequila, for many consumers, continues to remain supreme in its category.

The lesson here is simple: Brands need to learn how to integrate themselves better into popular culture (maybe even unpopular culture) so that they can become a part of powerful movements. Think about how the independent movie *What the Bleep Do We Know?* was so cleverly—and simply—promoted through e-mail and the organization of volunteer "street teams" in communities across America. This cheap, easy promotion worked so well that it became known as "the little film that could," as people began requesting that it be shown in their local cinemas, and this unusual, completely "anti-Hollywood" movie about quantum physics and deep spiritual questions regarding the meaning of life became an underground hit. It almost seems that today anyone with a few clever ideas can become an ace marketer through the power of technology. Of course, the most important element in all this is the product or brand—there has to be a culturally relevant brand that galvanizes people on an emotional level and connects to their lives in a real way for this spontaneous "brand explosion" to occur. And you guessed it, this requirement begins and ends with the consumer.

What I am saying is that to build and continue to strengthen great brands in the twenty-first century, you need more than clever grassroots promotions and cutting-edge, hip guerrilla marketing programs, more than brand loyalty programs that leverage a powerful lifestyle connection with consumers. You need more than a brand strategy based on building a brand's emotional equity. You need *all* these things—and more. You need to become a real, integral part of consumers' lives—a culturally evolved, *holistic* reflection of their physical, intellectual, and emotional worlds.

The dynamic "living brands" marketing strategy is the method and the medium through which a brand is brought to life—always in collaboration with the consumer—and it always should be based on a respect for consumer culture and existing need. This, I believe, is the only way to "harness" the power of *collaborative branding, the precursor to a living brand.*

CONSUMER CONNECT: ETHNOGRAPHY AND THE LOST ART OF SCHMOOZING

Over the past several years, ethnography has played an increasingly important role in our quest to break free of the focus-group mold and better understand the attitudes and behavior of consumers. While certainly not a foolproof approach, done correctly, ethnography can bring us closer to the kind of authenticity we are seeking because it studies consumers in natural settings, where they use products and services. This allows us to determine consumer attitudes about the products and the general activity (such as the attitude that "shaving is a hassle")—as well as nifty little hidden (and often surprising) facts concerning how products actually are used in real life.

In recent years, companies have assigned teams of researchers to document consumers (usually with video cameras) as they cook, shop, eat, clean house, shower, drive, and sleep. We have pried into diaries (to record attitudes and behaviors), conducted ethnographic interviews, and asked consumers to express their feelings and ideas through techniques such as building collages or creating their own videos. The idea behind all this is to create an intimate, face-to-face contact with consumers that not only will capture their behaviors but also will uncover their motivations and emotions and the contextual factors behind their behaviors.

The agency Ogilvy & Mather, for example, has a dedicated unit within strategic planning called "The Discovery Group" that successfully uses a video ethnography methodology in which members of the unit "live with" individual consumers (or business-to-business [B2B] targets as needed) for a given period, recording whatever transpires with a video camera to create a holistic picture of consumers' lives.

Bill Abrams, founder of the New York ethnographic consultancy Housecalls and author of *The Observational Research Handbook: Understanding How Consumers Live with Your Product,* agrees with this one-on-one approach, saying: "Knowing the individual consumer on an intimate basis has become a necessity. And ethnography is the intimate connection to the consumer."[2] One of the recent success stories of Housecalls is how the company created a new positioning and advertising strategy for Kodak's single-use cameras. Through observing how 18- through 24-year-olds relate to and use single-use cameras, the company identified the phenomenon of the "group camera," and this was the genesis for the "Pass Along" TV campaign that celebrated the fun that can be had by sharing these cameras with a group of friends.

The point here is that we get a chance to see how people actually use brands, products, or services in natural environments—and that is invaluable. Why? Because what we see consumers do is often quite different from what we hear them say—either because they cannot remember or because people sometimes do not tell the complete truth (including a few too many opinionated focus group moderators).

"Whereas focus groups often work in artificial settings for short periods, ethnography situates consumers within the larger social and cultural context," explains Donna M. Romeo, Ph.D., an in-house corporate anthropologist at Whirlpool. Ethnography looks not for opinions but for a 360-degree understanding of how a product might resonate with a consumer's daily life. For instance, Whirlpool recently asked Romeo to conduct a study for a line of luxury jetted bathtubs. Using a sample of 15 families from four different markets, Romeo conducted in-home interviews and filmed participants while they soaked. She also asked them to respond by creating a journal of images to such questions as, "When you think of your tub, what images come to mind?" What emerged was a consumer picture of bathing as "a transformative experience," says Romeo. "It's like getting in touch with the divine for 15 minutes. Those learnings—the emotional, cultural, symbolic meanings—are quite powerful." They also validated Whirlpool's working concept and name for the luxury tub—*Cielo,* meaning "celestial" or "heavenly" in Italian and Spanish.[3]

The real power of ethnography, however, lies at the front end of product development. Because every time a new product is developed, we have an opportunity for a new window into the consumer's reality and a new opportunity to reinvent not only the product but also the relationship, both conceptually and experientially, in relation to a newly forged shared reality. When I helped to position for adidas its aluminum-free deodorant for women that had cotton as an ingredient, it was based on the simple observation that cotton is a part of women's intimate health routine (i.e., tampons) and would be an added-value ingredient with a high trust factor for women.

Schick also clearly was paying attention to the daily discomfort and awkwardness most women face when they attempt to shave their legs in the shower (fumbling with slippery soap or the application of shaving gels and foams while bending over to reach their legs) when it created the Intuition razor for women, which has a soap attachment that surrounds the blade so that the razor lathers and shaves all together in one quick, easy motion.

The beauty of ethnographic methodology, says Patti Sunderland, an anthropologist and partner in B/R/S Group's Chicago office, is that it's inductive rather than deductive. "Part of the idea of going into peoples' homes or wherever it is that a product is important," she explains, "is that you're discovering from them what the meaningful categories are." Toothpaste marketing, for example, used to be about fighting cavities and whitening teeth. But ethnographic research found that consumers' concepts and concerns had changed, explains Sunderland. "People are really concerned with gums, their tongue—the whole mouth," she says. "When they're putting the toothbrush in their mouth, it's not just cavities that they're interested in anymore." Toothpastes such as Colgate Total, which purports to "continue to work even after you stop brushing," are designed to appeal to this broader concept of dental care. Meanwhile, in the face of all this research indicating that consumers want whitening toothpastes and much, much more, Procter & Gamble didn't think that even the whitening element was all that necessary, and the company ignored it. When Colgate jumped on this opportunity with the global launch of Colgate Total and its many brand extensions, the company overtook Crest's market position. Crest is now playing catch-up as a result of not listening to consumers.

But perhaps today P&G has truly learned its lesson. Recently, Crest let consumers decide what their new flavor of toothpaste would be—surprisingly, consumers chose lemon. Not a predictable choice and not one most marketers ever would have guessed. Overall, P&G seems to be undergoing a dramatic change in philosophy, perhaps owing to the consumer-centric approach of its new CEO, A. G. Lafley. The company, long famed for its rigid marketing techniques and product-development philosophy, where products were created first and foremost in the lab and then marketed based mostly on technical features (e.g., laundry detergent that will remove stains, etc.), is now finding its way into women's homes in order to watch what they do there—cleaning, caring for children, putting on makeup—first hand.

"We discovered that women don't care about our technology, and they couldn't care less what machine a product is made on," Mr. Lafley told P&G executives in Caracas during a recent tour of Latin America. "They want to hear that we understand them." In an effort to do just that, Mr. Lafley himself follows women shoppers around stores asking them questions and has begun personally visiting the homes of 10 to 15 women a year around the world to get a more intimate view of their daily lives and to learn how they use various products. So far he has found it very enlightening. Spending time with a young housewife in Caracas, he learned that browsing through her Avon catalogue in the evenings searching for beauty products is a valuable form of entertainment for her—and he deduces that perhaps this is one reason why Avon is the market leader there. Through similar initiatives, P&G has created smart consumer-sensitive initiatives such as the idea of packaging the extremely successful new Pearl Tampons in noncrinkle plastic so that teenage girls can open them in a bathroom stall at school without anyone knowing. Is this consumer-centric approach working? The numbers speak for themselves. Since Mr. Lafley took over, P&G's stock price has more than doubled. The company's earnings have increased, on average, 17 percent a year since he became CEO, to $6.5 billion in the most recent fiscal year, which ended June 30, 2004.[4]

Apart from visiting consumers in their homes, what are some other creative ways to learn about consumers? One of the best I've heard about is how Jeanine Recckio, beauty futurologist and CEO of Mirror Mirror Imagination Group, hosts slumber parties for teens in order to research their habits, attitudes, and preferences around fragrances and cosmetics. She rents large hotel rooms, supplies music, food, and lots of products, and sits back on the sidelines for hours to observe how the girls interact with the different products. A simple, intuitive approach perhaps? Brilliant? Definitely!

Another example is how Avon's recent initiative, "Girl Talk," demonstrated tremendous savvy not only by creating a platform to solicit consumers' opinions about a collection of soon-to-be-launched products but also by providing a forum for consumers to talk directly to each other openly about the products. Based on the belief that women respond better to beauty advice from other real women than from a celebrity, Avon created the "Girl Talk" platform via the normally static medium of magazines to engender a conversation between reader and product. "As a child, women remember the Avon Lady, this real woman coming into the house and connecting about beauty," says Janice Spector, vice president of global advertising for Avon. "Girl Talk" was an articulation of that relationship. The idea was for real women to become Avon's beauty experts, or "Avon Mavens." MediaVest ran ads in publications such as *Glamour, O,* and *Lucky* asking women to test the new products, promising to print their responses. The ads received a phenomenal 10,000 responses.[5]

There is no replacement for one-on-one interaction with consumers—which more and more will need to take the form of actual collaboration. In the following section, Kim Hastreiter, editor-in-chief of *Paper* magazine, tells us about her secret for staying in touch with the street trends and culture of a younger, ever-morphing generation.

(UN)COVERING TRENDS

by Kim Hastreiter, Editor-in-Chief, *Paper* magazine

I have been coediting and publishing *Paper* (www.papermag.com), a magazine that has built a reputation on (un)covering the most cutting-edge art, fashion, entertainment, and pop cultural trends. It has always been my job to present the newest, hottest, and most below-the-radar information authentically and on point. As a 50-year-old, I would never presume to know what a 21-year-old hipster-skateboarder would listen to on his or her iPod. And so I make sure that I surround myself with the most interesting young kids I can find and invite them to talk about what they are into on our pages. Even if I'm not sure I understand what they are saying, I trust my own instincts enough to trust that they know what they are talking about. It's all about that trust. A great editor finds great people and then trusts them to articulate what they know about.

This is the problem with corporations. There are so many layers put between what is authentic and what that eventually morphs into (something often unrecognizable). And there is so little trust in youth. Nothing is trusted until it's already been proven. This is no

way to stay ahead of the curve. To me, good marketing is about great instinct, fearlessness, and trust. And not diddling with a good idea. Keep it simple, stupid.

THE INTERNET AT ITS BEST: A LIGHTENING-FAST WEB OF CONNECTIONS

When it just isn't possible to have all those smart, trendy, and otherwise inspirational people in your actual office or to visit consumers' homes in person, today's technology can offer us new opportunities to be in touch with what's happening in people's lives on an unprecedented global level. Sputnik, Inc., has created a "virtual salon," recruiting cultural leaders, scientists, artists, business people, designers, and students from around the world as "correspondents" to participate in discussions on various topics. From this virtual salon, the company extracts threads of ideas that seem to be repeated in order to determine global trends. Of course, the Internet vastly increases the global range of the people the company is able to reach to discuss issues. These vibrant discussions include everyone from graffiti artists to distinguished scientists, resulting in an ongoing publication called *Mindtrends*—a cultural reflection and summary used by select businesses around the world.

Genius Insight, another agency featured in Secret #1, specializes in using elaborate electronic voting systems to elicit consumers' quick feedback for brand communications and the various phases of product development, such as determining design and color, the naming process, and packaging design. The company has created an online "focus group" of over 2,000 dedicated members to give immediate responses to a packaging design, for example. The power of the immense number of votes that can be collected quickly is astonishing and truly can result in a democratic brand that has been "voted into existence" by the people. These kinds of online voting booths are great for immediate "yes or no" determinations about specific questions: Red or green for the packaging? Nicole Kidman or Charlize Theron for the movie?

Genius Insight also has created what it calls the *StarPower Report*, which is a consensus of data collected from the company's ongoing queries of a huge database for quantitative responses about brands, celebrities, sports figures, and more. This gives a quantitative model for both brand and celebrity value based purely on consumer perceptions/affinity for certain specific celebrities and brands relative to specific psychographic groups. These "likability" ratings of celebrities or brands can show such things as which celebrity from a list conveys more masculine qualities or what brand of sneaker is most loved by teens.

Brands are rated by votes so that they can be ranked democratically and quantitatively according to how they are perceived by different groups of people. This, I believe, is the only true, objective measure of a brand or basis of a new brand's competitive benchmark. Certainly, technology will offer us increasingly better ways to answer these types of questions, but as yet we have only begun to scratch the surface. It is amusing to me, for example, that marketers are now beginning to turn to Internet blogs as the new "eureka" in consumer insight, yet rarely do they take the time to just sit back and watch the world go by.

Many agencies have been trying to learn how to "pan for gold" (i.e., valuable information about consumers) among the plethora of existing blogs with varying degrees of success. Some even hail "blog watch" (or eavesdropping, really) as the ultimate focus group because opinions are unfiltered and honest, and the nature of the content is often undirected stream of consciousness, which can give surprising new insight. Of course, there's no question that capturing unfiltered blogs specifically about your brand and written by your desired consumers is a million times better than the information gleaned from focus groups. For example, U.S. Cellular recently used blog watching to try to reach college kids with a successful ad campaign promoting its new calling plan. The company hired the youth-focused agency G Whiz to listen (using linguistic analysis) to a cell-related blog. G Whiz learned that what bothered these kids the most was unwanted calls eating up their minutes. When they reached the point of using up all their minutes near the end of the month, they had to shut off their phones, and the result was a sense of isolation from friends. U.S. Cellular then was able to craft its spots to address these specific themes.

While "electronic eavesdropping" hardly can be said to further an intimate relationship between brands and consumers, this sort of research perhaps does have its place in terms of achieving a basic level of authenticity. As these initiatives become more and more commonplace, however, it will be important to remember their limitations—and potential pitfalls. Case in point: Some brands even have infiltrated blogs with fake "brand bloggers" (much like those undercover guerrilla brand promoters on the street) in a desperate attempt to win over consumers, only to find that consumers became livid when the truth was revealed. For example, when Dr. Pepper recruited young bloggers to write online about a new product, the company drew widespread condemnation from its target audience. Mazda also was heavily criticized for creating fake blogs with "viral videos" that were sent out to people by a fictional blogger. The ethics of cultural intrusion are complicated and no doubt will be a subject of controversy now and in the foreseeable future.

INSTINCT AIN'T ALWAYS EASY:

KEY LESSONS ABOUT UNDERSTANDING CUSTOMER ASPIRATIONS

Everyone today is looking for a "silver-bullet methodology" for developing an ongoing understanding of our fast-changing culture and translating that understanding into actionable brand concepts. The truth is, though, that of course there is no silver bullet. In fact, as consumers move into a more participatory role of brand collaboration/creation and as they increasingly influence the evolution of the media, it will become more apparent what consumers want on an individual case-by-case basis because they will be involved in the process and in direct versus indirect communication with brands. In pursuit of this collaborative relationship, we have to continue to work hard to connect with consumers—from many different angles, using all our many different tools, and always remembering that just as in any relationship, the objective is to try to stay close and keep consumers happy. Take a look, for example, at the very ingenious methodology PUBLIC Restaurant in New York has developed to initiate an ongoing dialogue with its customers.

PUBLIC RESTAURANT: A PUBLIC DISPLAY OF CONSUMER AND CULTURAL AFFECTION

AvroKO, the cutting-edge architecture, design, and concept group, created PUBLIC Restaurant in New York City based on the concept of 1960s public utilities, complete with authentic fixtures from post offices and multiple details such as Camay-like soaps in the bathrooms (imitations of the artifacts of 1960s hotel visits), that combines to create a fun, multisensory ambiance that aptly reflects the culture of that time, as remembered and projected today. It is the

projected reality of something that is no longer real. It is perhaps better than the reality that was. It is superreality. It is genius.

Included in the dining experience is an actual mailbox program to both encourage the frequency of guest visits and to promote a direct dialogue between the chef of the restaurant and its patrons. Specialty condiments, wines, and all sorts of personalized gastronomic treats are personally selected by the chef, often reflecting local products and even introducing other local businesses—including unique value-added access to those businesses and their wares or services. In an era marked by both overstimulation and, ironically, high levels of increased isolation, this intimate dialogue becomes a vehicle of human closeness and a source of continual surprise. True to the notion of preserving the spirit of a beloved time, a comfortingly vintage library catalogue is a veritable time capsule of previous shared experiences at the restaurant, including an archive of menus and memories.

In addition to representing the concept behind the restaurant, the information in the archive can be used to influence catering options and tasting menus. It imbeds the consumer within the legacy of the restaurant, the brand. Guests can even shape the PUBLIC experience with others by arranging in advance for their (the consumers') guests to enjoy a personal favorite menu item and/or receive access to a mailbox with a secret key, just waiting to be opened. Members also receive special invitations to PUBLIC events and private tastings and coupons from a variety of other nearby local community businesses and culturally inspired events (see Figure 2-2).

FIGURE 2-2 ■ "You've got mail" takes on new meaning at PUBLIC Restaurant when combined with the idea of a brand biosphere.

ADDRESSING OUR PERCEPTIONS: WHAT IS THE LESSON LEARNED?

We must bridge the gap between what we think we know about the consumer and consumer culture and the reality of that culture as it relates to brands and brand messages. Before we begin, however, we must address our perceptions of what we think we can do individually and what we have the potential of achieving collaboratively. Think about it. This is the only way people will fall in love with your brand—it has to become a reflection of something already meaningful to them. Your brand must befriend culture, clad in its own fully developed, rich personality that could not exist without the influence of the consumer's tailoring.

A great example of this is how Absolut has created, through its innovative branding programs, a witty, playful, and constantly relevant personality based on its uncanny continuous cultural relevance. It is never the same and always the same. The famed long-running Absolut campaign, based on using the Absolut bottle as an inspirational centerpiece for artistic expression, exemplifies the concept of bringing a brand to life through culture. The Absolut brand personality has, in fact, become such a noted part of popular culture that artists such as Versace and Keith Haring have used the campaign as inspiration for their own "Absolut creations." What is so great about this is that it occurred organically as the branding became a part of the cultural landscape. As Goran Lundquist, president of Absolut, says, "Consumers drink the ads as much as they drink the vodka."[6]

In searching for cultural icons, your net must be cast wide to include celebrities, places, music, art, events, other brands, and specific experiences. Again, just look at the choices for the Absolut campaigns—everything from Andy Warhol to the noted graphic designer Jennifer Sterling, particularly well known for her ingenious integration of typography and design to create a new language of expression.

The rainbow-striped "Absolut Pride" ad for gay and lesbian consumers is another proof of the brand's commitment to ongoing cultural dialogue. Initially groundbreaking, the ad campaign, along with ongoing initiatives such as the "Absolut Out" promotions at gay pride events, now has become an established part of culture. Why? Because the ads reflect culture. They do not attempt to create it.

Another great example of what I am talking about is Cadillac's recent use of a Led Zeppelin song in its ads. For many of us men in our 40s, the idea of owning a Cadillac and becoming a rock star are parallel dreams. As younger men, we lived in an era when advancing our careers made us envious of our more rebellious brothers. We may have been earning MBAs, but very few among us did not dream of becoming rock stars rather than CEOs. Hence, in a brilliant move, Cadillac's agency, AWE, combined the music of Led Zeppelin with an accompanying promotion and musical backdrop in an advertisement for Cadillac, one of the few American luxury cars. The results were spectacular. Sales grew by 500 percent!

This really brings us back to the evolution of luxury. Because Cadillac really looked deeply into the hearts of consumers, it realized that one aspect of luxury is the fact that freedom and rebellion are part of today's definition of luxury. Certainly there are those cultural purists who might claim that the use of iconic musical references, such as the use of Iggy Pop's "Lust for Life" by Carnival Cruises or Quest cell phone's use of the Beatles' classic "Got to Get You into My Life," somehow disrespects the art.

I would ask those persons: Isn't art supposed to evoke emotion? And isn't positive emotion relevant within the context of even the most mundane human activities? Lucky enough to pose the question of whether or not his music, his face, his anything would be diminished were it to be used commercially, Nikki Sixx of Mötley Crüe fame (or infamy, depending on your point of view) summed it up perfectly: "When art, any art, is expressed in context, staying true to itself, bringing pleasure or personal expression into somebody's life, then yeah, it's real. It is authentic." When asked if he would endorse a brand, license his name, or allow the use of one of his songs, he replied, "Like I said, if it's part of something real to my fans, then it's real by me. Then it's good. No, then it's great."

Being on trend, however, is not always enough. In addition to being on trend, we also have to be able to see beyond the current trends and anticipate future trends. This is where the going gets rough and where real talent lies. George Lois is one of the very few marketers whose work always has provided a clear demonstration of a visionary genius. He has, after all, among many other brilliant coups, been credited with salvaging *USA Today,* rescuing ESPN, taking Xerox advertising directly to the consumer, and creating the concept of Lean Cuisine, which literally forced Stouffer's to create a breakthrough line of gourmet diet frozen foods. His thinking was (and is) far more modern than that of most of the 20-something consumer intelligence and/or creative "gurus" prancing around offices today. For example, take a look at the following section to see how—in a spectacular *tour de force* of collaborative branding well before its time—he saved (and created, really) MTV as a brand.

GEORGE LOIS TO THE RESCUE OF ROCK AND ROLL: THE "I WANT MY MTV!" CAMPAIGN

It's hard to believe today, but after its first year of operations, MTV was an abject failure. A 24-hour rock 'n' roll channel? The 2,000 people at the cable convention that announced MTV literally laughed the Warner American Express honchos off the stage. Music publishers insisted that the MTV concept could kill their business. Record companies swore that they would never produce music videos. Advertisers considered it a joke. Ad agency experts snickered. Cable operators scoffed. A fledgling concept faced crib death. Despite an introductory period of advertising, MTV was a total wipeout.

After a zero year, the whiz kids at MTV asked advertising legend George Lois to do an emergency "trade" campaign to change the

minds of the cable operators of America, most of whom believed that kids who rocked were into sex and drugs. But Lois had a better idea, the "big idea"—to go right to the rock-loving audience and shove MTV down the rock-hating cable operators' throats with his clarion call, "I want my MTV," delivered, hopefully, by a rock superstar. Guerrilla warfare at its nastiest. The young execs at MTV told Lois that rock artists thought that MTV was a bad idea and would never deliver his punch line, but the intrepid ad man convinced Mick Jagger to do so.

The clincher in each commercial was this windup sequence as a voice-over proclaims:

> *If you don't get MTV where you live, call your cable operator and say [then a quick cut to Mick Jagger, who bellows into a telephone] "I want my MTV!"*

"I want my MTV" ignited a firestorm of popular demand for MTV within minutes after the commercials ran in each market. In each city, thousands called moments after viewing the commercial and screamed for their MTV! Within months, MTV was in 80 percent of all households, record companies begged to have their videos on the channel, advertisers looked at MTV as a must-buy for viewers aged 14 to 28, and every rock star in the world pleaded with MTV to mimic Mick Jagger's plea in Lois's follow-up commercials. They flew to New York and lined up to go on film: David Bowie, Pete Townshend, Stevie Nicks, Lionel Richie, Madonna, Sting, Michael Jackson, and every other rock star who wanted to explode his or her record sales. Six months after the start of the campaign, *Time* magazine called MTV "the most spectacular pop culture phenomenon since the advent of cable television and, arguably, since the invention of the tube itself." Now owned by Viacom, MTV Networks is a financial powerhouse, among the most profitable companies in the world (see Figure 2-3).

FIGURE 2-3 ■ **Give them what they want already. The campaign for "I want my MTV" marked the beginning of a consumer-led revolution.**

Lois's MTV coup proves that drawing consumers into a dialogue/participatory relationship about a brand is the most powerful achievement of any branding initiative. But how exactly do we draw them in?

As marketers, we shouldn't forget either that cultural attitudes sometimes can be played with to create a very interesting, dynamic dialogue with consumers. One of the things this means is that companies can work with culture even if it includes playing on stereotypes. In fact, it's actually okay to be politically incorrect as long as the consumer is in on the joke and understands the cultural implications—the point is to create a dialogue. Culture is constantly changing around its perceptions of what is "politically incorrect"—suddenly, for example, since the popularity of the cable show *Queer Eye for the Straight Guy*, it is fine to use the word *queer*, but for a long time it was not okay unless you were part of the gay community. A brilliant execution of this concept is a campaign Jim Feldman created for the diamond industry, which he explains in the following section.

BLONDE DIAMONDS: REDEFINING A CATEGORY (AND A STEREOTYPE)

by Jim Feldman, Jim Feldman Creative Design

We at Jim Feldman Creative Design pioneered a movement in diamond jewelry advertising that clarifies and defines personal style versus conventional, traditional definitions of luxury. This is an idea we brought with us from other work we had done in jewelry and metals (gold notably) and from our work in fashion, cosmetics, and fragrances. When a client specializing in yellow diamonds came to us wanting to brand and market its stones, we saw a way to apply the idea of personal style and individual expression to the company's jewelry.

The very slim market for yellow diamonds consisted of women who were older than bridal age (35 and up), leaders in taste rather than followers, well informed, and with the financial means to act on their desires. While the client wanted us to market yellow diamonds to the bridal market, we saw a far greater opportunity, which was to let women of this segment know that they had another possibility to define their style with something truly rare and beautiful. As is everyone, we were aware of the cultural currency of being blonde and how for ages blonde has been force-fed as the standard of beauty to the American consumer. Not every woman can be blonde, although many try and many fail miserably. But give women the possibility to possess "blondeness," and you have another equation altogether. So we recommended to our client that rather than just brand their yellow diamond jewelry, we rename the category along the lines of calling copies "Xeroxes" and tissues "Kleenex." Ergo, "Blonde Diamonds," which conveys not only the nature of the stone but the idea of a certain glamour as well.

Knowing that the majority of Americans are increasingly anything but blonde, we built the campaign around "Portrait of a Blonde." The only blondes in sight are the stones; the models are all dark-haired and not typical. We wanted to speak to the real woman who will see the ad, not some fake version that is a product of advertising. We continued the campaign with "New Blonde in Town," "Meet a Natural Blonde," and "Blonde Becomes Her." The tagline for the brand is: "For the woman who lives life in color" (see Figure 2-4).

FIGURE 2-4 ■ Louis Glick brings a fantasy to reality with this "Meet a Natural Blonde" campaign.

Another fabulous example of a playful, intelligent twist on the blonde stereotype is a direct-to-consumer advertising campaign executed by the Paris-based ad agency Brune. This campaign was quite radical because it branded itself, thus soliciting consumers to intercede on their behalf with prospective clients. Brune understands the power of today's consumer. The spot—which played off a double entendre of the agency's name Brune and *brune,* the French word for "brunette"—was set up to be a sort of insider's practical joke. The TV commercial featured two receptionists: a blonde and a brunette. When the phone rings and the caller asks if this is "Brune," the blonde receptionist answers by saying, "No, I am not a brunette, I'm blonde. You have the wrong number," and then hangs up. Finally, after several calls, the brunette receptionist takes the phone, rolling her eyes, and says, "Yes, this is Brune. How may I help you?"

Following a direct-appeal entertainment model, the agency's credibility and a company's connectedness to consumers were reinforced by a direct alliance between an agency and consumers—the ultimate consumers of the client's product—by advertising directly to consumers and creating a buzz around the agency. Because its own strategy worked for Brune, potential clients were reassured that Brune's creative sensibility provided what consumers wanted—dialogue and shared wit between equals (see Figure 2-5).

FIGURE 2-5 ■ The advertising agency Brune has more fun, as seen in this still from its television commercial targeted at the end consumer rather than its potential client base.

STAYING TRUE TO YOUR ROOTS: THE POWER OF SIMPLICITY IN A COMPLICATED WORLD

Ketel One is another example of a brand that has looked to truly understand and satisfy existing consumer desire as opposed to trying to create artificial demand. This brand's personal approach, its advertising, choice of media, and long-term brand integrity all reinforce the major tenets of what define a modern brand. Think about it—an ad, without a model, minus hype, that promotes a superpremium product? Heresy, you say? With its quirky campaign that addresses consumers directly with intimate statements and questions, Ketel One has managed to do something truly unique in an extremely competitive category and challenge the current category norm—all flash and no substance. The company took a very "in your face," honest approach and directed its message toward an audience of one.

Ketel One, a brand that is over 300 years old, is a prime example of the type of brand integrity that defies the notion of what marketing textbooks define as brand life cycle. Ketel One remains relevant owing largely to its product quality (appealing to a growing expectation of perfection in products) and its intimacy, as reflected in its simple, yet highly sophisticated advertising. As you will see in the following section, rather than apologizing for the brand's lack of hype, in a brilliant move, M&C Saatchi's Ketel One campaign exaggerated it. William L. Eldien, president of Nolet Spirits U.S.A., gave M&C Saatchi one very specific challenge—to sound real and reflect the dignified, precious, yet playful brand experience. As Mr. Eldien puts it, "Discovery marketing has been the cornerstone of success for Ketel One. By making a connection with the consumer, Ketel One is able to create a dialogue with its consumers and be an active part of their decision-making process."

KETEL ONE'S NO FRILLS ADS: TALKING STRAIGHT TO THE CONSUMER

by Jason Riley, Account Supervisor, M&C Saatchi, Santa Monica

Perhaps one of the most profound cultural shifts of the past decade, at least as far as marketers are concerned, is the "luxflation" phenomenon. "Luxflation," a term coined, I believe, by Pamela Danziger in her terrific book *Why People Buy Things They Don't Need*[7] refers to the proliferation of luxury goods and services throughout our culture as the masses have looked to trade up in almost every aspect of their lives. Indeed, it was not so long ago that a $4 cup of coffee would have seemed a laughable extravagance, when heated leather seats in a Korean car would have seemed patently ridiculous, and when the very idea of a national chain of all-organic grocery stores would have seemed like sheer madness.

Yet advances in manufacturing and distribution have made quality goods easier and less expensive to produce and get to market. Globalization has helped to spread those quality goods to and from every corner of the earth; if you can make a quality good, somewhere in the world there is a market for it. Quality simply isn't a differentiator anymore; it's a prerequisite.

The aging of the baby boomer generation has given rise to a massive class of consumers with more disposable income than any generation before them. And while we may not all be able to afford the best of everything, almost all of us can afford the best of something, and what that something is tends to, for better or worse, determine our sense of place and self. Where am I if not on an Ethan Allen sofa? If not in a Hummer SUV? Who am I if not a Whole Foods shopper? If not a Starbucks drinker? We are becoming the sum of our brands, and perhaps more significantly from a marketer's perspective, they the sum of us.

Our brand, Ketel One, and the rise of ultrapremium vodkas in general are an excellent example. By definition, vodka is a colorless, odorless, and tasteless distilled spirit; the average consumer would be hard pressed to identify any vodka by taste. Yet Ketel One sold almost 1.5 million cases of its product last year. So what are all those Ketel One drinkers buying, then? Most would say that Ketel One is the smoothest vodka in the world, that it has the cleanest finish, that it has the best taste. In other words, most would cite some practical reason for their choice. But most ultrapremium vodkas are relatively good products, and for most people, vodka doesn't really taste like anything anyway, right?

The reason, of course, is the brand. Ketel One began as a very small imported vodka brand from Holland; no one had heard of it because it wasn't advertised, it cost a bit more than the rest of the bottles on the shelf, and the bartender insisted that it was a lot better than what everyone else was drinking. And so the brand grew, simply by word of mouth. One person telling a friend about this brand of vodka that they'd discovered all on their own, about the secret to actually enjoying (as opposed to tolerating) a martini, about this quirky brand with the funny bottle that no one else knew about. Of course, a lot of effort went into getting Ketel One into a position to be discovered—through a process we call "discovery marketing." But in the end, the success of Ketel One has been about a group of consumers with a bit more disposable income than most discovering for themselves a product that is in fact a bit better than most.

In a very real way, then, the Ketel One brand is practically formed from nothing but its drinkers; it is an amalgam of the entire lot of us. And I think that this may be true of a lot of brands. Any bartender will tell you that we drink what we drink because of what it says about us, because our choice of cocktail, our choice of jeans, our choice of perfume, our choice of carpeting, or our choice of charcoal grill defines who we are and what we believe both for our peers and for ourselves, at least for a time. A brand choice, then, either will include us or exclude us from a set of groups within a category; it's a bit like joining a club. When you drink Ketel One, you are a Ketel One drinker, forsaking (however temporarily) all other identities for the perceived benefits of affiliation with this group of people, these Ketel One drinkers: leaders and connoisseurs, eccentrics and rebels, confident and cool. It's a lot for a drink order, I'll grant you; but for most of us, these are less conscious decisions than unconscious reactions to the constant stream of input we receive from friends and family, from popular culture at large, and of course, from marketing and advertising.

So how do we advertise a brand like this? Better put, how do we advertise a brand like this without undermining everything that it stands for? We can answer part of this by looking in part at the category—full of brands staking claims to taste, or to image, or to sex, or to heritage—and in part at our brand and what made it a success in the first place. Leaving the competitive discussion aside, except to say that it was important to do something different, the key seemed to be to create a campaign that was as true to the birth of the brand as possible. Our success always has been founded in the idea of one-on-one communication, that human relationships are those that are most important and thus those that are the most influential to us. And so this is the genesis of the "Dear Ketel One Drinker" campaign; personifying the brand and speaking directly to *our* drinkers (see Figure 2-6).

The results, as one might imagine, have been polarizing: You either love it, or you hate it. But you know it's there, and in advertising, that's half the battle. And the fact is that

Dear Ketel One Drinker
Thank you.

FIGURE 2-6 ■ The honesty of this Ketel One ad cuts through the clutter of consumer-expected hype.

we're not for everyone; we're different. For a group of followers, the advertising may be a turn-off; for our group of leaders, that's exactly what they love about it.

KEEPING IT REAL: REAL BRANDS FOR REAL PEOPLE

In this "everyman empowerment" environment, it is clear that our notions of heroism and stardom have expanded to include the common man. The concept of the everyday hero is well expressed in a veritable landslide of recent ad campaigns featuring "real people." Using real people in branding efforts is a way to bring the brand to life on a more intimate level and to "share (or even give over) the hero spotlight"—traditionally reserved for the brand—with the consumer. This follows the everyman empowerment trend outlined in Secret #1 in terms of how it will demand that as marketers we change our approach radically to a new mind-set. Instead of attempting to take center stage, brands today need to establish themselves as props and stage sets for the consumer's performance of self.

The Dove campaign described in the following section has been discussed to death. However, it's worth revisiting. It's "breakthrough honesty" is both a model and a chastisement. We all should feel fairly stupid for not admitting and reflecting what we all knew was and has been true forever.

DOVE GETS "REAL"

Dove's "Campaign for Real Beauty," created by O&M Chicago, is a great example of using real people in a campaign for positive social effect. This now much-celebrated campaign used real women as models to convey an ideal of "natural," uncontrived, universal beau-

ty and to challenge traditional notions of perfect beauty by featuring a diverse group of women and, more recently, girls. The ads were a hit when aired during the Super Bowl.

The campaign attempted to involve consumers in a discussion of controversial issues of self-esteem and body image with a Web site set up to be a global forum for women to voice their personal opinions about beauty. Visitors are encouraged to vote for whether they believe Merlin, a 45-year-old artist with silver hair, is just "gray" or "gorgeous" and to join discussions taking place concurrently in different countries. The campaign's overall goal was to combat low self-esteem around body issues in women.

In 2002 Dove conducted an internal study on self-esteem in women, and the result revealed that 50 percent of women said that their bodies disgusted them. Dove also reviewed two other pieces of research: the "U.K. Teen Body Image Survey" (January 2004), which showed that 6 out of 10 girls think that they'd "be happier if they were thinner," and the British Medical Association study (2000), which showed that the body fat of models and actresses portrayed in the media is at least 10 percent less than that of healthy women. Shortly after this review, Dove established the Dove Self-Esteem Fund to support a myriad of worldwide initiatives to help educate and inspire girls on a wider definition of beauty. The Dove Self-Esteem Fund has established such programs as "Body Talk Workshops" in England, where schools across the country host workshops designed to help young girls (and boys) understand and deal with feelings about their physical appearance and learn how "ideal" images of beauty are created.

Apple was one of the first to use the stories of real people to bring its brand to life. The brand has long led a successful campaign using real people as a convincing and personal way to tell peoples' stories about why they converted from being PC users to Mac users. Apple recruits people from e-mails and letters it receives, printing the full text of their "testimonial" e-mails on the Web site. It is a perfect approach for the brand that tries to embody the concept of "humanized technology."

Yahoo! created an innovative campaign around real people for its Yahoo! Personals by conducting photo shoots that illustrated the personalities of the people chosen from the Yahoo! ads in the course of their daily lives. For the campaign participants, it was, of course, a fantastic opportunity to attain a great deal of visibility and attract dates. The company developed the campaign with promotional and media events that mimicked a reality TV show, with participants being followed by a camera crew on red-carpet dates. What all these campaigns really show us is that we are truly entering a new humanistic era in brand development.

CELEBRITY BRANDS: DREAMING BIG

In this new era of consumer collaboration and everyman empowerment, you may conclude that celebrities perhaps might lose some of their powerful grip on the popular psyche. In many ways, however, this era of everyman empowerment was itself inspired by the seismic cultural shift toward celebrity worship over the past several centuries. At the risk of blasphemy, *celebrity,* in its broadest interpretation, may be the foundation of an entirely new religion. The book *Life: The Movie—How Entertainment Conquered Reality*[8] describes this notion quite convincingly; one need only remember the deaths of Princess Diana and Pope John Paul II to realize that people are passionate about believing in something and long to have a hero to worship. While the enormous outpouring of grief for Pope John Paul II might be attributable to religious conviction, the global mourning of Princess Diana, complete with theme song, logo, and tagline "The People's Princess," all suggest that people are hungry for relevant archetypal icons—be they human or commercial. One need only look to the passion of sports fans or the clear-cut social division between Mac and PC users, which has recently provided inspiration for Mac advertising.

And so, in as much as they represent aspirational concepts, it is my belief that celebrities will continue to be an important cultural barometer for modern life. In fact, there is no reason to think that our passion for celebrities may not grow even stronger. But there will be one very big difference in how celebrities will be viewed. For consumers today, celebrities are fast becoming members of a *supporting cast*. In other words, the celebrity signifies aspirations that consumers wish to actively pursue in their own lives. In this new paradigm, the celebrity becomes a symbolic icon in the consumer's performance of self. When consumers buy a celebrity-created product, they are choosing the costars for their customized version of a movie starring—themselves! The celebrity is the consumer's costar, and brands represent the props for plots that are written, produced, and acted out by consumers. Modern marketing is quickly shifting toward an era of pure "art direction," and we are quickly assuming the roles of stylists versus writers in the grand and yet-to-be completed drama of twenty-first-century civilization.

Studying some very successful celebrity brands can give us some very interesting perspectives for understanding exactly what this drama will be about. They tell us an awful lot about ourselves and our dreams. When we see great celebrity brands, we have to ask ourselves, what is it about these persons or brands that connects with consumers so powerfully on the level of dreams?

Coty has used insights from several groups to identify cobranding and licensing partner opportunities. Celebrities such as Celine Dion and Jennifer Lopez clearly have attained the brand stature necessary for successful licensing and have developed enormously successful fragrance, cosmetics, and clothing lines because of consumers' aspirational affinity. In addition to appearing to be at the pinnacle of possibilities in terms of their tremendous talent, beauty, and success, they also exude an important element of accessibility. For some, Celine Dion, for example, may symbolize the positive power of big dreams and womanhood realized. Modern women are reclaiming their right to be glamorous. In the midst of uncertainty, changing sexual roles, and previous attempts to portray powerful women as unfeminine, women have come to realize that they can have it all. Celine's fans are so passionate about her positive message that they have created a club on their own called "Team Celine."

Here is a very simple way of looking at Celine Dion's Belong fragrance brand:

Reality. Human need for love

Trend. Movement toward personal expression

Result. Belong by Celine Dion—a fragrance intended to demonstrate the multiple dimensions of love and our ability to express it in our own way (see Figure 2-7).

FIGURE 2-7 ■ The sheer joy of love versus any notion of restriction expresses a natural human desire.

CONCLUSION: To Love Is to Be Loved

I would like to conclude this chapter with a case study on one celebrity and cultural icon who, surprisingly, is also one of the best marketers out there. Fabio. Yes, that's right Fabio—the Ford model who has appeared on literally thousands of romance novel covers. He is what I would call a *spontaneous celebrity* and subsequently a *spontaneous brand*—one that was created by the women who loved to see him on book covers and demanded to know more about him. As a celebrity, he is a product of a collective dream. But that is not all. It just so happens that he truly loves women and has translated that love into an extremely successful clothing brand—not through any kind of gimmick but through a genuine understanding and affection for his consumers—women.

THE EVER-FABULOUS FABIO: WHAT'S NOT TO LOVE?

Fabio has successfully parlayed his phenomenal rise to fame as a top Ford model, gracing the covers of thousands of romance novels, into many major advertising and marketing campaigns, as well as into an extremely successful fashion-brand venture, an outerwear garment line sold exclusively at Wal-Mart's Sam's Club.

Fabio's commercial success is attributable largely to the critical role women played in creating both the myth and the reality of the Fabio brand. In fact, Fabio is the very personification of a consumer-created brand. And because women created the brand themselves, they have a vested interest in seeing their brand prosper and grow. Yes, that's right. The Fabio brand model is indeed the wave of the future.

Consider the success of his outerwear line. Created from the concept of an outerwear line that warms both the body and heart, it sells so well that it can hardly be kept in stock. But this does not surprise me after meeting Fabio, the man. On meeting Fabio, one thing becomes immediately apparent (besides the fact that he truly is a hunk in real life!). Fabio genuinely respects and loves women as human beings. This has translated perfectly to fashion. Fabio clearly enjoys making women feel both appreciated and good about themselves.

Fabio gets it. Because he truly loves women, he has been able to embrace them (figuratively) and create a brand, as well as speaking for other brands in a common language—the language of love. It's as simple as that. It does not surprise me that his recent return to the classic "I Can't Believe It's Not Butter" campaign, his fascinatingly charming dual roles in Nationwide Insurance's hugely successful Super Bowl ad, and his "larger than life" role, which included his image featured on a 10-story building façade as part of Oral-B's feminine outreach efforts have only reconfirmed his star and brand power, proving once and for all that romance truly never goes out of style.

The connective thread of this chapter has been that great brands are built on great consumer interaction. I recently came across a press kit containing a reprint of an article in which one of America's fastest-rising celebrities was asked her opinion regarding her views relative to the type of brand she would see herself as. She compared celebrity careers to cars. Although beautiful and shiny when new, cars are known for rapid depreciation. This celebrity has no plans of becoming a car; instead, she would see her career and her brand becoming a house. She noted wisely that with regular maintainence and the occasional upgrade, a career—and a celebrity brand—has the potential to become a house. And, houses, unlike cars, appreciate over time. Frankly, I was very impressed by this insight. Sadly, however, when I asked whether or not she would want her name and quote cited, she respectfully declined. My point: A celebrity brand, like any other brand, can indeed be likened to a house. But beautiful houses, those that stand the test of time, typically include windows—the more the better. And, as we all know, with the exception of some tacky cars and houses created for the ultrasecurity conscious, windows were meant to be transparent. A true brand must be a window, a panoramic view including vistas both inside and out.

In the next chapter we will take a look at exciting emerging technologies as new mechanisms for interaction and ponder how each might bring us closer to our ideal of meaningful consumer dialogue and collaborative brand creation. We will learn more about windows and how to see beyond the glass.

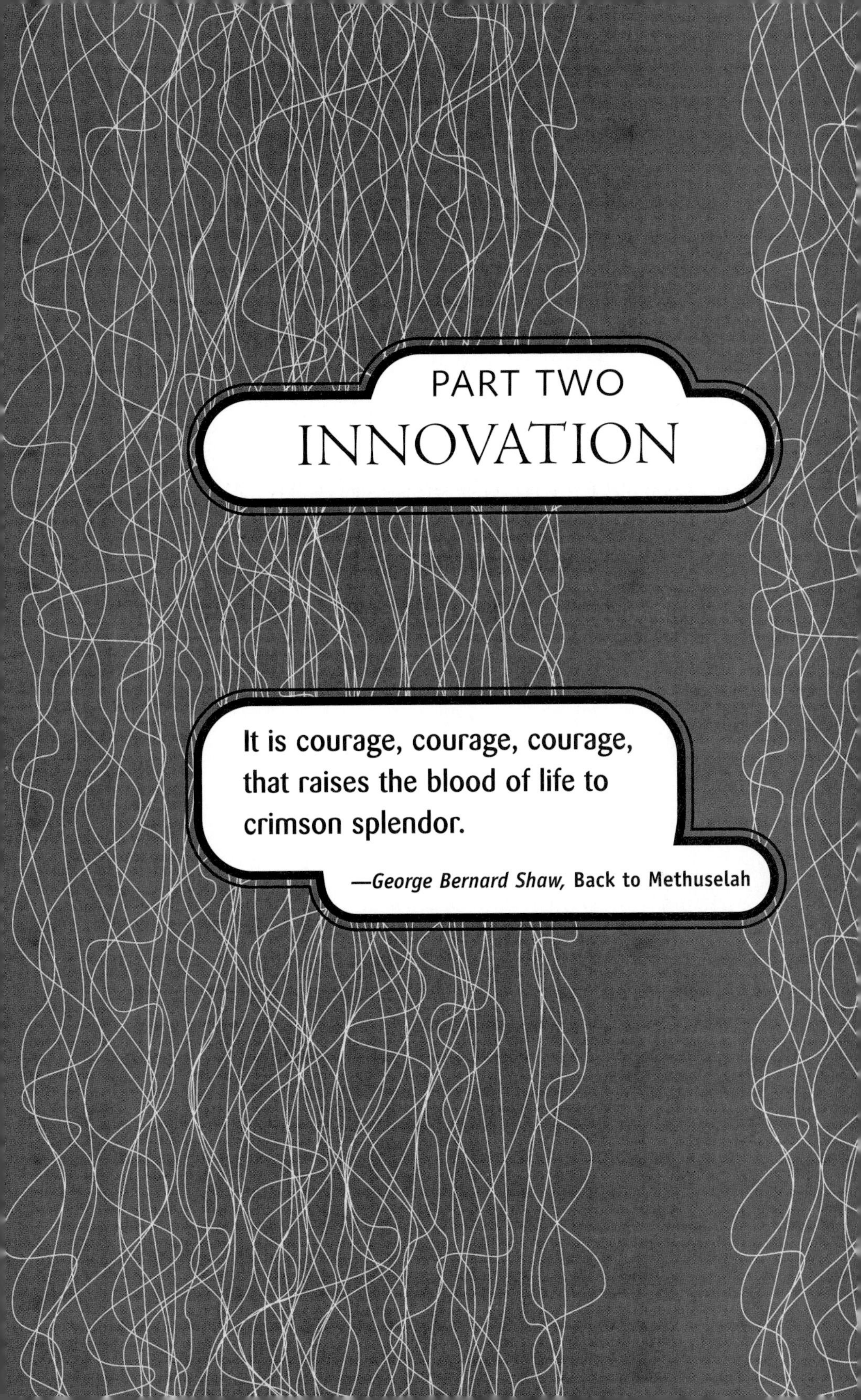

PART TWO
INNOVATION

It is courage, courage, courage, that raises the blood of life to crimson splendor.

—*George Bernard Shaw,* Back to Methuselah

SECRET #3

BE INTIMATE

ENABLING REALITIES IN THE IMAGES OF THEIR MAKERS

Everything you can imagine is real.

—*Pablo Picasso*

INTRODUCTION:

INTERACTIVE TECHNOLOGY AND VIRTUAL REALITY—DISCOVERING THE NEXT GENERATION OF BRANDING

Because consumers do really want to be surprised, delighted, and connected continuously in new and innovative ways, technology is an ever more important part of the Living Brands Living Media® strategy. It is also the medium that will allow exactly the kind of far-reaching "brand web" and direct consumer input that will accelerate the consumer-as-creator marketing transition I am predicting. Put simply, a heightened use of the most cutting-edge technologies will be crucial in creating tomorrow's great brands and is perhaps the last hope for established brands to reinvent themselves within the context of a technologically enabled brand-new world. Being on the cutting edge of technology is not just a way for today's consumers to self-define as being hip—it is fast becoming a real baseline necessity for cultural relevance. We live in an age of technology. Our brands must fully address our age and harness its advances.

In his book *The Wisdom of Crowds,*[1] James Surowiecki provides an insight that most of us should have grasped intuitively; that is to say, the wisdom of many informed minds is better than the will or wisdom of one individual. While this chapter addresses this phenomenon from a marketing perspective, it is interesting to note that even the financial markets are capitalizing on this technologically enabled truth. Gold-standard institutions such as Goldman Sachs, Deutsche Bank, and Hewlett-Packard are using group wisdom to refine and forecast everything from projected sales to the impact of future economic indicators. Consumers already can access a similar phenomenon via Web sites such as www.ideosphere.com, www.hsx.com, and www.longbets.org, all predicated on the notion of group wisdom and collective consciousness.

This transition is here to stay and certainly is not just about the latest and greatest things we can do with new gizmos—it reinforces the advent of virtually complete consumer empowerment. Consumers are empowered increasingly through technology to live out their greatest fantasies, converging real fantasies into actual realities. We thrill at the expertise and control over our lives that we can acquire through technology and marvel at the power of being on the cutting edge of new horizons. Until now, however, marketing mistakenly has viewed technology as a mechanism for perfecting marketing and not as a means for perfecting the art of need fulfillment. The collaborative branding approach focuses on individual persons, not abstractions of persons or the consumer caricatures commonly reflected in demographic or psychographic profiles. It is technology that ultimately will open up entirely new realms of brand and experience customization by truly making one-to-one collaborative marketing a reality rather than merely a theory or goal.

This chapter will delve into interactive, experiential technologies, most of which are available right now. These technologies will both allow for new levels of consumer intimacy and connection and enable retail experiences and the creation of "brand worlds" the likes of which we have never seen. Many of the breakthroughs outlined in this chapter will have an enormous effect on product design and development, brand messaging, and even the redefinition of how media forms are created to reinforce a brand image. David Polinchock, CEO of Brand Experience Lab, a think tank that helps companies to create engaging brand experiences for twenty-first-century audiences, will provide a glimpse into the burgeoning worlds of mixed and augmented realities and the reasons why consumers are attracted to them.

In addition, this chapter features interviews with two of today's most intriguing and visionary technological voices, cultural creatives and entrepreneurs Les Neumann, director of the Globian Institute, and Victor Chu, CEO of MIL. Digital Labeling. Both Les and Victor are veritable trailblazers. They will reveal fascinating case studies of exactly the types of technologies that will enable consumers to collaborate increasingly with brands to invent consumer cocreated worlds.

This chapter is organized in two parts according to the two primary themes. In the first part we will explore true customization and interactive technology, explaining how technology will provide the missing link between consumers and brand, which will lead to true customization that some brands (particularly in the health and beauty, nutritional, media, fashion, and pharmaceutical categories) have already begun to explore. The second part will delve into virtual reality and brand immersion, where I will show you how these futuristic technologies will allow for the ultimate expression of the concept of living media with media forms that envelop the consumer in worlds of his or her own creation. Through these new media creations, consumers' experiences of brands will reach a previously unheard of dimensionality, and truly living brands will be born.

PART 1:
TRUE CUSTOMIZATION AND INTERACTIVE TECHNOLOGY

THE DNA OF CUSTOMIZATION

I am convinced that in the market of the twenty-first century, the only way to create emotionally relevant brands is to focus on unearthing and responding to consumers' real dreams in the most direct one-on-one ways at our disposal. While it may not always be possible to create multiple, simultaneous dialogues, we owe it to our consumers and to our brands to maintain this as our goal. After all, it is a goal we are getting closer and closer to achieving in a variety of ways. As we saw in Secret #1 in the section reflecting on the humanized technology trend, daily advances in biological research are allowing us a deeper understanding of human nature—both physical and psychological—broadening the potential repertoire of brand communication "languages." Many of the latest developments in technology are moving brands in the direction of customization through methodologies such as "DNA marketing," where products are tailored to each consumer's unique biological needs.

Overall, technology is bringing us a new kind of customization based on reconnection with our own essential human nature. We are gaining a deeper understanding of the consumer as a biological entity, allowing for true, not just topical, customization. Call it the *DNA of desire* (which is linked directly to the real DNA of a person). It comes as no surprise that some of the first concrete signals of things to come emanate from medicine and the health and beauty (HBA) segments. Dosages of medication have and will continue to become increasingly customized. For example, not only will there be modified dosages for children, but there also will be modified dosages or even completely different medicines for each genetically profiled individual. Just imagine that once upon a time there were "one size fits all" vitamins, and now a vast industry of specialized vitamin preparations addresses every age group for every demographic (women/men, women/men over 50, pregnant women, the young/active segment, etc.). And as recognition for biological differences between persons grows, it will continue to fuel the increasing desire of consumers for individualized treatments, influencing their demand and further defining their specific needs across virtually every other category of product.

At Coty, realization that genetics and nanotechnology are the future of luxury led to the development of such brands as Lancaster's 24-Hour Cellular Elixir based on new cellular technologies that provide ingredients that conserve cellular energy (versus expending it to ward off the damage inflicted by free radicals), thus retaining energy to reinvest in improved DNA replication—leading to more perfect and younger-looking skin. Lab 21 Skin Care is another brand that is completely tailored to each consumer's unique biological needs and actual DNA composition. Similarly, recent advances in microencapsulation technology now also have created products that are responsive to the wearer's chemistry and the environment. These products allow for the release of different amounts of active ingredients throughout the day depending on where you are (a fragrance, for example, could emit a little in a plane or an elevator or a lot on a dance floor).

Science and culturally adapted messages will be the key to creating and communicating personalized brand messages; moreover, technology ultimately will be the enabler of truly customized branded products and their respective consumer benefits. The Smart Molecule® Technology created for adidas, where active ingredients in products themselves are engaged in response to specific situations (i.e., more deodorant released in warm conditions, etc.), is an example where this notion already has been built seamlessly into products in consumer-friendly and understandable ways. This idea of products being malleable to the influence of the momentary needs and moods of the consumer is one that we will see over and over again because it is gaining tremendous momentum. The invention of intelligent fabrics follows the same idea, and such fabrics are another area where this kind of technology lends itself to amazing new products. In this burgeoning new category we see brands such as Gunze already delivering such products as its fat-burning Beauty Shape VIFA Pantyhose with caffeine and other natural essences (e.g., grapefruit, pepper, fennel, and tarragon) infused into the spandex fibers that interact with the wearer's perspiration and body oils, dissolving into skin and activating fat-dissolving enzymes. Or take the example of Bonnie Glogover, who in partnership with Bossong Hosiery Mills, Inc., actually has created and recently launched Pain Manager hosiery, which combines traditional benefits of fine hosiery with the added dimension of wellness. By integrating conductive carbon technology directly into fashionable, comfortable wraps, bands, and hosiery, aches and pains are minimized or totally relieved (check out the company's Web site at www.glogoverhosiery.com).

Many other manufacturers are beginning to design products with intelligent fabrics that provide sun protection factor (SPF) or mosquito repellant custom responses to climate—heating or cooling properties and other benefits. Evidence the fabulous work of designer Jeffrey Grübb, whose groundbreaking fashion designs are created with his own special intelligent fabric, MicroSilver, which is pure silver combined with other fibers (in this case, polyamide and elastaine), rendering garments that are 99.96 percent antibacterial-antimicrobial (odorless and germ-free), as well as thermoregulating (keeping you temperate and comfortable) and antistatic (no shock value), again demonstrating the fusion of fashion and technology. We are only on the ground floor of a trend destined to explode. Technology, performance, and branding will never exist independently again—even in the hyper-image-driven fashion arena (see Figure 3-1).

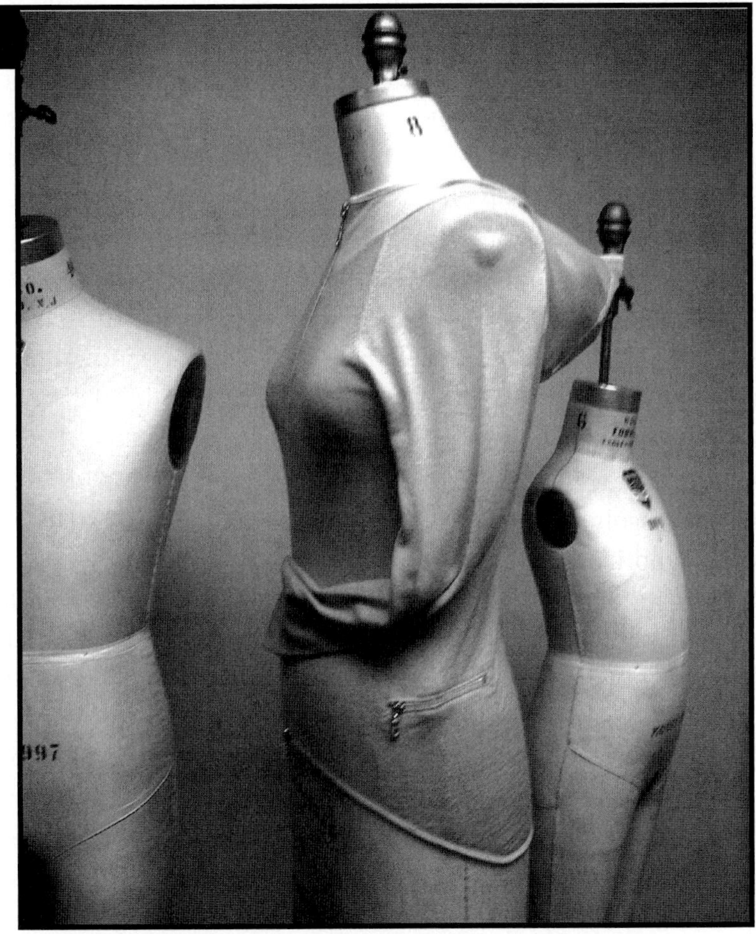

FIGURE 3-1 ■ As fashion and technology merge, style will continue to move toward an ideal of form and function, as seen in this hoodie from Jeffrey Grübb that includes antibacterial MicroSilver fused into the fabric.

Today we see technology empowering consumers across every industry and category. For example, many architects are currently using new cutting-edge lighting technology in stores, restaurants, and clubs in which the light intensity and hue are highly malleable and can change according to the mood, time of day, and so on. The current trend in packaging is toward "active packaging" that self-heats or self-cools. A remarkable example is Nescafé coffee that heats up as soon as its container is opened. And we will see in the next section just how far active packaging can go—to the ultimate in interactive and intelligent packaging that is intimately customizable in ways that go beyond mere function. In every category, brands will need to explore the product-development possibilities suggested by this type of "humanized technology" with the consistent objective of creating more personalized and emotionally fulfilling brand experiences.

Looking into the future—even the very near future—we will see technology making brands more integral to the actual physical self to the point that brands/products begin to work as extensions of the consumer, almost as if products and brands were additional limbs or organs. This is the future of branded technology, which, like branded entertainment, will integrate into the very fabric of human existence, perhaps even helping to stretch the boundaries of what is considered human. Wearable or implanted computers and intelligent sensors are already a reality, and the possibility of memory-enhancement chips inserted in the human brain (which can be downloaded at will) is just around the corner. Rapidly developing nanotechnology (the reduction of interactive media to microscopic size and even perhaps someday to subatomic size) and the burgeoning phenomenon of bioeconomics (a new category already being included in some nations' economies, based on products enhanced via their coordination with the human body, such as touch-screen identification based on fingerprints) are clearly the wave of the future. The implications for marketing are utterly profound. We are truly on the eastern edge of the new Wild West.

Imagine a time—not far from now—when microscopic robotic immune system repair devices can be injected via a syringe into the human body to protect us from disease. These astounding technologies most definitely will be part of commerce and will make us rethink everything. An excellent exploration and outline of possible future scenarios, filled with this uber-futuristic technology, can be found in the book *The Age of Spiritual Machines: When Computers Exceed Human Intelligence* by Ray Kurzweil.[2] Certainly the technology is fascinating and potentially empowering beyond all imagination. The question remains: What will we do with it when it arrives?

THE ADVENT OF CONSUMER COLLABORATION THROUGH INTERACTIVE TECHNOLOGY

Many other recent developments in technology, such as the Internet and interactive TV, also are moving brands closer to true versus fictionalized customization by allowing a direct dialogue and collaboration between brands and people. The launch of Fox's Me Network presages everything that is to come. Every network ultimately will become a "me network," as consumers take ownership of programming the content of their lives. One early indicator of this trend already being used by marketing involves the sorts of de facto electronic consumer preference census takers/quantifiers, such as the databases created by Genius Insight, one of the agencies mentioned in Secret #1. Consumer feedback is quantified and used by marketers during every phase of product development, including determination of elements of packaging design and brand names. While this "democratic" form of customization often does not allow consumers direct one-on-one interaction with brands, it does give consumers a tremendous sense of empowerment because they play a vital role in the design and creation of brands prior to their launches and throughout their entire life cycles. Ultimately, these kinds of collaborative brand experiences can foster strong emotional brand bonds because they offer a more personal investment in a brand's future.

Who wouldn't want *their* brand to succeed? Who would not take extraordinary measures to ensure that it does? This is part of what I am referring to when I present the heretical notion of consumer as creator—because far beyond democratic customization, interactive technology will make it possible to create brands in direct collaboration with consumers. Today we have branding scenarios that easily can include many, many more voices—from the several thousand consumers of traditional surveys to the possibility of reaching several million people concurrently—we are already shifting to a more collaborative mind-set. But beware. Just as these technologies can and certainly will be used to create brands, they also will be used to bring about their demise—the flip side of the consumer as creator theory is, you guessed it, *consumer as destroyer.*

If you are still feeling the least bit skeptical about the power of technology-based consumer control, just think about Amrit Srivastava, a Californian who brought Coca-Cola India to its knees merely through blogs about some of the company's alleged unethical activities in India. See the following section for more on this fascinating story.

HOW ONE MAN AND HIS COMPUTER ARE CONQUERING COKE

Amrit Srivastava, a one-man nongovernment organization (NGO) armed with a laptop, a Web site, and a telephone calling card, has played an integral role in coordinating the activities of far-flung protesters of Coca-Cola's activities on a global level and has emerged as a key figure in Coke's travails in India. Using the Internet, Srivastava and his allies have managed to affect how a huge multinational corporation does business in its global markets.

In 2002, Mr. Srivastava began a "fax action" initiative through Corp Watch to protest the practices of a Coke bottling plant in a poor tribal area in Kerala, where locals accused Coke of extracting so much water that their wells either dried up or yielded brackish, undrinkable water. Web site visitors were urged to send a fax to Coke via the Internet. More than 1,400 people responded. Subsequently, Mr. Srivastava discovered many more problems with

Coca-Cola in India, and he started his own NGO focusing on these issues. Coke officials report that Srivastava has relayed more than 9,000 faxes to date, and his Web site gets about 20,000 visitors a month. Activists throughout India credit Srivastava with helping them to link together.

Mr. Srivastava has uncovered some very serious issues for Coca-Cola's business practices in India. Overall, Srivastava has cost Coca-Cola millions of dollars in lost sales and legal fees in India and growing damage to its reputation elsewhere, including the United States and Europe. Coke has been forced to fight legal and legislative battles all across India—including challenging a court order in the northern state of Rajasthan that would require soft-drink makers to list pesticide residues on their labels. In 2004, Kerala local officials shut down the US$16 million bottling plant. Coke has been trying to regain the plant's license; the case has gone all the way to the Indian Supreme Court. After a visit from a *Wall Street Journal* reporter, Coke acknowledged that it had violated its own global safety standards by failing to conduct toxicity tests on a dump site used by its biggest Indian plant.

Mr. Srivastava is now rallying college students in the United States and Europe to take up the NGO's cause. While speaking on a tour of U.S. college campuses, he accused Coke of stealing water, poisoning land, and selling drinks laced with dangerous pesticides. At least a half dozen colleges, such as Bard College in New York, Carleton College in Minnesota, and Oberlin College in Ohio, now have decided not to renew their contracts with Coca-Cola or to boycott the product. To further publicize the pesticide issue, some NGOs began spreading stories online that Indian farmers sprayed their crops with Coke as a pesticide. Srivastava admits that the whole thing was a publicity stunt by a local activist. This proves, however, that not only are consumers wise to our marketing techniques, but they also have figured out how to use them against us. The case of Mr. Srivastava clearly illustrates how the role of social activist increasingly is played online, where the power of one becomes the

power of many. "The moral high ground seems to be anyone with a Web site," complains David Cox, Hong Kong–based communications director for Coca-Cola Asia, who has spent months in India trying to combat the NGO's allegations. According to Cox, Srivastava and his activists are "making false environmental allegations against us to further an antiglobalization agenda."[3]

To its credit, Coca-Cola at least has responded to culture's complaints (out of necessity, not necessarily altruism), and more important, it has taken them seriously. While I can't speak for Coca-Cola, I find it gratifying to see an almost immediate, modernized return to its classic advertising campaign, a campaign that literally encourages the world to sing in perfect harmony and, hopefully, in the way it chooses to do business.

Consumers cannot and will not "fall in love" with a lie—unless, of course, they help to create the lie themselves. A lie that a consumer creates for himself or herself becomes a myth. Myths are acceptable. Lies are not.

In the end, I believe that consumers will tolerate and even forgive exaggeration—or well-intended honest mistakes—just as long as the "dialogue" between the brand and consumer is based on a relationship between equals and framed by mutual understanding and respect. Increasingly, technology can and will be used for purposes of social change, and as consumers discover and make use of it more and more, business will need to understand this new culture of connection. In order to create sufficient consumer trust and connect with consumers, brands will need to fully reveal themselves through a campaign that literally encourages the world to sing in perfect harmony and be brave enough to risk a certain amount of vulnerability and even potential criticism.

Just as with any long-term relationship, you have to be open to constructive criticism and ultimately to change. There is no shame in being seen naked—in fact, it is often the foundation of deeper intimacy and emotional understanding. The following section explores this consumer empowerment "culture of change" enabled by technology via the types of technology chronicled in the amazing book *Smart Mobs: The Next Social Revolution—Transforming Cultures and Communities in the Age of Instant Access*[4] by Howard Rheingold, one of the world's foremost authorities on the social implications of technology.

This book is a must-read for anyone who wants a glimpse into the future and a deeper understanding of digital culture. It discusses how technology today, such as wireless organizers, wireless networks, and community supercomputing collectives, is enabling people to act together and create a very powerful collective force.

SMART MOBS RULE THE WORLD

"The people who make up smart mobs cooperate in ways never before possible because they carry devices that possess both communication and computing capabilities. Their mobile devices connect them with other information devices in the environment as well as with other people's telephones. Dirt-cheap microprocessors embedded in everything from box tops to shoes are beginning to permeate furniture, buildings, neighborhoods, products with invisible intercommunicating smartifacts." Here are some examples showing some of the far-reaching implications of the "smart mobs" phenomenon:

- **Street demonstrators in the 1999 anti–World Trade Organization protests used dynamically updated Web sites, cell phones, and "swarming" tactics in the "battle of Seattle."**

- In 2001, the people of Manila overthrew President Estrada by demonstrations organized via forwarding text messages on cell phones.
- A Web site enables fans to follow their favorite celebrities in real time through Internet-organized mobile networks and provides a similar channel for journalists to organize citizen-reporters on the fly. The site makes it easy for roving phone tribes to organize communities of interest.
- In Helsinki and Tokyo, you can operate vending machines with your telephone and receive directions on your wireless organizer that show you how to get from where you are standing to where you want to go.
- Lovegety users in Japan find potential dates when their devices recognize another Lovegety user in the vicinity broadcasting the appropriate pattern of attributes. Location-based matchmaking is now available on some mobile phone services.

As Mr. Rheingold observes, "The same convergence of technologies that opens new vistas of cooperation also makes possible a universal surveillance economy and empowers the bloodthirsty as well as the altruistic." Clearly, the opportunity for consumer/manufacturer collaborative branding initiatives is tremendous. (For more on smart mobs, visit www.smartmobs.com.)

The first fast-acting consumer/brand-connecting technology was the Internet. The Internet has provided people with an amazing tool—one that can be used to create massive positive change. People in any community now can come together and organize around any and every issue. I am impressed by programs such as Worldstudio's FEED ME project that encourages and assists students and parents in protesting the poor nutrition of school lunch programs by offering posters, buttons, stickers, and T-shirts with the FEED ME graphics from the Web site. Parents and students can download the graphics along with information on how to use them to mount campaigns geared at pressuring school administrators to improve food quality. Imagine if you were able to convince consumers to rally around a brand or brand cause in a similar fashion? There will come a day when, hypothetically speaking, an organization such as FEED ME will partially take over the roles of governments and businesses, demanding that every food brand deliver on nonnegotiable nutritional standards. The message: Make the move before consumers force you to make the move, because when they do—and they will—they will remember your arrogance. The resulting damage to your brand no doubt will be irrevocable.

For the first time, in 2004 we saw a very strong use of the Internet in a presidential election by both Republicans and Democrats. There were sites such as the Blog on America Democratic site, where an interactive Web log journal allowed anyone and everyone to contribute their ideas in a chat-type format. The MoveOn.org site also continues to grow as a grassroots phenomenon that attempts to bring ordinary people back into politics, supporting a nationwide network of more than 2 million online activists through e-mail outreach and other initiatives. MoveOn.org was created in 2000 by two Democratic Silicon Valley entrepreneurs as a way to combat a political system that they feel "revolves around big money and big media, leaving most citizens out." Of course there are many more everyday examples of Internet empowerment—the organization of the "Do not call" lists via the Internet is a good one in that with just a few clicks it provides consumers relief from annoying sales calls. The fact that the law upheld this consumer action shows that we have, indeed, turned a corner and that consumers are in many ways beginning to take control of the corporations often accused of attempting to control them. This is only just an early signal of the consumer-as-creator revolution and yet another reason to think of marketing in an entirely new way.

In addition to providing a new powerful forum for social action, the Internet also provides us with a vast forum for social *inter*action. Yes, this is a networking age! This is what is behind the success of eBay—a site whose format allows people to have direct contact with one another and collaborate to achieve their goals. Again, it is about empowerment. We see a continuing flourishing of social networking Web sites, such as Friendster, which is set up as a free online service that helps people to connect with their friends and discover new friends and share interests. Some brands are using social networking Web sites such as Friendster to promote themselves and are attempting to deepen their relationship with consumers.

For example, the TV show *The Apprentice* posted in-depth bios of all the show's participants on Friendster, providing users with a chance to learn more about their favorite contestants than the information available on the show. The bios, of course, inspired a blog on the site, with people voicing their opinions about the contestants and about the latest happenings on the show. Other sites, such as Recycle.org, allow people to network around shared interests and hobbies and even trade used goods for free (think of it as the world's largest yard sale/nightclub/auction!). The extremely popular Craigslist.org operates in a similar manner—as a community bulletin board for everything from finding your dream house to used refrigerators to potential mates and activity partners. Still, in the business world, the question asked over and over again is: How can Internet technology be used to create a positive, win-win relationship between brands and consumers?

In books such as *Commodify Your Dissent: Salvos from The Baffler*,[5] the bestseller by Thomas Frank and Matt Weiland, multiple arguments are made in favor of empowering consumers to express their discontent with brands via technology, but they never really propose a positive practical application of this empowerment. Clearly, the Internet has enabled a new channel for consumer-to-brand feedback, but few brands are really listening. Web sites that operate as stores are a great venue for consumers to vent, rave, and question brands—and most important, to talk to one another. Here, the power of one unhappy customer is tremendous. For example, if you read that one person's son in Florida had a nasty spill off the bike you're planning to buy for your daughter because the seat is poorly constructed, chances are that you're not going to buy it, no matter what the safety ratings are. Or if you hear a couple of people complain that the new CD you were dying to purchase is boring and repetitive and not as good as that band's previous release, won't you reconsider? You bet.

Of course, eBay was built on the power of consumer-to-consumer salesmanship. Above all, however, eBay allows people to build a reputation through product and service quality ratings, and that is what makes the whole thing work so well. If you have a bad experience with a seller or an item purchased, you can blast them, and this will affect their rating and their business. Of course, the thrill of the hunt and the networking are part of the draw, but ultimately, it is the trust enabled through the transparency of the whole system that keeps people coming back for more.

Few brands are really leveraging this word-of-mouth vehicle for new opportunities to build intimacy with consumers. Why not create brand Web sites that facilitate consumer-to-consumer interaction relative to your brand—not the brand hype but the actual infrastructure, planning, historical practices, performance, and future direction of the brand? For example, why not encourage consumers to rate products and post their opinions and helpful insights about the products on your brand's Web site? Why not allow complaints to be aired freely for all to see? Yes, you might lose some customers, but think of what you would gain in terms of understanding consumers' desires and building trust! Why, at the very least, aren't new technologies being used more as new and improved versions of the age-old "suggestion box"?

The Home Shopping Network long ago understood the power of consumer-to-consumer referrals, and the company has built a very successful brand by taking common technologies (the phone and television) and using them to allow consumers to interact and network with one another. People also seem to use the Home Shopping Network as a form of entertainment, which proves that the social aspect of this kind of interaction can be even more compelling than getting insider's information about a product or the promise of a "deal." Acknowledging this phenomenon and the role technology played in it is a first step toward humanizing the vast array of communications technology already in our hands.

Since technology as a means to connect in a more intimate, one-on-one way with consumers is still and will continue to be one of the best uses for the Internet, the following example demonstrates its power at its best. There is a fascinating National Geographic Web site called Novica, which was created as a global network of artisans of third-world and developing countries, that allows consumers to have direct contact with the artisans themselves. This means that a much greater share of the profit—traditionally cut out by a "middle man" purchaser who buys the goods very cheaply and instigates a steep markup progression—goes directly to the artisans. The site provides the personal story and photograph of the artisan who has crafted a given item, and when you purchase something, it arrives directly from Bali or Nepal or some other faraway location with a personal handwritten thank-you note from the artisan himself or herself! Think of all the other ways layers between brands and people might be stripped away by such a direct, intimate connection between human beings.

Another really wonderful example of the power of exactly this kind of technology put to good use by enabling collaboration between people is an organization called DKMS, a nonprofit global organization dedicated to promoting awareness of leukemia and related blood diseases that was begun on a grass-roots level based on the very personal experience of one family. From that, the Internet has enabled 1.5 million volunteer donors and their many supporters to create a very powerful brand. I believe strongly that this type of connective technology will fuel a proliferation of similar brands in the public and private sectors. I will talk more about the DKMS project and its branding campaign in Secret #5.

Today, technology is providing us with so many new ways to create a dialogue between brands and people—we are truly limited only by our imaginations. Take a recent Nike outdoor billboard advertisement in downtown Manhattan, for example. The ad featured a phone number where people could use their cell phones to request that the ad change colors, and it would respond by changing for 15 minutes—a brilliant way to coax consumers to pause on a busy New York street to participate in the Nike brand expression. Another great example of technology getting people involved with product and related communications development is an initiative called NY1, undertaken by a local TV news channel in Manhattan. The channel has created a system where viewers can log on to the channel's Web site and "produce" the 9:00 p.m. news show, *The Call.* People are able to determine which stories they'd like to hear reported and in which order using the same tools the newsroom producers use. And, of course, the incentive to actually watch the news is then much greater when you know that you've had a hand in creating the program.

The more consumers are offered this kind of fun, interactive feature, the more they will come to expect it in all areas of their daily lives. In the United Kingdom, the company I-Vu has had tremendous success installing screens in hundreds of styling stations in hair salons. These fully interactive touch screens allow customers to view hairstyles and purchase products to complement their look while they are in the stylist's chair. Thus they can play a more active role in determining their look. The products purchased then can be waiting for them at the front desk when they leave.

The following section explores another exciting potential for interactive communication between a brand and its consumer via an incredible patented interactive labeling technology that has the ability to change virtually any product into an interactive communications device, an honest-to-goodness advance in living media.

THE FUTURE OF BRANDING AND THE REVOLUTION OF DIGITAL LABELING

an Interview with Victor Chu

Victor Chu, CEO of MIL. Digital Labeling Technologies (www.mildigitallabeling.com), is both an engineer and a talented designer with an exquisite aesthetic sensibility. He views technology as another artistic medium. He defines himself as a "fashion tech-

nologist." In this interview, he discusses the role technology plays in creating brands in the fashion industry.

QUESTION: As a designer who uses technology in his work, how do you describe what you do?

CHU: For the last 12 years, my professional design and marketing experiences have been drawn from the fashion and technology industries. The fashion industry and the technology industry share similar traits, yet they are still worlds apart in culture. Both industries are driven by creating new and exciting products. One industry is driven by beauty and women and the other by machines. Fashion now needs technology to advance and grow. Technology now is utilizing fashion and beauty to sell more electronics and technology. The two are finally converging in a major way. As a fashion technologist, I believe that technology is an accessory. Technology will never live your life for you. It is a tool, an accessory to life, work, or literally it is a fashion accessory that matches an outfit; an expression of status, culture, and anything else. Expressing relevant fashion includes understanding changing standards of beauty, culture, and consumer trends. Relevant technology must reflect the same understanding. Technology is about advancing computerization for more function, communication, efficiency, and effectiveness. In other words, creating better tools to enjoy life, which is also applicable to fashion products.

As a designer I have created designs for brands such as Polo Home Collection, Tommy Hilfiger, Brooklyn Mint (Puffy's first fashion venture), Sean John, G-Unit, Reebok, Jansport, Nautica, Rocawear, Pro-Keds, American Express, Dow Chemical, Tommy Boy Records, Tenba/Mamiya, Urban Outfitters, Case Logic, Living Doll, Giant Step, and many others. In the '90s I started mixing technology with fashion. Cell phones and digital cameras just became affordable; the Internet boom was about to start. I became the design director for the Modo wireless information device. I taught computer fashion illustration and cell phone design at Parsons and, most recently, started up MIL. Digital Labeling, Inc.

In 2004, our first digital labeling customer was Davis, a high-end women's fashion shoe brand. Davis wanted us to take the girl in the logo and make her dance, so we produced the first "dancing digital Davis label." The labels are used as charms on very sexy and teched-out fashion high heels for women (www.davisfashiontec.com). Our first consulting customer was a high-tech Dow Chemical spin-out called Aveso. Aveso has an innovative thin and flexible display that will eventually replace paper and ink. In working with Aveso, we had the intention of creating a partnership to utilize its flexible displays for digital labeling applications.

Today, we are licensing and selling our digital labeling technology to shoe, apparel, soft goods, and hard goods companies.

QUESTION: **How do you see the evolution and application of technology affecting consumer-to-brand communication? Do you foresee the day when labels and other technologies such as yours will directly influence how products and brands are created?**

CHU: Very much so. Most packaging is still the ink-printed paper wrapped around a product used for thousands of years. In the twenty-first century, we should expect the ink to do something for us. It should move and attract our eyes, entertain us, and provide dynamic function. Even today, the only way we can personalize a product with data such as name, weight, age, height, sex, allergies, and any kind of preferences relevant and important to the effective use of the product is only through writing it on the product with ink or etching it. But the ink cannot mix and instruct a person to take this product *x* amount of times per day and warn against consuming with *y* because it will create an allergic reaction. And the ink cannot send a message to a preferred retail account where a replacement will be shipped automatically for delivery in one day. MIL.'s digital labeling technology will enable this scenario.

Our plan and product development will take product data and individual user data to create consumption data and consumption function. Today, everything is going digital. Products with MIL. digital labels will be able to communicate with each other, with other devices, and with larger computing systems. Companies/brands/manufacturers can push and pull all these data plus dynamic marketing and branding content such as advertisements, video clips, coupons, animations, personalized logos, product updates, and new software that enables more product functionality and features.

QUESTION: How does the technology work? Is it primarily decorative, or does it have the capacity to eventually become an interactive device?

CHU: Refer to the photo of a Davis shoe with a digital branding label and story board of the animation sequence (see Figure 3-2). The technology comprises an LCD display powered by a microchip and button-cell battery. The animation is programmed into the chip, which activates the crystals in sequence to create the animation. On the back panel of the display, DAVIS is screen printed so that when the battery dies and the girl stops dancing, the label still will display DAVIS. This digital label is decorative. It adds a cute and cool factor because the girl is dancing/posing; animation motion attracts the eyes for increased shelf appeal. MIL. is talking to other customers about interactivity such as motion-activated animation, touch-screen illumination, transmitting data, stats, and marketing to the label.

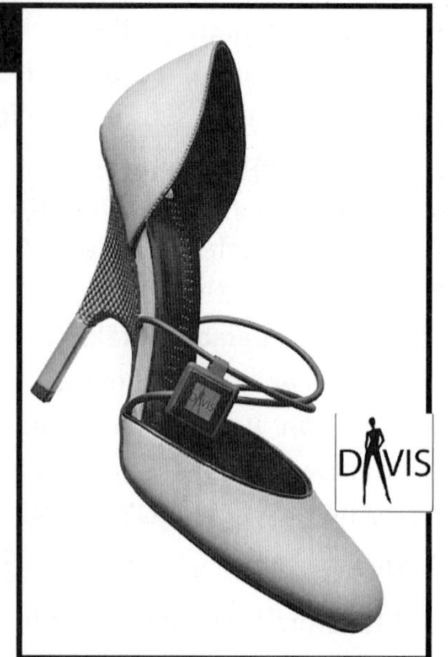

FIGURE 3-2 ■ Davis shoes—meant both for walking and dancing—use advanced label technology to deliver an entertaining message like never before.

QUESTION: Might consumers see a day when dietary suggestions could be put on the back of products? Or, when detailed assembly instruction might be included in 10 languages? What are the limitations of the technology today?

CHU: Absolutely! You could also display styling suggestions such as, "Use this lotion with specific shampoos and conditioners to create the hottest new looks." For example, a popular look for girls now is the trampy, overtanned, underfed, overfashioned heiress style, i.e., the Paris Hilton look. To achieve this look, the digital label on a product can suggest using this lotion along with a skin-bronzing agent with a certain shampoo, conditioner, and styling gel to achieve the hair style. For the face, the label can instruct the consumer to use very specific makeup, eyeliner, mascara, hand and nail care, and even perfume and a teeth whitening regime—all with animated icons and pictures and text. Consumers can choose the look they are going for by selecting the celebrity endorser, or the digital label can select a look based on input of personal user data. Either way, for a Cover Girl product as an example, a user can select the Eva Mendes look, the Milla Jovovich look, or the Halle Berry look, and the digital label can display the entire beauty regime through product suggestions. This is displayed through a mixture of icons, images, and text that can be communicated in any language and dialect. How many languages depends on the memory of the digital label. Memory is very inexpensive.

QUESTION: What limitations exist currently to the practical application of this technology?

CHU: All the technology is available right now to make this happen. The biggest limitation is imagination and boldness. Executives have forgotten that their companies were founded on innovation and the commercialization of new products, which tend to be expensive at first. However, the average consumer can recognize and appreciate true innovation, which will always translate directly into successful adoption and sales. This leads to costs dropping and profits rising. It's naive and arrogant to think that all of this is craziness and too expensive and that it will never happen. It is not about it never happening; it is about who will do it first, second, and third. The first to do it will establish a market-leading position. The second time around will profit. The third will standardize and profit more. It is a natural progression and evolution of products, culture, technology, and events in modern consumerism. Just in the last 150 years there has been incredible progress through innovation and market competition. The prevailing advancements, such as the airplane and electricity, resulted from bold ventures created by the partnering of inventor and entrepreneur. Innovation happens when there is trust between business and visionaries.

QUESTION: What motivated this concept? What is your vision of its ultimate evolution?

CHU: I realized that if everything is going digital and electronic, then eventually we will need "digital labels." The main points of interest for us at MIL. are (which are also current macro issues/trends) (1) authentication/secure identity and (2) consumption data.

In the first point, brand and product authentication is a huge problem for luxury items and people's identity. We are creating digital labeling solutions that work for immediate authentication in parallel with net-based authentication systems.

For the second point, consumption data = product user data + product/labeling data + product consumption history + user preferences. The ultimate evolution of the digital label will be a labeling device that will process dynamic consumption data on the product and provide more features for the product user. Going back to the lotion example, with all this input of data, such as how much water you drink, weight, sex, how often you shower, skin type, and so on, the digital label can process all these data and create a personalized mix of lotion at the precise amount per pump, dispense the lotion electronically, and advise the user as to where to rub it in and when. The ultimate version of this digital label will be made of recyclable electronic components and printed onto the bottle.

QUESTION: Do you agree that in the future the creation of brand biospheres will mandate a more participatory consumer culture? Do you agree, at least in theory, that products such as yours might one day truly blur the lines between consumer and creator?

CHU: I cannot tell you how happy I am to be living in the twenty-first century! I have waited all my life for this! Also, yes to a participatory consumer culture. The current American consensus suggests that no matter what you do for a living, you can still be a star and celebrity. The consumer groups age 19 to 35 have all been exposed to the explosion in fashion, hip-hop bling culture, reality shows, and plastic surgery, instant status through affordable luxury and material goods, and making the average-looking girl into a cover girl. This group is extremely celebrity-driven, so their participation is based on the culture of celebrity and how they can interact with or become a celebrity. So, if these types of consumers can "create" or have their stylists remix their own versions of celebrity-endorsed products through choice or input, then they will buy, buy, buy.

For example, with a digital label, a consumer can input her name into a designer handbag and her name will be interacting on the same label with names such as Louis Vuitton and Prada. The consumer also can choose what type of animations, logos, graphics, and features that the label will display. For consumers 12 to 18, they have grown up exposed to but are less affected by celebrity culture. They value the computer and Internet as tools for knowledge and really know how to use all kinds of electronic devices and computers quickly and efficiently. They want to continue on to college and challenge themselves intellectually; they want to create and produce. These consumers will be able to program their products with digital labeling. For them, a modern product of, let's say, 2010 will be a product with a digital label that prompts the user to upload user data and preferences by placing it near a laptop or cell phone. The laptop or cell phone sends the data wirelessly, and the product calculates the most effective usage plan for the product and the consumer. The product and computer also will prompt the user to select certain upgrades or features that also can be uploaded into the product for more features and functionality.

QUESTION: **To conclude, where are you now with the project, and where would you like to take it?**

CHU: **Currently, MIL. Digital Labeling is selling our digital branding labels. These labels display animated brands and logos for any type of product such as shoes, outerwear, and hard goods. We are also about to finish our first digital authentication prototype for luxury handbags. These digital labels will display authentication data inside the handbags for consumers. Consumers also can personalize the bags by entering their names, other personal information, and digital monograms, and by choosing what animation or graphics to display from a selection of art. The big picture is to digitally label everything and have all products communicate and interact with other devices and systems—and with consumers too, of course!**

What Victor Chu shows us is that the new possibilities presented to us by developing technology are prodding us in the direction of beginning to think outside the box about everything, including the most seemingly mundane media. For example, look at how Stefan Sagmeister, the renowned designer, recently created a book printed in electricity-conducting ink that lights up when touched for an exhibit at the Deste Foundation for Contemporary Art in Athens. He says that he believes in "involving the viewer in the design with any means possible." Just think of the potential applications of this technology for print ads and packaging!

PART 2: VIRTUAL REALITY AND BRAND IMMERSION

Now let's explore another kind of brand intimacy that comes from the cocreation of brand worlds through recent cutting-edge advances in holographic technology. Today, holographic virtual reality is giving us a way to revolutionize the whole notion of brand experience in a way that up to now was thought to be only a distant possibility—more science fiction than fact. This technology has created the possibility of simulation booths that provide multisensory experiences for people through sound, visuals, scent, and even pressure-sensitized apparatus. It has been used in the medical field to help people to relax prior to surgery and in the military to create simulated instructional environments. Commercial application of this technology could come in many forms—most interesting is the possibility for the user to manipulate and create his or her own customized versions of brand experience.

You will see that once you enter the realm of holographic technology, your mind will begin racing with possibilities. Already some brands have used this technology to create exciting brand experiences—Kirin Beer has used holographic technology to project holographic images of dragons careening down the streets of Tokyo, and in Soho, New York, one cutting-edge store, the Monastery, provided a guided tour of the store by a "virtual monk." Surprisingly, though, virtual reality retailing still remains a largely unexplored branded experience tool.

One of Coty's brands did use a form of holographic projection for the launch of the Isabella Rossellini fragrance Manifesto. The fixture involved a holographic projection device that showed the package floating above the aisle—literally merchandising the last frontier of available retail real estate—the air—both enhancing the shopping experience and garnering considerable public relations coverage.

Closely linked to this type of innovation, Les Neumann is a true pioneer of emerging technologies and has been at the forefront of creating exciting applications for virtual reality technologies for some time. His latest invention—which, based on its different potential commercial and noncommercial applications, Les has labeled, among other names, "personal relaxation space," "orgasmatron," and "immersive virtual reality pod"—has truly amazing potential for the creation of powerful brand worlds. Apart from this latest invention, the following section discusses another of Les's inventions, an intriguing consumer-empowering concept called the "virtual makeover kiosk."

VIRTUAL REALITY—COMING SOON TO A STORE NEAR YOU

by Les Neumann, Director of the Globian Institute

In 1999, the free-standing kiosk was starting to have a dramatic influence on our society, and touch screens were becoming all the rage. But who was using them, who was engaging them, and for what purpose? The most frequent users of touch screens were the 18- to 34-year-old demographic, and their most frequent application was the automatic teller machine. Since 18- to 34-year-olds in the cosmetics field are the most sought-after demographic, it became logical to me that this age group almost would rather interact with a machine than be confronted by a direct sales person, and by presenting such an opportunity, the kiosk would become the preferred medium to experiment not only with the application of cosmetic products but also with a host of accessories and accoutrements such as glasses, hair styles and colors, and jewelry.

This led me to invent the virtual makeover kiosk. The unit could sit on a retail counter or as a stand-alone unit in almost any venue. I incorporated a digital camera at the top of the unit. The camera clicked the consumer's image and in a matter of seconds displayed her image on the screen. Then the consumer was encouraged to experiment with lipsticks, blushes, eye shadows, and other cosmetic items from a series of color palettes, which then appeared on the image of her face in real time. Each color was accompanied by sound effects to the rhythm of upbeat music. I also incorporated a series of scents that were emitted from the system along with an indicator stating what exact color the consumer was using and what branded fragrance she was smelling. Once the customer had made up her face exactly as she wanted it, she received a printed slip that

compiled a list of the products she decided were perfect for her. The printed slip included the SKU number, price, and manufacturer of each item. The system received rave reviews from the media but never met with commercial success. And yet I still feel that I accomplished some significant breakthroughs that one day will manifest themselves in other iterations. The concept of using digital photography and being able to map a subject's face instantly in order to allow the products to be applied accurately is still revolutionary.

In 2001, my business partner and I invested in and managed a virtual reality development company that was focused on immersive reality simulations for military and industrial applications. The company made tremendous strides in the area of immersive virtual reality and translation of computer-aided design files that were seamlessly optimized as working components within the simulation. I recognized an opportunity to create an immersive virtual reality relaxation pod. My concept pulled together and integrated several existing types of hardware and mated them with proprietary software and proprietary high-definition audio and video that would permit a user to define his or her ideal relaxation destination. In a unique enclosed personal environment, the user is transported into a multisensory environment of his or her choice.

Imagine, for example, that you're on a secluded beach hearing the sound of the ocean's waves lapping against the shore and smelling the aroma of nearby orchids amidst swaying palms stirred by a gentle breeze. Ah, doesn't that sound great! Now come to the realization that it's 20° outside, you're in a mall, and bundled to the max. This is "escapism" at its best and the concept behind the most revolutionary personal relaxation product since the invention of the beach, piña coladas, and babysitters.

This immersive virtual reality pod or personal relaxation space is a collection of existing hardware, including hemispheric display screens, sensory-stimulating seating, location-matched electronic olfactory delivery, specially shot high-definition video, and high-definition sound and unique music combined in a proprietary spherical (shaped like a giant egg) personal relaxation environment. The personal relaxation space provides the methodology for a branded series of entertainment-based consumer-activated products designed to promote a brief bit of relaxation or escapism. For some, it may be a beach; for others, a secluded rain forest; and yet for others, an underwater adventure filled with wildlife and flora. Each personally selected venue provides a noninvasive multisensory environment whereby the mind becomes totally immersed in the on-screen activity, and the stress and anxiety that brought you here is placed on the back burner—at least for the moment. The regeneration and reinvigoration possible through relaxation become a reality.

This technology is in its prototype stages, and I estimate that the impact on the stress and anxiety markets will be dramatic. The pod can mitigate the tortuous indignities of dialysis or chemotherapy with a sense of peace and tranquility, enhance a spa visit by transporting the mind to a relaxed state, or become a mental stimulator back into another time for an Alzheimer's sufferer. All noble goals—and the best news is that they are achievable.

This experiential technology is, of course, susceptible to a multitude of incredible experiential branding opportunities. We will give you the chance to be where you never thought you could be and to experience the essence of the location.

I also see the potential to work with clothing, jewelry, and hair care manufacturers and destinations to interact with subjects by placing them, virtually, in any of their products or destinations. Using my methodology of employing existing technologies, such as body scanning systems, and coupling them with proprietary predictive metric software, we can repurpose such systems and integrate them into dynamic new markets. Logical extensions also will occur in the video gaming markets. Anyone who has experienced new video games can testify that they are getting more real every day. Video games themselves are a transporting mechanism into another place and another persona and also provide escapism—a total multisenso-

ry experience where all your senses are committed to keeping you alive, winning the race, or traveling to other dimensions.

And let's not be puritanical and ignore one of the most profitable and often-visited online experiences—pornography. The porn industry takes in over $9 billion annually. Some of the best-known worldwide firms are involved in porn at arm's length. I'll let your imagination take over here.

Yes, we can customize life. We can transform everyday life into our own personal fantasies with just the click of a mouse or swipe of a credit card. Innovation or intervention? We're not cloning sheep or humans but merely providing a place to relax and take your mind off the trials and tribulations of everyday life.

I believe that widespread use of Les's awesome technologies, and others like these, is just around the corner—it will only take a few maverick corporations to start the ball rolling, and soon we'll find ourselves in an entirely new world of virtual branding. You may well wonder what other similar virtual technologies are coming our way. There are companies such as 3D Mirage (www.3dmirage.com) that are using holographic technology in the market today to create display devices that project three-dimensional full-motion images into space. These displays can be used in shopping centers, airports, and other public spaces, and since they are fed via the Internet, advertising content can be changed quickly to suit the time of the day, the weather, or current events. Beyond the flexibility of featuring coffee ads in the morning and movie trailers in the evening, this also means that there is a potential here for brands to speak to people in a more meaningful way—responding to real events occurring in real life. Surely someone also will find a way to make this branded content useful to people—offering an entertaining distraction at a bus stop or information in a branded format, such as directions. However it is used, there can be no doubt that the use of this technology will become more widespread very soon. 3D Mirage is currently working on holographic technology that will be broadcast into people's living rooms through satellite and broadband.[6]

The following section comes courtesy of David Polinchock, CEO of Brand Experience Lab. This company educates corporations about emerging technologies that either enhance consumer experience, enable direct collaboration, or even potentially allow for product cocreation between consumers and brands. The project represents some of the most highly trained, brilliant minds committing their genius to one thing: creating worlds in the image that humans would have them be and giving rise to experiences that lend relevance to the mundane act of consumption.

DON'T CAPTURE, CAPTIVATE

by David Polinchock, CEO of Brand Experience Lab

It's not just a cliché, it is a new world. The changes in the advertising world today are like no other time in history. Never before have we been able to reach an audience in so many ways and places. And never before has the audience had the power to turn off that advertisement in so many ways. Today, the language of advertising and marketing is the language of a hunt. It's about capturing the audience, capturing "eyeballs." So much of our efforts today are about merely being able to claim that we are in the consumer's face. The hunt continues onto the street and sidewalks. Guerrilla campaigns are hot today, but do we really want to create a world where people are worried that everything they do could really be a paid-for advertising message? Street team marketing has become so ubiquitous in urban landscapes that it now borders on street pollution.

What will happen if we don't make the changeover from marketing on functional benefits to creating an emotional experience with consumers that is perceived as truly unique and personal? The answer is easy. People in captivity always revolt—you can take that to the bank. If we don't start looking for ways to captivate rather than capture, then we need to start fortifying the barricades, for the revolt

will come. And sadly, many people in this business will be yelling, "Let them watch commercials" as they're led to the guillotine.

John Hayes, CMO of American Express, had this to say: "Brands are not being built on advertising. If you fly JetBlue, you talk about the experience. That's how you build brands today, through experiences. . . . Ultimately, it's going to be about creating experiences for people." And American Express has been putting that into action. Today, less than 40 percent of the company's total advertising budget is spent on network TV, whereas the company is increasing its budget for *experiences.*

In today's world, it takes more than a creative commercial, a cool product, or a fun, interactive store display to create a compelling brand identity for your audience. We now have an audience that has come to expect dynamic environments in everything they do. They watch content and receive information when they want to, and when they are bored with our content, they make their own. If traditional marketing campaigns no longer serve as the key differentiating factor in this commodity marketplace, what will truly set your brand apart? How do you ignite passion and inspire loyalty for your brand now and into the future? The answer lies with the experience of your brand. A product or service is nothing more than an artifact or an act around which customers have experiences. Over time, your brand will be defined by a total impression of those experiences rather than by the products or services themselves. The right experience set creates a strong and consistent emotional connection with the consumer. Never underestimate the degree to which your customers and consumers will go out of their way for a better experience. In today's world, the consumer has too many choices to put up with half-hearted or inauthentic efforts. Brands today must explore innovative ways to create a stronger identity, bringing the brand story to life in ways that have not been thought of before.

WHAT IS BRAND EXPERIENCE LAB?

Brand Experience Lab is an experience think tank that helps companies to create engaging brand experiences for twenty-first-century audiences. Technology meets media at our loft in Soho. The lab offers hands-on experimentation with technologies that have never been used commercially before. There is no other place where you can interact with this wide array of technologies and discover practical answers to your marketing questions. We look at the messaging about your product and compare it with the experience of your product to look for the gaps and disconnects. Using this information, we then ideate and create compelling, authentic, and relevant brand experiences.

We believe first and foremost in total narrative and integration—as such, we are not married to any one solution, nor do we believe that there is one specific solution. And as a result of our university partnerships, strategic alliances, and board of advisors, marketers gain the best understanding of what technologies are available and possible in the field of experience marketing.

EMERGING TECHNOLOGIES

Technology is now part of every aspect of our marketing lives. We have VOD/TiVo, interactive billboards, Webisodes, podcasting, SMS/MMS, and video on our cell phones. In the future we'll see wearable computers, gender recognition, mixed and augmented reality, brain scanning and behavioral targeting, gesture tracking, and a bunch of technologies that haven't even been thought up yet. And in-store you add digital media, radiofrequency identification, dynamic pricing, smart technologies, and even tools for people to check pricing using the cameras on their cell phones.

We've divided some key emerging areas that might have the greatest impact on the "experience economy" into two areas.

Mixed Reality (MR)/Augmented Reality(AR). The idea of combining the real world with the virtual is not necessarily new, but the technologies available today give us a much greater opportunity to bring it to fruition. In the early days of the Internet, when everyone was talking online and offline (and many still are), we talked about creating "oneline" experiences—experiences that moved you from the online to the offline world and vice versa. People don't live online or offline, they just live. MR/AR lets people live in the real world but gather information as an "overlay" to the world.

- *Mixed reality (MR).* Mixed reality is the merging of real and virtual worlds to produce a new environment where physical and digital objects can coexist and interact. In an MR experience at the Institute for Simulation and Training at the University of Central Florida, participants enter a battlefield simulation environment that combines the real and virtual worlds together. While the audience sees just a blue screen in the doorway, the participant in the head mount sees video content. Initial consumer uses for MR experiences probably will be focused in the out-of-home entertainment field, where this could lead to the next generation of theme park attractions. By combining the real set with the virtual experience, this creates the first "holodek" of the *Star Trek* series, something that has intrigued people since the first time they saw it. It creates great opportunities for repeat visits to these attractions because content can be updated or modified based on previous visits, as well as personalized so that each guest receives some slightly altered information.
- *Augmented reality (AR).* Augmented reality is a field of computer research that deals with the combination of real world and computer-generated data. At present, most AR research is concerned with the use of live video imagery, which is digitally processed and "augmented" by the addition of computer-generated graphics. Advanced research includes the use of motion-tracking data, marker recognition using machine vision, and the construction of controlled environments containing any number of sensors and actuators.

On the spectrum between virtual reality—which creates immersive computer-generated environments—mixed reality, and the real world, augmented reality is closer to the real world. Augmented reality adds graphics, sounds, haptics (tactile sensations), and smell to the natural world as it exists.

In the next decade, researchers plan to pull graphics out of television screens or computer displays and integrate them into real-world environments. Video games are expected to drive the development of augmented reality, but this technology will have countless applications. Everything from tourist maps to military field information delivery systems will benefit from the ability to place computer-generated graphics and information in the field of vision. Augmented reality displays, which eventually will look much like a normal pair of glasses, will allow informative graphics to appear in your field of view, and audio will coincide with whatever you see. These enhancements will be refreshed continually to reflect the movements of your head.

In the future, when wearable computers are in much greater use, AR will play a more significant role in our daily lives. Many universities have developed wearable computer labs, exploring everything from full computers with heads-up displays to clothing that can monitor our health. These wearable systems will create a network of technologies that all "talk" to each other, sharing information about what is happening to us in real time. Currently, there are a number of very practical business applications using AR, and we certainly see that trend continuing. In the retail world, for example, planograms might be part of an AR experience with product information projected onto the actual store shelves. For consumers who wish to receive such information while they walk through the grocery store, product information can be projected right onto the actual products themselves, including the easy information such as pricing and/or specials but also more detailed information such as nutritional information. The system also could be programmed to let you know which products go together while you're creating a specific recipe or perhaps if you're shopping for a specific diet (e.g., low salt, etc.). This kind of visual information could be extremely helpful to today's time-starved shopper and is made even more valuable by the fact that it is an "opt in" service.

AR also will allow us potentially to have a more creative interaction with the real world. Think of the variety of new experiences possible through virtual characters being placed in the real world. Could Sesame Street characters help my four-year-old daughter learn no matter where she is? Could the Count help her learn to count right there in a store? Once we move from the technologists to the storytellers, both AR and MR will open the door to experiences that we've only dreamed about!

Synthetic Environments and Characters: Examples of Tomorrow Today. Virtual interview technology allows you literally to ask questions and carry on a real-time conversation with an actual or virtual image of a person, whether it's on a Web site, kiosk, store front, or other device. The fact that consumers feel that they are engaged in an actual question and answer session and that their needs are being directly and promptly attended to create a much more fulfilling experience. Researchers at Carnegie Mellon University's Entertainment Technology Center created one of the first synthetic interviews as an interaction between a human and a sophisticated multimedia database. They used an actor to portray Albert Einstein and answer people's questions. Imagine chatting with Einstein himself—now that's an experience!

Guests can use either a drop-down menu or a natural-language search to ask questions and receive responses from the database personality. If a question not covered in the database comes up, the guests will be asked if they would like to be contacted when the answer is available, creating an opportunity for ongoing dialogue with the audience. The synthetic interview allows you to look at an image of a person and watch him or her answer your question in real time. In some instances, the synthetic interview helps users to feel as if they are getting private "face time" with a person. In addition to more traditional uses (i.e., an updated version of FAQs), synthetic interview technology can be used to help companies create a deeper *emotional* connection with their audience. For example, in a post-Enron world, letting people have access to the CEO or other C-level execs can create a sense of transparency and inspire trust.

There are also ways to use synthetic interviews to allow children to speak to historical figures (such as Einstein), whom they would not have the chance to engage otherwise. Think of the learning that could be accomplished by having children speak with Dr. Martin Luther King about his life in the 1960s.

While much work is being done to better connect people who are already connected, a greater challenge is to create tools for people who are currently "unconnected" and allow them to enter the networked world of the twenty-first century. One example of those efforts is the PCtvt.

The PCtvt is designed to be an "Internet appliance" and is being created specifically to help with a largely illiterate audience. Its menu-driven interface allows people to interact with the networked world without needing to know how to read or write. This is creating extensive challenges for the designers of the systems because it actually requires more computing power than a computer using a keyboard for access.

While this project is still in development, it will open up an estimated audience of over three billion people to the connected world that we live in today. And that could provoke some very significant changes in terms of how information flows and is used in the future.

As with changes that have occurred throughout human history, our job is to explore the new tools available to us and see how they can be used to create a better experience for our audience. We must be extremely consumer-centric in everything we do to ensure that we put their value chain front and center. Only then we will create value for ourselves.

WHAT ARE WE WAITING FOR?

It's Time to Enable Dreams

So I ask—what are we waiting for? Marketing already has access to tools beyond our imaginations; I challenge us all to use them. The whole notion of consumer insight has become quaint—the fact is that the concept of insight itself is antique. Today we are increasingly equipped with nothing less than the potential for nearly complete, permission-based, two-way consumer interaction. However, as we hurl head first toward this thrilling, seemingly limitless technology-enabled world, we must remember that knowledge and wisdom are different. Insight comes from wisdom. Wisdom comes from real-world understanding.

The more wired our culture becomes, the greater the value of human touch. Think, for example, of the success of what seem to be "antitech" companies, such as Approche Sur Measure, which offers its high-end clients personalized, one-on-one customer service via the phone—a phone answered by a dedicated, live, expert human being—a human being with both a name and a human voice. People today are clearly frustrated with the lack of human contact. We are lonely. In the very broadest sense, *brand clubs,* as they have been called, may in fact be yet another method of easing twenty-first-century loneliness. Can this need ever be fulfilled through intelligent "synthetic characters" or other highly responsive interactive technologies that allow us every opportunity for customization? I don't think so. The future holds a place for both human and technological consumer intelligence and interactive models.

And as we experiment with getting the proportions of techno versus human touch just right, we must acknowledge that complete knowledge of anyone or anything, under any circumstance, is a powerful, potentially dangerous tool that can wreak social and cultural havoc in the wrong hands. Consumers as well as marketers will need to remain sensitive to one thing: Be careful what you wish for. Chances are you'll get it. And once you get it, what if you don't like it? What happens then? Where will we go from there?

BE INSPIRED

CREATE WONDER, PROVOKE FASCINATION

> **You ride astride the imaginary in order to hunt down the real.**
>
> —*Breyten Breytenbach,* Return to Paradise

INTRODUCTION:

Exploring a New Era of "Brand Habitation" (Instead of Consumer Manipulation!)

This chapter is where the great leap happens—where you'll begin your creative journey into consumers' lives and realize the power of your new role as cultural liaison and style provider. I guarantee that this may be just about the most dynamic, important, and fun thing you have ever done. Despite the challenges of new cultural and psychographic complexities, rapidly shifting competitive environments, and more discerning consumers, this is truly an amazing time to be in marketing, a time like no other in history—ripe with opportunity.

Today, mature brands are clinging to life, and births of relevant new brands are simply much too few and far between. Rose Marie Bravo, the former CEO of Burberry—a brand brought back from the brink of extinction—was quoted recently in *The Economist*,[1] saying that she sees the future of brand experience to be not only a proliferation of licensing and endorsement, which instantly identify a brand to a set of values, but also a greater number of (heretofore unlikely) collaborations between like brands within different categories (e.g., Burberry and Dr. Scholl's). Burberry always has had a style—the company simply took that style and applied it to what was going on in the world, and voilà, a great turnaround occurred. But Burberry, it would seem, is still only halfway there. What Bravo claims to be a revelation is merely stating the obvious.

Partnering with other brands and branching out into other product categories are only a small part of what needs to happen for a brand to reach consumers on a myriad of levels. Once a brand has applied the model of (1) really seeing people's lives and (2) creating a brand that enables and augments consumers' lives, then it also must seek out every mechanism possible to create a multidimensional "brand web" that touches consumers' lives in numerous ways. And, like a web, the design of consumer interaction will no longer be one-sided or linear. That's the beauty of a web; it appears both random and deliberate. It is nearly impossible to determine where it begins and where it ends.

The aim of this chapter is to conduct an in-depth exploration of how to create new worlds of brand experience through lifestyle participation. I will show you exactly how to create a "living brand" by developing a never-ending, nonintrusive brand web that reaches all consumer touch points in the most exciting, emotionally vibrant ways possible. As we will see in this chapter, to perpetuate a living brand is to evolve continuously. To change, change, change and then change again. Classical branding was all about consistency. Life-enabling branding is all about evolution. Life is never static. So, too, is a living brand. It must continue to actively seek out original, relevant, and consensual vehicles of its expression. And when a brand becomes outmoded, it quite simply must redefine itself or die. Brands are not gods. And consumers have embraced a new era of enlightenment.

In this chapter I will show you how any brand—from "mass market to prestige"—can achieve an amazing degree of aliveness for consumers. Even with a modest budget! We will look at a plethora of examples of innovative brand presence programs culled from around the world from such brands as Ketel One, Selfridges, iPod, Barbie, Virgin, adidas, Target, Baby Phat, and more.

WELCOME TO THE NEW WORLD: A LAND OF "BRAND BIOSPHERES"

Entertainment, fashion, travel, leisure, restaurant, and hotel brands historically have demonstrated the best grasp of the absolute necessity for consumer brand habitation and cocreation. Overall, however, relatively few marketers outside these categories have yet taken the phenomenon of consumer empowerment to the next level—to develop a fully collaborative branding strategy that really *embraces and focuses* "consumer power" to create/propel multifaceted, multilayered *living brands* that are capable of enabling and augmenting consumers' lives in truly meaningful ways.

Bernd Beetz, CEO of Coty Inc, formerly of Christian Dior and Procter & Gamble, had the following to say to other CEOs in observation of this phenomenon.

THE GEEKS HAVE GONE GUCCI

by Bernd Beetz in a Speech at the *Women's Wear Daily* (WWD) Beauty CEO Summit in 2004

Traditional marketing using traditional media forms is no longer sufficient. Traditional media forms do not really connect with consumers' lifestyle orientations. And they no longer deliver the kinds of audiences they once did. More important, they aren't "sticky" enough. They don't allow consumers to inhabit the brand in a way that's required in today's marketplace. The electronics industry certainly has gotten this message. It's as if the geeks have gone Gucci. Olympus, the Japanese camera company, recently linked with designer Esteban Cortazar as a nontraditional way to reach consumers and reposition its digital cameras in a way that is more lifestyle-oriented.

Olympus sponsored a recent Cortazar show and had the designer create a one-of-a kind silver "Esteban Cortazar for Olympus" camera bag. Estaban himself emerged with a digital camera strapped to his jeans. At a recent Baby Phat fashion show in New York, models strutted down the catwalk with new Motorola Baby Phat phones clipped to their clothes. The phone is actually a limited edition of one of Motorola's new phones that will be available only at Bloomingdale's. Clearly, these phones are not intended to be a big revenue source. But they do create an aura of exclusivity and relate to a high-end, fashion-oriented target.

Or take adidas, one of Coty's partners. The company has a promotions unit dedicated to communicating with trendsetters who influence other end customers. The philosophy of the group is based on the premise that consumers won't stand for being coerced. But they will respond if the outreach has something to do with their interests, lifestyles, and values. This is particularly true in marketing to trendsetters in the youth market, who are very sensitive to perceived manipulation.

In light of Beetz's observations, which reinforce my own thoughts, Disneyland, the Disney and Warner Brothers stores, the ESPN store, the Discovery Channel store, the REI store, Planet Hollywood, the island owned by Jose Cuervo Tequila, the Hershey theme park, the Gaudi House owned by Chupa Chups in Barcelona, and the unbranded European Levi's stores (more lifestyle artifact aggregation than branded Levi's specialty stores) all have hinted at things to come for virtually every brand category. But they are only the beginning. Despite their innovation and creativity, they will, in the very near future, find themselves challenged by products, brands, and innovative new methods of retailing and direct consumer collaboration bordering on what previously may have been considered variations of science fiction. The future is no longer distant. The future of marketing is now. And our challenge is not only to catch up to culture but to constantly surpass the most daring, exhilarating expectations of consumers. In return, consumers not only will embrace the result but also, in fact, will support our efforts as together we create brands and branded lifestyles that satisfy on the level of collective dreams, a concept I refer to again and again. This will result in the proliferation of meaningful relationships not only between brands and consumers but also between consumers and their like-minded peers—peers who may share no demographic attribute other than a single common interest or shared value.

If one traces the evolution of the Turner Media Group and how it has created "media real estate" in which thematic "media building lots" (various themed channels and branded media) are created and populated based on psychological location (or lifestyle), it becomes quite clear that consumers and visionary media providers are ready to build. What they ultimately build is anyone's guess. But the fact that marketing and advertising will function in the capacity of a pseudoarchitect is a foregone conclusion. When it comes to the notion of branding and my analogy of media as the newest form of cultural architecture, I asked Jim Morrison, the former general manager of Turner Media's Fashion and Beauty Network, his opinion. Jim replied, "It's not a mistake that great beauty and fashion brands have historically been referred to as houses. Perhaps what we have done at the Turner Networks, by creating different channels for different sorts of consumers, is to create homes for content and commercial messages that house not only brands but also their consumers."

I couldn't agree with Jim more. Consumers today want brands that are custom created according to their desires and lifestyles. They want brands they can "live in." The living brands strategy gives dimension to a brand so that it can—sometimes quite literally, as in the case of the Versace hotel—be inhabited. Let me explain.

The Palazzo Versace Hotel creates what I call a *brand biosphere*—a completely evolved brand world designed to give people a visceral multilayered experience of all that is Versace. It is a great example of creating a living brand because it is done so well—to perfection, with every small detail taken into account.

The hotel, located on a private marina on Australia's beautiful Gold Coast, exudes the dazzling over-the-top, indulgent elegance the brand is so well known for, incorporating the same opulent Italian Renaissance design aesthetic in the architecture, decor, and furniture that permeates the fashion collections. The result is that visitors can actively participate in the Versace fantasy through every aspect of their sensory lives for a few days—from the artfully selected fine-china tea cups they sip from in the morning to the very "Versace-esque" mosaic tile designs of the walls of the beautifully appointed bathrooms where they soak in tubs at end of day. The brand itself has become a real, tangible destination—an exclusive, luxurious place existing in multiple dimensions—the physical and psychological. This is what I call *lifestyle enablement* and a prime example of the living media that naturally results as an extension of living brands.

The fact that these ultraluxurious branded hotels are on the rise—as evidenced by Armani's, Bulgari's, Missoni's, and Byblos's recent developments of spectacular collections of worldwide branded hotels, all reflecting in extravagant detail the design aesthetic of their respective brands—is further evidence that the age of the brand biosphere truly has arrived. In the marketing of the future, marketers still may provide the style, but it will be the consumer who will provide all the substance in a world constructed of branded experiences.

Brand biospheres are physical or psychological spaces where like interests, desired experiences, and happy cohort consumers come to dwell. Really it's all about fusing consumer desire with an identifiable brand mark—a brand geography or an implied emotional street address. After its acquisition by L'Oréal, Redken moved to New York. Suddenly, the California-bred brand assumed by osmosis the sophisticated glamour and contemporary street style of its new 5th Avenue address, merging that "sense of place" with Redken's established prowess as a technologically superior brand. Redken changed its name, officially morphing into Redken 5th Avenue NYC. This mature brand is now stronger, more dominant, and far, far hipper than ever before. That's the power of place establishing a precedent for emotional real estate valuation—both real and invented real estate.

FIGURE 4-1 ■ **Not only will the future require consumer collaboration, but brands also will unite to reflect a shared ability to address consumer needs, as seen in the LYCRA "Has It" campaign, overlaying the message of all its cooperative advertising.**

The brilliant branding effort that led to the creation of Hotel LYCRA in São Paulo is another case in point. How do you build awareness and foster a "sexy" design-conscious buzz around a fiber brand? The answer: Create a conceptually focused "faux hotel" (there are no real rooms to check into) as a shopping, restaurant, and cultural venue showcasing innovative interior design, art, food, and fashion with the aim of allowing people to experience LYCRA, the brand, in many nontraditional ways.

Although Hotel LYCRA has closed its doors due to zoning issues, it contained boutiques featuring up-and-coming designers' cutting-edge interpretations of LYCRA (from apparel to chairs stretched with the fabric and even flexible dinnerware!), several gourmet restaurants, and a LYCRA Museum where interactive exhibits were ever-changing and always exciting, making this hotel a trendy destination among both locals and tourists. It and the other amazing efforts by LYCRA undeniably have transformed a fiber into an emotionally rich brand biosphere. When it comes to fascination, LYCRA "has it," and more important, LYCRA knows what to do with it (see Figure 4-1).

The LYCRA story is a great example of creating a living brand that reaches consumers by responding to their lifestyles with unique, fascinatingly authentic offerings. The lesson here is that if LYCRA "has it," your brand can have it too. All it takes is a little imagination, some daring, and a great deal of cultural sensitivity.

THE MEDIA IS THE MESSAGE: REDEFINING MEDIA FOR A NEW GENERATION

Today's consumer has very clear ideas about what he or she wants and is increasingly adamant about getting it. Consumers demand that brands deliver on their promises. Media is an implied or actual promise—whether it be functional, psychological, or experiential. Traditional media has been so codified, sanitized, monopolized, and aggressive that most of us, having grown up viewing it, now see it more as a necessary evil than as anything useful or pleasant; hence, while it still can help to generate sales, many of us wonder how and why it does. Furthermore, when asked, most people would readily admit that most commercial messages are simply not to be believed; lies not only have redefined reality, but they also have usurped its very space. However, without alternatives, consumers had little choice but to sit back and bear it. They're not sitting back anymore—thus defining a new consumer-empowered age, as well as a new brand emancipation proclamation—establishing new rules for marketing.

The biggest opportunity for relevant, truthful brand contact in this new age is through action and emotional *location,* not words or vapid images. These actions will occur organically over the course of consumers' daily activities, respect their space, and speak only when spoken to. The question becomes why it is that many of us in marketing resist accepting the inevitable. We all know that consumers today are much harder to reach. They are busier, more distracted, and have more media from which to choose (a euphemism for bombardment and sensory overload). They lead lives that are more complicated and less predictable. Yet, surprisingly, even today, the bulk of marketing budgets are spent on traditional interruptive advertising. The tides, however, are shifting. American Express, for example, has dared to seriously examine its media strategy and, as result, although it spent 80 percent of its marketing budget on TV in 1994, by 2003, that number had fallen to 35 percent. The company now spends the other 65 percent on product placement, sponsoring music concerts with celebrities such as Sting, various festivals, and other grassroots marketing initiatives.

As I mentioned earlier, Procter & Gamble, another major corporation with long-time ties to TV advertising, also reexamined its strategy. In 2004, the Cincinnati-based company was the number one U.S. advertiser, spending roughly $2.5 billion on TV—more than 80 percent of its estimated $3 billion ad budget. But P&G announced that in 2006 it will cut TV spending and look for new venues. Its commitments to cable channels may fall by as much as 25 percent, whereas its spending on broadcast networks will be cut around 5 percent. It also is expected to reduce spending on syndicated daytime talk shows such as *The Oprah Winfrey Show* and *Ellen.* As P&G's global marketing officer Jim Stengel put it at a conference of media buying executives in 2004, "There must be, and is, life beyond the 30-second TV spot." He also declared, "We must embrace the consumer's point of view about TV and create advertising consumers choose to watch."[2] Perhaps models such as those promoted by Turner Media will be the evolution of the 30-second spot Mr. Stengel seeks. More likely, it will be a combination of branded entertainment platforms seamlessly interwoven with breakthrough retail experiences and, of course, the power of consumer-to-consumer dialogue enabled via the Internet and new mechanisms of connection already on the horizon that, combined, will fuel this shift, led, of course, by the consumer.

Meanwhile, the advertising industry only recently has been waking up slowly to the fact that traditional advertising is (1) worst case—dead, or (2) best case—morphing. The past decade has seen advertisers frantically reinventing their business models, becoming overnight experts in nontraditional media, and exploring new ways to reach consumers through outdoor media, increased product placement, sponsorships, and events. But what they are not always getting is that what's needed is more, far more, than an old-fashioned "plug" slapped onto a new media form.

The collaborative branding model proposes that the media often is the message! This is not a new phrase. It has been used for years. It has meant that, for instance, if an inexpensive brand runs advertising in a prestigious magazine such as *Town and Country,* the product immediately takes on the aura of what that magazine and other brands contained within that magazine represent. This was and remains true. However, the notion of media as message is evolving—and has now come to mean something far more encompassing, far more direct and profound. Consumers are now media. And their lives constitute the messages that to this day still seem to remain largely unheard.

To top this off, media and reality have merged. What does this mean? It means that all media, like brands themselves, now quite literally *belong* to consumers. I'll give you an example. In the 2005 holiday season, some of the most talked-about new gifts were various devices enabling individual consumers to broadcast their own personalized "podcasts." As podcast superstars inevitably emerge from the ranks of consumer/creator podcasters, how long will it be before companies start paying the more successful podcasters for commercial time on this new form of consumer-created media? Chances are that there are clever (if not underhanded) media planners already working out strategies for this. We will be paying consumers to broadcast brand messages (imbedded in highly personalized, allegedly random podcasts) to other consumers so that companies can, in theory, "earn" the right to create brands that give the impression of being consumer-created, with the existence of these brands being noted by the actual voices of fellow, allegedly unbiased consumers and lifestyle cohorts. The concept is astounding—as long as the voices remain coercion-free. Otherwise, consumer cynicism will only escalate, not diminish—the negative result of slapping an old branding model on a new media form, the danger I mentioned earlier.

I am not suggesting that the future of media will be limited to a single form. However, whatever media form you choose for your brand, it should be a vibrant, honest representation/reflection of current culture, perpetuating a lifestyle and set of values that already exist—free of brand intervention. The now-famous and very successful iPod outdoor ad campaign embodies this idea in a very simple manner. These outdoor print ads were created for iPod by OMD in 2004 to build a broader awareness of Apple's then-niche product. The challenge was to attract new consumers while maintaining the cool factor for the earlier adopters—to find a way to invite people in to the iPod culture, which is really about the culture of music. The simple, brilliant idea behind the effort was to celebrate the common bond between people in their love of music by showing people dancing and grooving with their iPods in a very kinetic, graphically stylized way. iPod made a direct connection with different youth music cultures and conveyed a clear understanding of how to use—and enjoy!—the product. However, living media sometimes even assume a life beyond a living brand, meaning that the aggregation of emotion related to a product or collection of products often takes on the collective attire of cultural reflection, inspiring, but not creating, extensions and evolution of that culture.

A WORLD WITHOUT CATEGORIES: FLUID, CONCEPTUAL, ALL-EMBRACING

One of the best examples of the kind of lifestyle/cultural affinity that brands need to develop today is how some brands have been able to stretch their product offerings to previously unheard of limits—far beyond the confines of their traditional categories. The truth is that today, traditional categories often are misleading or meaningless. Marketers really need to think purely in terms of lifestyle and intangible, emotional benefits in order to place their brands accurately in terms of category. As long as you stay true to a brand's promise and keep the emotional quotient strong, your brand can have enormous elasticity. It depends quite simply on how far your mind can stretch and, above all, how much people really love a brand—which ultimately is linked to how well your brand enables consumers to love themselves and the way they choose to live.

Virgin's love of its consumer has been reciprocated by its loyal fan base, which is why Virgin, originally a record label, has been able to move seamlessly and successfully into such categories as airlines, trains, finance, books, travel and resorts, health clubs, beverages such as wine and soft drinks, personal electronics, cars, cinemas, cosmetics, and even bridal wear (called Virgin Brides, of course!). This innovative, much-imitated brand has captured a modern, fun, edgy entertainment-focused brand equity that consumers themselves have adopted and shared with their cohorts. Meanwhile, Virgin has been careful to make certain that the brand stays true to its roots as it morphs into new forms—product areas are linked through the overall Virgin lifestyle that is conveyed—funny, edgy, irreverent, urban, and above all, premised on "entertainment everything."

Virgin has also succeeded because it found ways to become a part of its consumers' lives—*and to help make things more fascinating, fun, or easy for those consumers.* In the early days, Virgin became renowned for its surprising menu of perks, such as massages or manicures on transatlantic flights. And Virgin has shown some real understanding of the power of brand collaboration. For example, a company-sponsored student Web site (www.virginstudent.com) is an open forum for students to use and express themselves and communicate with one another. There is a matchmaking service and lots of information about music, concerts, and fashion, with sections that focus on Virgin products cleverly woven into the content as special offers and deals. Virgin in all its companies and Web sites is clearly focused on becoming a resource for the consumer—the company wants consumers to look to it as a partner in their leisure activities.

Another example of cultural affinity and cohort marketing is how in some markets Nike has been able to expand into products such as urban (but still active-focused) fashion and accessories and portable consumer electronics such as mobile phones. The idea here is that the brand, Nike, supports a busy, modern, on-the-move lifestyle where physical activities and sports may be blended into many different daily activities (your workout could be sprinting up the stairs to your office!), and there may not always be time to change clothing before heading to the gym. This is how Nike's consumer is living in his or her daily life, and the evolution of the Nike brand offering is smartly reflecting this reality.

A multifaceted evolution for brands in every category is increasingly possible today because lifestyle-oriented brands can capture an entire emotional territory and satisfy multiple consumer needs on multiple levels. But this needs to be done intelligently—and it's not easy. Some brands, such as Coca-Cola, have been struggling for some time to move beyond their particular category in the hearts and minds of their core consumers (teens) in order to embody a more multifaceted fun, young, urban spirit. Coca-Cola has created teen fashion lines such as Coca-Cola Ware and programs that seek to leverage Coke's brand equity in an interactive and original way that involves consumers and helps to develop and expand their world, such as the Coca-Cola Youth Partnership Programs.

The Youth Partnership Programs in academics, the arts, and athletics offer a wide array of sponsorships for everything from encouraging literacy among first-generation immigrant children to corporate internships, and from college athletic scholarships to creative endeavors such as a filmmaker's award. Coca-Cola clearly has understood the importance of becoming a part of the consumer's everyday life in a meaningful way. An entire section of the Coca-Cola Web site is devoted to music, with interactive features such as the one that allows kids to play D.J. by mixing and then downloading their own music. But whether these efforts are successful in deepening a connection with consumers remains to be seen—results from Coca-Cola Ware were less than stellar.

While Coca-Cola remains a huge, truly global brand, and despite its obvious efforts to reflect culture, perhaps it is still experiencing a decline in its cultural relevancy, as reflected by the failure of its clothing line to take off. Perhaps it is not impossible that a time-honored, iconic megabrand such as Coca-Cola could be vulnerable to serious decline. This is the price you pay for defining a market or consumer need rather than allowing real life to define it for you. A great example of this is the New Coke fiasco, which Sergio Zyman, former marketing head at Coca-Cola, actually touted ironically as a success in his book *The End of Marketing as We Know It*,[3] based on what to me remains an unfathomable rationale. Rather than reflecting the true need behind consumers' affinity for Coca-Cola, Mr. Zyman and Coca-Cola tried to impose a new one. The lesson here is very clear: We are, indeed, witnessing the end of marketing as we knew it, as well as the birth of a brand-new consumer-empowered marketing prototype.

But, of course, this is not to say that some degree of marketing intuition is not valid and needed. In today's market, if you are not searching constantly (including the search from within yourself) for intelligent ways to expand the relevance of your brand into new realms, then you also may be missing real opportunities to deepen your connection with consumers—and if you are not moving toward your consumers, you are moving away from them. There really is no status quo anymore, just ultimate survival or disintegration.

Ultimately, a brand is as much an idea as it is a product. What, for example, do the movies *Toby McGuire, Spartacus,* and *Rebel Without a Cause* have in common? On the surface, not much. But they are all linked by the fact that they explore the theme of righteous indignation. They share an archetypal emotional appeal. Once you can begin to make this kind of leap in thinking relative to your brand and follow that thinking through, you can find yourself on the path to a potentially very exciting brand evolution. You'll find a really great example of what I am talking about in the following section entitled "Colorstrology," a new brand based on a brilliant concept created by Dann Gershon, president and founder of Product Lounge, a Miami-based licensing and marketing firm.

COLORSTROLOGY: THE COLOR OF MEANING

by Dann Gershon, Product Lounge

Dann Gershon has come up with some really amazing brand concepts for his clients, from one of the most successful ad campaigns in the history of the Partnership for a Drug Free America to Colorstrology, a revolutionary concept that he created for Pantone, the world leader in color communication. In order to bring a new emotional element to the Pantone brand and increase consumer recognition for its licensing program, he conceived and created the Colorstrology brand and then brought in a renowned spiritualist, who combined the ancient traditions of astrology and numerology with the emotional essence of color.

Colorstrology filled a void by producing an emotional layer to Pantone, allowing for increased emotional stretch and broader related licensing opportunities in a wide variety of consumer product categories, as well as a rich content base for both traditional publishing and the new digital media market. This brilliant concept allows consumers to interact with and engage color in a very unique and personal way. Although unexpectedly personal and dynamic for a company associated with precise color specification, Gershon's approach to marketing color to the consumer has infused Pantone with increased brand equity and has differentiated it from a sea of self-proclaimed "color experts" around the world.

The marketing concept of Colorstrology now has turned into a brand unto itself and has attracted the interest of several top retailers around the world. Gershon was one of the founders of Product Lounge and recently has founded and operates Danger Management, a Miami-based lifestyle marketing consulting and licensing agency also serving as a key provider of cultural and entertainment content to a broad range of industries and clients.

Colorstrology's fusion of consumer collaboration and cultural inspiration was the result of serendipitous alignment of both external forces and the razor-sharp ability of Gershon to connect the appropriate dots. Fortunately, this sort of brilliance is not necessarily a process beyond replication. In fact, in a process not that much different from the think tanks I conducted for Coty, the following section outlines a proven model developed for Mattel by Ivy Ross that empowers both consumers and creators. Ivy, a true innovator and creative visionary, has worked for over 25 years in design management for such companies as Swatch Watch, Calvin Klein, Liz Claiborne, Avon products, and Coach and currently is the executive vice president of design and development for Old Navy, The Gap Inc.

PROJECT PLATYPUS: CARVING A NEW PATH TO INNOVATION

by Ivy Ross, Executive Vice President of Design and Development for Old Navy, The Gap Inc.

It was 2001, and I had been senior vice president of design and development of the girls division at Mattel toys for three years. The words *innovation* and *creativity* had started appearing in annual reports. Businesses were struggling because it was no longer about how quickly or how cheaply something could be made, but instead, the quality of the "idea" was becoming equally important—not just any ideas, but new ideas that excited and delighted the consumer.

Mattel restructured its development design cycle for more "creativity" and looked to hire more "creative people," thinking that that was the answer. I looked out over the sea of 200 creative people in my division working individually in little gray boxes on items identified as "needs" by the marketing department. I knew intuitively that there was a better way to unleash the talent we already had. We were not giving employees the gift of experience and stimuli before

we asked them to generate something new. Creativity is in part about freedom. The problem in large companies is that your creative flow of possibilities is constantly being stopped in order to be observed, reviewed, or measured, thereby turning an idea or design into an ordinary thing before it has a chance to become extraordinary.

It became clear to me that we needed to create a process to explore the possibilities for Mattel rather than working "against" realities. In a training course I had spoken with Mukara Meredith about how living systems theory can be applied to groups. I had learned how in a group, when members reach a certain level of interconnection, they form a web or matrix where the resources, talents, and expertise of each member become available to the whole group. I realized that I needed to have a group of people working together in an immersive way, giving them the gifts of information, stimuli, and time to allow for interconnection to occur. I asked for 12 volunteers to conduct an experiment.

I set up a "What if?" scenario to explore: "What if there was a building toy designed just for girls?" There was none. The only attempt from Lego, the largest brand in the category, at the female market was creating pink Legos. None of the volunteer designers had ever designed a building toy before. I believe that sometimes your greatest strength lies in the very thing you have not yet done. Once the group was formed, we immersed ourselves in questions— "What are the different ways to connect things?" "What do girls think about first when they begin to build something?" "What do girls build in their minds?" I brought in architects and mechanics that gave the team lectures and workshops around these issues. We then set up playgroups with girls. Unlike traditional methods, we did not watch them through one-way mirrors but engaged in conversations with them while they created not with other toys but with raw materials. From leading experts we learned about how females versus males tend to think and play. Rough prototypes were put in front of kids, and we made refinements based on observations. The winning direction became clear. The product concept, along with the brand name, packaging, merchandising, advertising, and business plan, was presented to upper management, who were extremely impressed. The brand called Ello was launched on the market in late 2002. "It blew me away," said Chris Byrne, a long-time industry analyst and a contributing editor at *Toy Wishes* magazine. "You rarely see something as original anymore in this industry. Usually everybody copies everybody else's ideas." Consumers rewarded this originality and collaboration with their dollars.

I then created an ongoing program, calling it "Project Platypus" because a platypus is a totally unique being in the animal kingdom. The program took 12 people from their jobs for three months. The deliverable for each session was a viable new brand or new big idea for an existing brand. I found the perfect partner to help run the program, the brilliant David Kuehler, who at the time was working at Disney. David added his eclectic background as an engineer, designer, teacher, and theatrical director to the mix, bringing in theatrical processes, improvisation, and storytelling. After an initial immersion period, the group began to form a living system with trust and passion at its core. Egos and titles were checked at the door, and people related to each other in new ways. In most companies, when you have a task, there is a strict time line throughout the entire process, not just a deadline. But creativity needs to happen more organically. Each group had a different rhythm, but they all came up with remarkable brand ideas by the end of the twelfth week. Project Platypus maximized individual positive skills, and instead of creating a competitive environment, the program fostered strong personal relationships. Platypus went on for approximately two years, creating many new opportunities for Mattel.

BRAND MASTERS:

Celebrities as an Ultimate Expression and Indigenous Population of Brand Biospheres

As we saw in Secret #2, celebrities can create powerful brands that resonate with consumers as living reflections of their dreams—because celebrities often are direct creations of and contributors to culture. Celebrity brands, such as Oprah, are the original masters of "lifestyle affinity" because they are seemingly infinitely able to parlay their popularity across multiple categories. Today, Oprah is a talk show, a magazine, a production/film company (Harpo Entertainment), and a book club, among other things. Oprah clearly has enormous power on a cultural level. She has played a huge role in spearheading an entire movement toward self-actualization in the United States. The Oprah brand has been able to cross over into a myriad of categories because Oprah is actually interested in finding ways to contribute to people's lives on a variety of meaningful issues. And we obviously can't talk about Oprah without also talking about Martha—another pioneer in the creation of multifaceted brand biospheres built on the edifices of celebrity personality. The name of Martha Stewart's company—Omnimedia—says it all and certainly gives a good indication that Martha understood precisely what she was doing when she originated her vision. The strength of her company surely will be tested now, post prison, but there is no reason to think that people will give up their love of the brand if Martha is sufficiently contrite and continues her brilliant branding strategy.

Another American cultural and entrepreneurial leader, Russell Simmons, has led a virtual revolution as one of the very first to recognize the significance of the hip-hop music movement and enable it to inspire entire industries—capturing the essence of how this musical genre influences the ways in which many persons dress, talk, and think. Russell Simmons truly demonstrates the convergence of multiple categories under a single aspirational, humanistic, entertainment-inspired brand. He not only created the Def Jam record label and the Phat Farm fashion brand, but he also now has created a new company, Russell Simmons Music. He is behind countless cultural events such as his HBO show, *Def Poetry Jam*, a hip-hop poetry slam, *Def Poetry Jam on Broadway,* and *Hip-Hop Summits,* which is a venue to involve young people in social causes.

Like Oprah, Russell Simmons remains committed to giving back and enriching the community through generous donations to a multitude of charities, as well as his ongoing political and social activism. Russell Simmons's Hip-Hop Summit Action Network is a nonpartisan, nonprofit national coalition of hip-hop artists, record industry executives, and community activists that attempts through concert summits to galvanize youth toward a more active role in politics and social issues. The concept behind the Hip-Hop Summit is youth empowerment and how participating in the political process is a part of empowering oneself as well as effecting social change. In 2004, Simmons supported the "Get Out the Vote" effort that mobilized America's youth to register and vote in a way not seen in many years. Like Martha Stewart, Russell Simmons truly has embraced the notion of omnimedia.

Through the creation of the Baby Phat brand, Kimora Lee Simmons, the fashion designer and entrepreneurial former wife of Russell Simmons, authentically reflects the lives of consumers just as legitimately as Russell does; she simply reflects it from a different mirror, a different angle. Her lavish hip-hop–inspired interpretation embraces a "glamour for all" philosophy that reinforces the notion that all women deserve to dream big, live large, and enjoy the best regardless of race or social status. She has a massive and quite unique appeal across racial, social, and cultural lines, with endorsements from old-guard glamour designers such as Carolina Herrera and Karl Lagerfeld. There is inherent consumer recognition of their own power in Baby Phat's brand positioning. There is validation that even within one audience (the cohorts of the hip-hop lifestyle) there is the opportunity to satisfy the desires of subsets of that audience. This shows us that even within the context of a similar brand theme, addressing similar if not identical lives, one style of marketing does not fit all. Some people fail to understand why Kimora can lead what seems to be an ostentatious lifestyle and still be an authentic link to hip-hop.

The answer is very simple. Perhaps you have seen young people (black, white, and everything in between) wearing T-shirts that say, "Don't hate the player. Hate the game." This is a secret code of sorts—what it means is that the trappings of luxury do not really conflict with the power-to-the-people philosophy of hip-hop. The T-shirt's slogan (which seems harmless enough) is really part of an underground, pseudorevolutionary movement of sorts. The beauty of it is that most parents probably think that it's just a silly slogan referring to baseball or some other sport. And it explains why idols such as P. Diddy and Kimora are celebrated despite their lavish lifestyles, with no stigma of "selling out" to the corporate world attached; in a world filled with oppression, we all have to play a game we may secretly hate just to survive. Young people use this insight to reconcile their own convictions with their identification with these icons. This new crop of young people is nothing if not earnest—earnest with a taste for the good life.

I was fortunate enough to be part of the creation of the Baby Phat fragrance Goddess, and when I first met Kimora Lee Simmons, I adored her immediately. She was unapologetic, proud, strong, brilliant, beautiful, and smart. I understood immediately how she personified and projected culturally inspired dreams. It's not difficult to understand her personal appeal and the power of Baby Phat, which began as an almost accidental flanker of Phat Farm.

Russell Simmons and Tony Austin, president of Russell Simmons Music Group, along with Coty, indirectly, deliberately, or through pure luck contributed heightened relevance to the launch of the fragrance Goddess, the first fragrance from Baby Phat, by Kimora Lee Simmons. Concurrent with the 2005 launch of the fragrance, Russell

Simmons Music signed with a talented group of female German pop/R&B urban musicians called Black Buddafly. The fortuitous simultaneous debut timing of Black Buddafly's musical release "Goddess" and the launch of Baby Phat's fragrance of the same name supported a more profound cultural connection to the word *goddess*, a product name, that otherwise might have been perceived negatively as being pretentious and self-absorbed. Let's admit it, the name Goddess for any product also might have been perceived as, well, a joke. Yet the launch of the fragrance Goddess was anything but a joke—perhaps, in part, due to the lyrics and added dimension of the Black Buddafly song. The song's simple message included this universal truth: Because women are the vessels from which life begins, all women are goddesses.

And while Kimora's supermodel looks certainly conjure up the glamour of Hollywood-created goddesses, her reputation as the devoted, supportive mother of two adorable daughters is a culturally entrenched *idea* (positive archetype) with the potential of outlasting something as ephemeral as physical beauty. Coty responded by using the song in advertising and was inspired to cocreate Goddess street teams to promote the dual notions of ultimate glamour and a deeper, more meaningful message of universal feminine power.

DRAMATIC, PLAYFUL, ENGAGING: GREAT BRANDS ARE PERFORMANCE ART

Marketers must create a dynamic (and hopefully interesting, fun, and meaningful) forum in which brands and people interact directly—not just experientially, but in the form of mutual dialogue, of collaborative brand creation. Theater is a good model if you include the impromptu dynamics of improvisational and street theater. One of my favorite examples of treating brands as performance art is the now-classic Barbie promotion that took place in England in 1998. In an effort to create a new brand impression for Barbie, Mattel painted an entire street in Manchester (buildings, street, lampposts—everything) "Barbie pink."

The result was a playful, *Alice in Wonderland*-like, almost surreal place that appealed to both children and adults. People could experience the brand in a visceral way. It was fun! It was creative. It was not unlike Cristo's Gates, which were constructed in Central Park in 2004 to create a startling new impression of an "everyday" place. The difference: The gates were fine art; Barbie's efforts were a fusion of art and commerce. Another example of this was the great promotion created by OMD for the launch of the new Nissan Maxima. The cars were parked in various busy streets of New York and Los Angeles with nearby everyday curbside urban fixtures—street signs, meters, locked bikes, and lampposts—appearing to be melted by the car's "hotness." The promotions created the desired buzz, drawing thousands of curious spectators and, eventually, the attention of even the mainstream media, with features on *Dateline* and write-ups in publications such as *New York Magazine*.

While it's true that the bar is raised for marketers today because it is so very easy to bore consumers who've already "been there, done that," it is also true that the raising of the bar makes our job that much more fun. A big part of creating a living brand means taking anything that is ordinary in marketing—any traditional media form or promotional event—and turning it completely on its head, infusing it with inspiration and ultimately enveloping it with renewed consumer fascination. One nontraditional and very creative slant on a media form was an adidas billboard ad in downtown Tokyo that featured two live soccer players engaging in a real one-on-one match every day during rush hour. Of course, you cannot help but look at something like that—it's so unusual—but the truly wonderful thing about it was that the match took place at the same time every day for several days running, and one day, one of the players would win, and then, perhaps the next day, the other would win so that people became involved in the game in the same way that you pick and begin to follow a favorite sports team. The living advertisement represents a brilliant variation of what might be termed *accidental* or *spontaneous marketing.* Refer back to the Preface by Creed O'Hanlon and reconsider what you thought he meant.

Other similar examples of truly out-of-the-box living ads are Target's fully vertical fashion show (off the side of a building in Manhattan) in July 2005 and a recent Yahoo! Personals promotion with people inside giant haystacks in Times Square that invited single passersby to search through the haystacks to find dates.

The true litmus test for creating a living brand is how well it draws the consumer inside the brand world—and this ultimately is based on the strength and authenticity of its foundation. When Coty bought Rimmel, it was an established (and somewhat dusty) English brand, strong in certain markets, but not really a global powerhouse brand. As part of Coty, I witnessed and contributed to the rebranding of Rimmel London cosmetics in order to leverage its London heritage in a new and trendy way that would appeal to youthful, fashion-conscious American women.

The brand is all about the fun of swinging, irreverent London—underground parties and edgy street fashion. Coty launched the brand nationwide in the United States at Wal-Mart stores using, among other things, London double-decker buses. The buses appeared at selected Wal-Mart parking lots with London D.J.'s and makeup artists inside to attract Rimmel's potential new North American consumer. It was a huge success—women of all ages (and even a few men) lined up to get a chance to go inside the buses for autographs and makeovers. The Rimmel "tour" hit 300 Wal-Mart stores and several college campuses, giving close to 21,000 makeovers and distributing approximately 150,000 product samples. Sales of Rimmel products increased as much as 24 percent for four weeks following the promotion. And the return to its London roots has bolstered Rimmel's market share even in Europe, where it already was one of the leading brands of color cosmetics (see Figure 4-2).

FIGURE 4-2 ■ **Rimmel double-decker bus: the solution to brand integration.**

Living brands is not just about image; it is, as the name implies, about life. Sponsoring the Grammy Awards is not, in my opinion, a particularly fascinating example of living media. We (both professional and lay) have seen it many times before. Figuratively speaking, it has been done to death. Remember, consumers are alive and, as such, completely spontaneous. Sometimes involving consumers in a brand means provoking, even shocking them—the way real theater often does. Regardless, great marketing, even great living media, is no longer a voyeuristic, formulaic exercise. Remember, more persons watched the conclusion of *American Idol* than the Grammys. Consumers increasingly chose to watch themselves—not dated exercises in celebrity self-congratulation and pathetic glamour-by-association branding.

A great example of fascinating, brilliant promotion/living media is a "reality play" the London department store Selfridges staged. As part of a promotion called "Body Craze" in 2003, the store had 500 naked people line up along several floors of escalators. Of course,

Londoners are a bit more comfortable with the reality of naked bodies than consumers in some other markets, and this would not have worked everywhere. However, it was pretty clever and certainly unveiled the brand in all its glory. Selfridges clearly understands its consumers and is trying hard to connect. The store has created an entire floor called "Spirit," designed expressly to become a destination for young fashion-savvy shoppers and featuring up-and-coming designers, ongoing unique events, D.J.'s and sofa areas, body piercing and tattoo parlors, and a "customization zone" where shoppers can create their own designs with the help of a high-tech design duo "dialogue box."

In looking to create dynamic, powerful living-brand presence initiatives, we would do well, as always, to look to culture for inspiration. And again, using theater as our model, we can find some of the most exciting examples in the form of spontaneous street theater and staged protests. Here is another manifestation of consumers mastering marketing communications methodologies—often with a great deal of savvy. The following section entitled "Show, Don't Just Tell" by writer and branding expert Alisa Clark Ackerman provides the story of how powerful the personal impact of an encounter with a very well-executed street protest/performance can be.

SHOW, DON'T JUST TELL

by Alisa Clark Ackerman, Founder of Brand Circle Creative, a Collaborative of Freelance Brand Consultants and Copywriters

The truth must be shown, not just spoken about. This is what great artists are able to do. Through vivid experience, they reveal to us the deeper truths of ourselves, of our culture, and of society, shaking us sometimes to our very roots. Because of its powerful emotional immediacy and magical ability to draw the audience into the heart of the truth, I have always loved theater best of all art forms. And at times it seems that some of the most dynamic and interest-

ing "theater" happens in the street—in the form of spontaneous performance art and passionate protests.

I believe that brands could achieve a tremendous integration with culture not only through using a traditional theater model in their brand presence initiatives but also through learning from the power of participatory "street theater" to captivate and even transform its audience. In other words, it's not just about creating the next outrageous, visionary spectacle (à la Cirque de Soleil) to halt consumers in their tracks; it's about using the sometimes subtle, ingenious magic of the "fourth wall" (the audience as part of the show) to draw them into the experience. This can be through either direct or indirect (via the imagination) "participation." Sometimes the best way to do this is simply to drop a bit of theater magic into the fabric of everyday life in a way that asks the "audience" of passersby to join your imaginary journey and believe it too—if only for a moment.

A great example of what I am talking about is an excellent staged protest I saw at an outdoor Christmas market in Union Square in New York several years ago. The best part of it was that I did not even realize at first that it was a protest. Intentionally and elegantly, it had been created to lure the audience in and then offer its true meaning as a surprise. It was like this: Walking through the crowd, I suddenly heard beautiful women's voices singing what sounded like old-fashioned carols. I scanned the crowd to find the singers and saw a group of women clad in fine velvet turn-of-the-century dresses. They were wearing historically accurate gloves, hats, shoes, jewelry, and capes and looked perfect—as if they had been neatly lifted out of one time and dropped into another. "Hmm, how charming, how *nice*!" I thought. I couldn't hear the words to the songs they were singing, but it sounded great. As I passed closer by, just as one of the women handed me a pamphlet, I also caught a line from one of the carols (sung to the tune of "Tannenbaum," I believe)—something like, ". . . . and we shall all suffer as victims of our president's ignorance. . . . " I stopped and looked down at the pamphlet, which read:

Ladies of Liberty: Removing the Bodice of Ignorance, One Clasp at a Time.

December 18, 2004—"Sirens against Silence" demonstration in Union Square, NYC

And then I read the mission statement:

> *The Ladies of Liberty exist to defend and demand reproductive and sexual rights. Although women gained the vote in the 1920s and therefore possess a voice, they and all people who demand the right to self-determination still do not possess their own bodies. Through creative and theatrical protest, the Ladies of Liberty draw on the tactics and imagery of the last phase of the women's suffrage movement to fight the current backward slide in our ability to choose.*

And then, at last, I understood. I was incredibly moved. Frightened even. What if they are right? Are we really going so far backward? So fast? Their perfect period costumes now had an eerie quality. Talk about a "wake-up call"! I could have read 10 articles in the newspaper, clicked through five Web sites, or watched as many shows on TV, and none of them would have had the same emotional impact as this demonstration, which did just that—demonstrated its point in the most powerful, direct, and human way possible. See? I am even still talking about it.

BRAND PLAYGROUNDS:
THE ANYTHING AND EVERYTHING "WONDER STORES"

The retail environment offers a prime opportunity to bring brands to life in some very unique and dramatic ways and is, of course, one of the first places to demonstrate the true impact of brand biospheres. Many stores today are, in and of themselves, experiences equaling a visit to a museum or an amusement park. And with the development of branded amusement parks such as Kellogg's Cereal City and the Lego theme parks, the lines of distinction between all of these are fading rapidly.

Anytime you create a physical "place" designed to be an expression of your brand, you have an opportunity for the aesthetics and interactive nature of that place to become the embodiment of consumer-created life projection. This is branding at its most profound, albeit esoteric level. Stores such as the Prada store in Manhattan, designed by Rem Koolhaas, are virtual tours de force of cutting-edge architectural genius that create a conceptual statement about the brand on the level of the finest art exhibit. In fact, the progressive, unconventional design devotes little of the store's enormous space (23,000 square feet) to commerce—instead of merchandise, the focus of the space is a huge concave wave shape that extends the full length of the store.

Prada managers say of the space: "Our ambition is to capture attention and then, once we have it, to hand it back to the customer."[4] The space is meant to house and become a magnet for cultural events in addition to fashion collections. The store houses events such as Programs at Prada, an ongoing collaboration with the Tribeca Film Festival that includes film screenings and panel discussions about the art of filmmaking with up-and-coming filmmakers. The store also makes intelligent use of high-tech innovations such as an electronic customer identification/service system that can track shoppers and their needs and dressing rooms with simultaneous, digitally produced front, back, and side views; phones for requesting another size; and walls you can shift from translucent—so that you can model for your friends—to frosted for privacy.

On a much less grandiose scale, we are seeing this trend toward artistic expression in retail in virtually every genre of store. Stores such as the Diesel Denim Gallery are creating innovative events such as the live audio/video performance and installation featured in its New York store. This exhibit by the Art Collective Fictive contemplates architecture and the nature of shopping so that the store's shoppers have an opportunity to take in interesting and thought-provoking artistic impressions as part of the retail experience.

This ultimately allows for a very different kind of experience and interaction with the brand. And this is really what it is all about—allowing consumers to have a new interaction with brands while also providing a venue for social interaction and cultural reflection.

PLACES OF CONNECTION: WHERE WE'LL ALL WANT TO BE

GDR anticipates that increasing numbers of leisure operators and retailers will take steps to facilitate social interaction and even interest or friendship networks, adding a whole new dimension to their service offerings and filling some of the gaps in our increasingly atomized lives. One example of this phenomenon is the Lloyd Hotel and Cultural Embassy (www.mvrdv.nl) (see Figure 4-3).

FIGURE 4-3 ■ Where once criminals were punished in order to be rehabilitated, a comfortable library at the Lloyd Hotel and Cultural Embassy now liberates minds.

Yet another brand biosphere, confirming this phenomenon is the Red Bull Interactive Bar (www.checkpointmedia.com). The Austrian design consultancy Checkpointmedia created this bar in a hangar-turned-gallery/bar/restaurant/event space at the Salzburg Airport. The horizontal surface of the curved bar displays a continuous digital projection of a miniature fantasy landscape, complete with circling Flying Bulls aircraft (because the bar is sponsored by Red Bull drinks). The aircraft react to touch, so if a drink is placed in the path of an oncoming plane, it will maneuver to avoid it. Hilariously, a miniature Douglas DC-6B functions as a messenger aircraft, stopping when touched and then offering a selection of messages. It then continues its flight until intercepted by another visitor, who can select his or her answer. It then returns to the initial sender (see Figure 4-4).

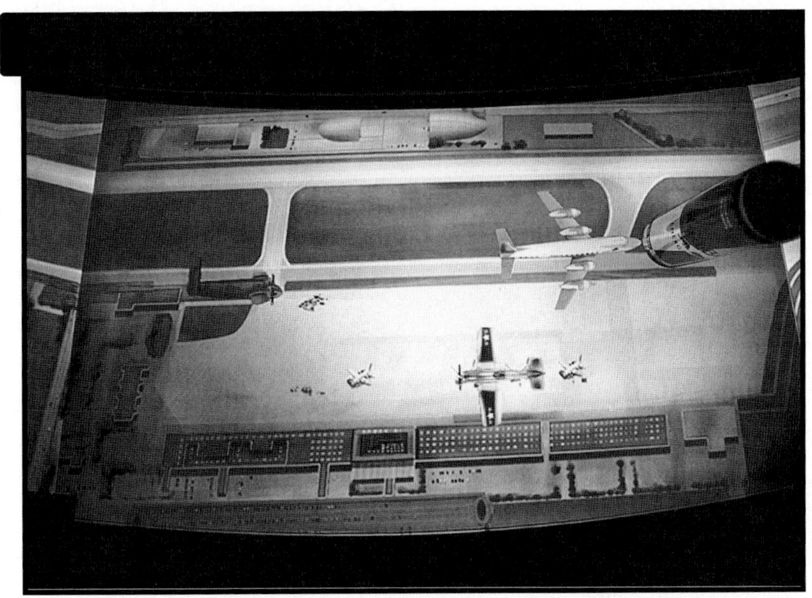

FIGURE 4-4 ■ Simulated reality at the Red Bull Interactive Bar is a true facilitator of human interaction.

Perhaps one of the most dramatic examples of this movement toward cohort collaboration and a potential mechanism of aggregate brand sharing is a developing concept that ultimately may prove to be a prototype for all human interaction and the mechanism ultimately bridging both the digital and the geographic divides.

Not yet launched, this circular building concept enables virtual audio and visual contact between individuals in different cities in real time. The cameras and projectors mounted inside will be in operation 24 hours a day, and the directional speakers and microphones ensure that conversations remain private. Maintenance costs will be met by advertising, which will be interspersed with videoconferencing mode, educational programming, news, entertainment programming, and tourist information. The potential applications for this technology are immense; imagine how a store would tap into people's need to be connected with their friends and relatives in other

countries if these were positioned in every Niketown in the world. The store would be providing an emotional, as well as practical, service to its customers. Check out Tholos at www.tholos-systems.com/htm/hom_fe.htm (see also Figure 4-5).

FIGURE 4-5: FOTOMONTAGE ■ Here, with this innovative device by Tholos, tourists in Paris can observe tourists in Pisa—imagine the branding opportunities.

The future of branding dictates that we will need to think about providing so much more in "brand spaces" than traditional retail venues have provided. We will need to build, per consumer specifications, the types of technological wonderlands we discussed in Secret #3, as well as simple, elegant, and "noncommercial" concepts, such as Tokyo's Relaxation Theme Park, which, unlike other types of amusement parks that are built to thrill, dedicates itself to nothing but tranquility and experiences geared at decelerating versus accelerating the velocity of sensory overload. We will, in fact, need to look to every conceivable form of human reaction for inspiration in creating an entirely new kind of brand world.

LIFE IMITATES ART: Where Culture and Commerce Meet

Just as we see a blending of brands with "reality" today in terms of their integration into real people's lives, we are also seeing a blending of art and commerce—or brands with artistic or pop-culture elements (i.e., reality-television worlds). Unlike others, I don't see this as the death of culture as long as the commerce remains subordinate to the culture driving it. I believe that we must accept this new reality because it is a true reflection of what people want.

Culture and commerce always have coexisted, and my hope is, that in our age commerce finds its legitimate place in culture, benefiting both and, more important, enriching individuals' lives. Some brands already have become such a part of popular culture that, in some cases, they have become beloved artifacts of cultural expression. Think of how Smucker's jelly glass jars with comic-strip superheroes have become such a part of popular culture that they are now considered to be collectors' items. And in Spain, large outdoor advertisements for a brandy called Black Bull had to be reinstalled after being removed because so many people protested vehemently against their removal. The beloved bull symbol literally had become a part of the local cultural landscape! A great example of recognition of the need for brands to move into the artistic arena is the recent opening of the two-story 65,000-square-foot Byblos Art Gallery in Verona, Italy. This fashion brand created the gallery to "converge art, design and fashion in the same space," says Masha Facchini, director of the gallery.

Another way to express a brand's personality in an artistic manner is to make an unexpected (and unobtrusive) artistic contribution to a public space, as opposed to a garish scar on the face of otherwise pristine roadsides, as in the case of many outdoor billboards and environmental signage. The Bombay Sapphire Gin Aquarium at JFK Airport is a prime example. This beautiful blue aquarium provides a calming, relaxing brand experience in the midst of a harried environment. The glass transitions from opaque to clear, revealing a school of live, incredibly beautiful blue fish. You are treated to a moment of surprising beauty and repose. This branding effort not only succeeded in creating a physical brand presence that brought the brand to life, but it also actually provided me with a level of delight I shall always remember. This is living media at its best.

On the other hand, cases such as the Fay Weldon novel for Bulgari, in which the author integrated the brand (for an undisclosed sum) into the storyline, don't seem to be the best form for brand/content partnerships. Efforts such as this may create some awareness but do little to create a real emotional connection with the consumer. Because the risk of gratuitous brand integration is so great, marketers always must ask whether or not they are contributing to or subverting culture before they dare to attempt to actually assert themselves into it. The ability to address this challenge sensitively will define tomorrow's great marketers and differentiate legitimate from fraudulent brands and brand messages. Hallmark, another legendary brand, has long promoted the association of its brands with strong emotional, yet fictionalized entertainment but often has done so with nary a reference to the Hallmark brand in any of it—apart from sponsorship credits. Hallmark got it right.

Another contrived living media flop was the FedEx/*Castaway* movie (for those who missed it, the unlikely plot of a castaway on an island with a stack of FedEx packages as his only line to civilization—and life!). We have to be able to do better than this—there is a certain contrived, consumer-obvious clumsiness in such endeavors.

They have the concept of moving toward branded entertainment right, but the execution simply is too blatantly commercial and contrived. The same can be said for the recent advent of pop songs with so many commercial messages embedded in them that they have become a joke. In the future, as this kind of brand plug becomes more and more commonplace across all forms of artistic expression, we will need to be more clever and much more connected to culture in order to make the brand-content marriage more meaningful—because, above all, brand habitation is more than building a house; it's about building a home.

BMF Media Group was founded in 2003 by young entrepreneur Brian Feit. Take a look at what Brian has to say in the following section that explores, among other things, how "brands need sound tracks." Brian instinctively understands the largely untapped power of music as one of the best common cultural threads to connect people to brands, places, and experiences. With an instinctual knack for identifying eclectic and innovative talent, emerging-marketing trends, and cutting-edge technologies, as well as a growing database of lifestyle-oriented contacts (boutique hotels and shops, celebrity clientele, A-list fashion houses, music supervisors, club and event promoters, corporate sponsors, and much more), Brian successfully combines these diverse resources to develop dynamic, inventive, and often unconventional cross-promotional and cobranding opportunities for his array of artists and projects, including the acclaimed *Operatica* series and electronic music visionaries Waldeck and Jay Jay Johanson. Achievements such as these garnered him recognition in *Advertising Age*'s esteemed "Marketers in Their 20s to Keep an Eye On" A-list.

THE ADVENT OF "ADVERTAINMENT"

Of course, it can reasonably be argued that great entertainment for entertainment's sake is a real contribution to people's lives. One of

the best examples of this is the series of digital short films called *The Hire* that BMW has been creating since 2001. This series of now eight films was the first to take the quality of feature-length movies to a format designed for the Internet. The films are directed by top directors such as the Oscar-winning Ang Lee (*Crouching Tiger, Hidden Dragon* and *Brokeback Mountain*) and feature stars such as Madonna.

The films are great because the brand plays a role in the film—each film involves a car in a fashion integral to the story (such as a dramatic car chase), and as the story unfolds, there are certainly some "eye candy" shots that "sell" the car—but overall, the branding is subtle, and the films could be captivating to anyone whether or not they care about cars. The whole of the film, in all of its edgy artful glory, serves to encapsulate the BMW brand and create a very cool brand biosphere that brings to life BMW's tagline, "The Ultimate Driving Machine," which is an experiential leap from BMW's previous, more staid brand image. The result? BMW has since become a more youth-oriented cultural icon, showing up in both the lyrics of many rap songs and the driveways of a more diverse range of consumers.

The trend toward branded entertainment is definitely moving forward. Another well-executed example is the series of movie shorts Amazon.com launched in 2004 to subtly promote items available at its e-commerce site. The shorts were produced by and starred major Hollywood talent and were available for free on the Amazon site. The shorts were based on the concept of "karmic balance"—the idea that in the long term those who do the right thing are rewarded. One film, starring Minnie Driver, tells the story of an overbearing fashionista who learns a lesson on inner beauty. Other films star Daryl Hannah, Blair Underwood, and Chris Noth. Items for sale on Amazon's site appear subtly in the films and in the credits.

Jeff Bezos, CEO of Amazon, says that the films are a "great example of Amazon's relentless commitment to finding new and innovative ways to surprise and delight customers and deliver an unparalleled online experience." The films also provide multiple links to other movies by the same directors that are available for sale on the site. In addition, there are "bio pages" on the actors with links to all their other movies, their favorite books and CDs, and any special causes they wish to endorse. For example, there is a link under Minnie Driver to Oxfam, a nonprofit organization for which she is spokesperson, encouraging rich countries to remove the barriers to imports for all low-income countries and for an end to the practice of attaching conditions to IMF–World Bank loans, which force poorer countries to open their markets regardless of the impact.

Today we find ourselves faced with the bizarre reality of corporate CEOs hard at work on "brand scripts" (no kidding!) as brands seek to woo Hollywood with plots created around their own brand concept. We are finding scenarios such as the Meltin Pot fashion brand placing an ad in a magazine in search of a perfect script. The company eventually chose a dark drama called "The Lives of the Saints" and is now filming it—with the entire cast dressed in Meltin Pot gear, of course. As this trend grows, we will surely find a mix of "the good, the bad, and the ugly," and in the end, of course, it will be the consumer who will decide who gets the rope—and who gets to be sheriff.

And what about brands genuinely offering their consumers opportunities to experience culture (as opposed to attempting to co-opt cu,ture)? Is the very notion too good to be true? Apparently not. Just look to the example of how Mountain Dew recently financed a snowboarding documentary called *First Descent* that attempts a more subtle "buzz by association" method for brand building. John Galloway, vice president of sports and media for PepsiCo, said, "Our goal is for this to be the seminal movie of snowboarding—we didn't want to go overboard with the product."[5] Smart move. Stella Artois's efforts in film are another great example of a more authentic approach to branded entertainment. In Europe and the United Kingdom, the Stella Artois brand has become extremely well known as the champion of film. Ten years ago—long before the branded

short-film trend—Stella Artois began making ads in a cinematic style. The company made "short-film-esque" ads with a plot and storyline and a high-quality-film feel. Based on the tremendous success of these ads, the company decided to make film an integral part of the brand culture. Instead of rushing out to make Stella Artois movies, though, the company made the decision to support cultural initiatives related to film by creating a wide-reaching long-term sponsorship of a film channel, developing a Stella Artois Screen Tour in order to give as many people as possible the opportunity to come and watch films in outside locations, such as Brighton Beach; creating Certificate 18, a short film competition to showcase new talent; and sponsoring events such as After Dark, a multimedia event dedicated to the future of cinema that brings together cutting-edge film, music, and art. "The return for us is recognition by consumers of what Stella does for cinema. In this day and age, it is important to show that we do sponsorship and events like these not just for commercial reasons," says Kevin McQuillan, sponsorship manager for Interbrew UK (Stella's parent company). And that just about says it all, doesn't it?

CONCLUSION: All the World's a Stage

Hopefully, this chapter has enhanced your appreciation of how many brands are already following and embracing culture. And perhaps you have even been inspired by the possibility for your forging new "mechanisms" for real culture-to-brand osmosis to occur, providing a fascinating direct consumer connection and a dazzling array of entertaining, engaging, and almost startlingly real yet simultaneously virtual brand worlds such as those discussed in Secret #3. Even now, Burger King's "subservient" chicken Web site, a Web site where consumers literally choreograph every movement of a chicken, is drawing millions upon millions of new consumers, introducing them to a new chicken sandwich. And, if that were not enough, the Web site www.secondlife.com is attracting consumers who literally create themselves as virtual characters in a virtual world, consuming everything from virtual homes and virtual versions of branded products, but paying in real cash. Think about that for a moment.

As a new breed of true brand architects, you may come to a point where even you will need to be reminded that while the creation of a brand biosphere will be essential, it is not the financial objective of a brand. Profitably satisfying consumer desire is the objective of a brand. Brands, as they are currently defined, still need to make money; they are not nonprofit amusement parks. And when you get right down to it, even the nonprofits still need to make money. What you really should be taking away from this chapter is that it's not good enough just to satisfy desire, create brands based on real need, and allow consumers to have their say in product development—you need to actually foster the media and brand experience for the mise-en-scène on the chosen stage of consumers' lives for, in the words of William Shakespeare, it is still true that "The play's the thing." It always has been. It always will be.

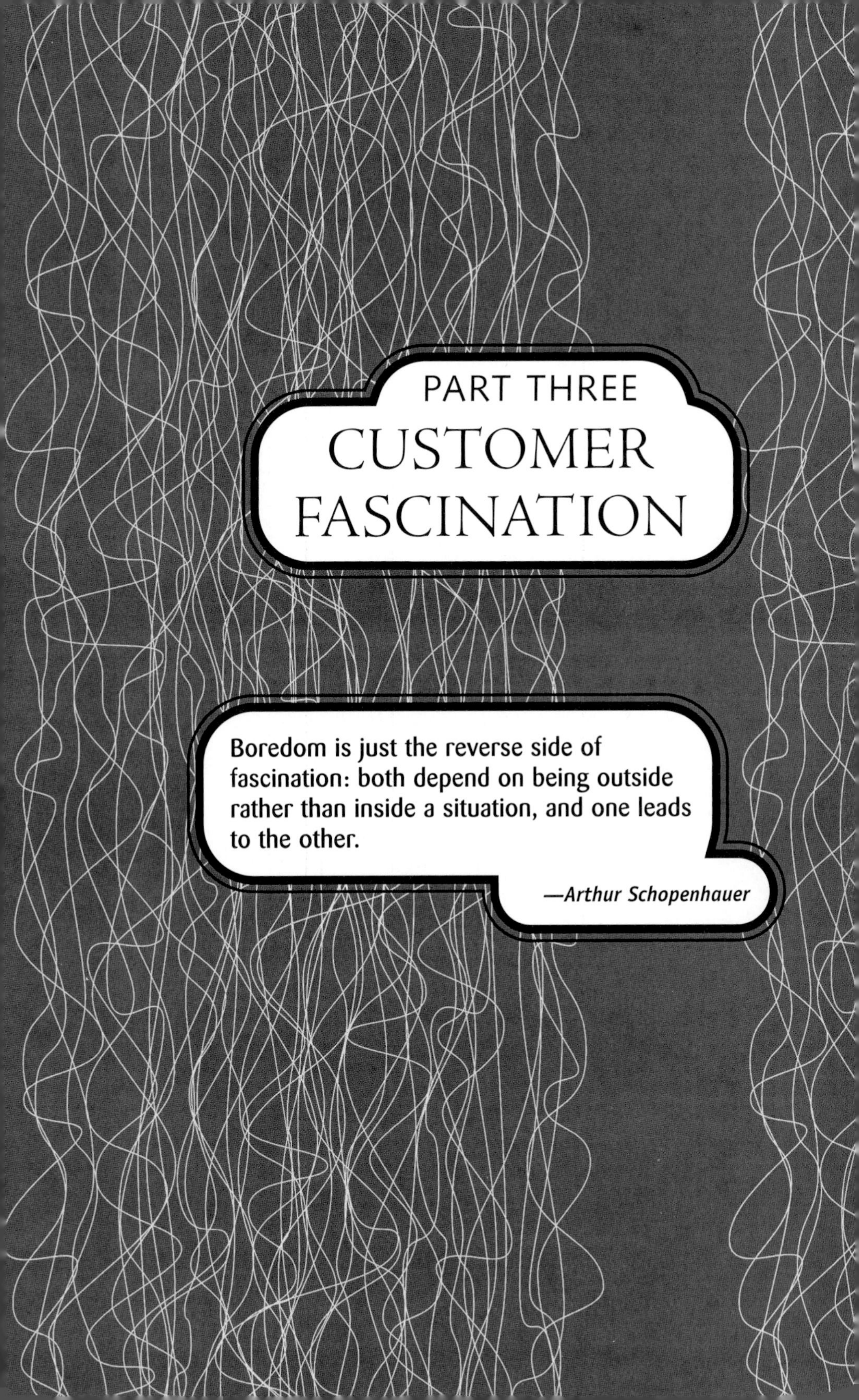

PART THREE
CUSTOMER FASCINATION

Boredom is just the reverse side of fascination: both depend on being outside rather than inside a situation, and one leads to the other.

—*Arthur Schopenhauer*

Be Good

PRACTICE ETHICAL BRANDING

> Men have torn up the roads which led to heaven, and which all the world followed; now we have to make our own ladders.
>
> —*Joseph Joubert,* Pensées

INTRODUCTION:
Give as Good as You Get

Today, we find many brands and companies using ethics as a means of differentiation, the "good brand" versus the "bad brand" so to speak. In the future, as consumers increasingly call the shots, being an ethical brand simply will become the minimum cost of doing business and will not constitute a point of difference between one brand and another. In short, unethical brands will be driven into extinction. This chapter deals with preservation of brand as species.

Given the enormous cultural and individual influences, variations, and misinterpretations of even just the definition of the word *ethics,* a discussion of "ethics" can easily break down. Heightening this complexity is its use within the context of business in a free-market economy. Apart from good corporate citizenship, I submit that the truest measure of ethics is and will continue to be the degree to which a brand or product satisfies a real versus a fabricated consumer need and reflects contemporary culture. However, to the degree that we allow ourselves to confuse brand identity with cultural authenticity and ethics, we become players in a potentially dangerous game of imperialistic branding and cultural abdication. Together these two killers could spell the death of free will, tradition, and soul. It is no less than the best of what it means to be human that is at stake.

Just as brands will be cocreated by consumers, so too will consumer ethics become, not a marketing point of differentiation, but an absolute minimum cost of doing business.

The lesson we can learn from ethics is: Keep your eye on the bottom line, but remember to be good—with *good* being defined not only in terms of consumer satisfaction with your product/brand but also by the acuity with which you perceive and honor consumers' authentic needs. Yes, do the right thing to survive. But don't count on just being good as enough to propel and differentiate your brand. Being good soon will be the norm, the minimum cost of entry. In the area of business ethics, the consumers' role and rights will become increasingly apparent as consumers become more and better equipped to express their approval or disapproval.

Along with the benefits they will enjoy in this new era of consumer/brand collaboration, consumers now also will be held partially to blame for potential corporate misdeeds. The famous lawsuit of the families of several obese teens against McDonald's lost, but the incendiary documentary film it inspired, *Super Size Me,* was a resounding success both as a film (it won at Sundance) and as a vehicle for imposing "brand conscience" (subsequent to the film, McDonald's did away with its "supersized" portions and introduced healthy alternatives, such as McSalads). *Thank You for Smoking,* a new film based on a parody of public relations and lobbying is bound to have similar effects. Smarter consumers demand more ethical brands. It's that simple. The jig is up.

Yet there still are many companies and governmental agencies that pay vast sums of money to create consumer crisis-control programs. Why not invest in doing what's right the first time?

What's most important here is understanding the difference between practicing business ethics and ethical branding. Being a truly ethical brand and using ethics as a marketing device are two very different things. For example, renowned luxury watch brand Baume & Mercier teamed up with Kiefer Sutherland, fusing Kiefer's celebrity, Baume & Mercier's luxury, and no fewer than three important causes—curing cancer, caring for children, and protecting the environment—in order to promote watch sales. This is all well and good. But does it say anything about the quality of the brand? Or does it suggest that the brand is doing the right thing for the wrong reasons? Does it mean that the brand, because of its enhanced image, will be able to charge consumers more so that Baume & Mercier can donate funds back to arguably good charities? Is it the equivalent of marking goods up an additional 80 percent so that you can discount them by 60 percent? For the time being, the answers to these questions probably don't matter much. At least charities are benefiting. And whether or not brands that donate to charity are being altruistic or manipulative, at least good causes are reaping the rewards.

Yet, while nobody can argue against altruism, from a branding perspective, altruism used as a method of differentiation is not a long-term marketing strategy. For one thing, it lacks propriety. There is little barrier to entry. What stops Rolex, Cartier, Swatch, and Timex from doing exactly the same thing Baume & Mercier is doing? Could the statement "My watch is better than yours" take on almost ridiculous new meaning?

Here is a potentially controversial observation: The virtue of a brand should not be measured by the degree to which it is able to differentiate itself emotionally via philanthropy; rather, a virtuous brand is one that is in tune with the culture and consumer needs/desires of its time. Certainly, environmentalism, humanitarianism, and cultural respect are givens, but emotional exploitation via philanthropy, a device that worked well in a more naive world, will come to mean less and less as culture and consumers decide for themselves the causes that mean most to them. Consumers will define a virtuous brand as one that delivers on its promises.

Nowhere are the violations of cultural interference and unethical behavior more clear than when a brand or company interferes in politics. Commercial manipulation in the political arena is perhaps the worst, most dangerous business sin. A business or brand is not a person, although it can be inspired by a person or persons. A brand does not have the right to govern, and brands should not interfere with the natural evolution of culture. I rue the day when government and the very definition of what is socially right or wrong, just or unjust, will be brought to us by the makers of laundry detergent or any other product, brand, or industry. When and if this time does come (and some would claim that it already has), we, in the broadest sense, will be lost. Culture, as historically defined, will be dead or left bloodied and dying.

I am not predicting doom and gloom or painting a future scenario of brands inheriting the earth. In fact, I am predicting the exact opposite. In the very near future, ethical branding will devour unethical brands, and hopefully, tomorrow's marketers will wake up and realize that they inhabit the same, albeit branded, world as the consumer. Wal-Mart, the company we seem to love and hate, surprisingly has conceded this by creating a new CEO position. No, I am not referring to a new head of the company. Rather, it has created an entirely new executive position, chief ethical officer. And lest any brand or any company choose to test the hypothesis that ethics doesn't matter and the consumer catch wind of it, that company or brand most assuredly will become the object of quick justice—consumer-inflicted justice. That brand will hang by the neck until dead.

Free will means that it is up to good marketers to actually use their brilliant imaginations to focus on more appropriate things than merely leveraging brand "goodness just for show." Consumer free will prompts our discovering new, more fascinating methods of satisfying the real desires of consumers and lending a touch of stardust to their daily lives during the course of satisfying even mundane basic needs. The good news, which this chapter explores, is that you are in control of how you use your brand.

CREATING LIFELONG CUSTOMERS: WHY ALL THIS EMPHASIS ON ETHICS?

I passionately believe in the value of brands and repeatedly have created some pretty memorable ones. Yet I know that unless we pay attention to ethics, the future creation of brands is doomed. It is sad to admit that I have learned more about the profound importance of my vocation from sources such as Naomi Klein's now-famous book and antibrand manifesto *No Logo*[1] than from recent marketing books—many of which are self-serving, deliberately cute, unnecessarily technical, or overtly manipulative. At the risk of sounding critical, I ask you, should a brand really ever become a love mark? At what point does an emotional brand become a manipulative one? We are at a point in cultural and commercial evolution where we must choose either marriage or a lifelong career as courtesans. And beware, a beloved partner can age, suffer through bad times, and even stumble, whereas a courtesan loses power the moment a prettier "face" comes along. The revolutionary idea I propose is that in the twenty-first century, marketing must turn itself around and discover new ways to truly love and commit to the consumer, who, in return, will reciprocate as a devoted partner in a veritable marriage of equals. This notion flies in the face of many recent branding experts' books and philosophies emphasizing seduction of the consumer versus the cultural fidelity of brands.

FROM DARKNESS TO LIGHT: HOW TO TELL THE DIFFERENCE

Despite the sometimes sordid history of marketing (particularly public relations, or propaganda, as it was known previously), today's balance of power only now has begun the shift in favor of the consumer. To understand this shift, perhaps we should look back to the beginning of marketing. The fascinating award-winning BBC documentary *The Century of Self* by acclaimed producer Adam Curtis provides a harsh criticism of Edward Bernays, the inventor of public relations (the precursor to all areas of modern marketing) in the 1920s. There are many of us unfamiliar with Bernays's name or impact. However his dark legacy continues to be felt via the deliberate style of manipulation, often bordering on deceit, still used by some marketers and quite frequently by politicians. Make no mistake, the "Bernays" method is still going strong, relying on Freudian extrapolations of fear, guilt, and the almost invisible border between rational and irrational decision making. This is not a particularly motivating state of affairs for those of us working in any discipline related to marketing. Critical reviews—combined with the fact that the television series was viewed with great interest, outrage, and dismay by a broad cross section of consumers—signify that the entire area of consumerism, ethics, manipulation, and marketing is now officially under the microscope. Clearly, we had better watch our steps.

WHAT CAUSED ALL THE COMMOTION?

From the dark recesses and mysterious philosophy of repressed desire, Sigmund Freud's daughter, Anna, and his nephew, Edward Bernays, created a pseudoscience embraced by the U.S. government (particularly the CIA), fascist Germany, and big business. Although alleged to have been an innocent attempt at improving order and influencing behavior for the greater good, the theories suggested that just beneath the facade of every civilized man or woman is a mindless easily manipulated being ruled by self-interest, fear, and barely controllable barbarism. Fear lay at the foundation of Bernays's technique and theories, and the approach to it was an appeal (or control) leveled at our primal, baser instincts and the manipulation of perceived reality. The result was the application of mass manipulation and the invention of not only public relations but of its more sinister-sounding sister, propaganda.

Even great talents, such as the legendary cinematographer Leni Riefenstahl, became pawns in this new world of twisted reality. Some would argue that Riefenstahl allowed her talent to be manipulated by the Nazis, indirectly aiding and abetting one of the twentieth century's greatest human atrocities. The lesson: Many of us in the marketing professions are among the world's most creative, loving, and tolerant people. Don't allow antiquated marketing to turn you into another Leni Riefenstahl. The end never justifies the means—even in the most competitive of categories or the most difficult economic environment. In short: Don't sell your soul for toothpaste. You are better than that.

Look, for example, at the heinous impact of marketing on politics, or observe how potentially dangerous pharmaceutical products are marketed as though they were completely harmless, benign panaceas for everything from cancer to impotence. You must at least consider the fact that despite the marketing industry's self-proclaimed hype regarding socially responsible messages and honesty, many of us are still promoting or using strategies and tactics based on half-crocked, archaic, dangerous theories. The important question here is, How much longer will consumers tolerate our manipulative folly and continue to purchase products/brands generated by our self-interests?

Let's take a more recent example that shows how some marketing groups still feel that they can get away with half-truths. Throughout the summer of 2005, virtually every car company offered "employee discounts" to consumers. Consumers are not employees. Yes, the campaigns attempted to make consumers *feel* as though they were part of companies, but they did so in such obviously false ways that the ads became parodies of themselves. Unfortunately, calling these promotional discounts employee discounts was seen by many as a transparent, inane trick, more a demonstration of "sleight of hand" than a reflection of consumer insight. They were no doubt designed to foster an inclusive relationship, bonding between consumers and a variety of brands, yet they resulted in a clear demonstration of corporate condescension.

Did anyone viewing these commercials actually feel like an employee as a result of the commercial? How much more convincing might it have been had actual potential buyers been screened/hired and asked to actually drive a particular brand of car for a weekend and then be *compensated* for services rendered for providing suggestions relating to potential product improvement? Part or all of the consumer's compensation might have been a real employee discount that he or she could have shared selectively with family and friends. The entire premise could have been built on amazing truth versus innocent deception. Remember, deception is never innocent. And being clever is simply no longer enough.

Yet, in our attempts to be clever, some of us continue to develop "viral" marketing schemes such as those using actor "plants" to secretly promote products in real-life scenarios (i.e., your new "friend" sitting next to you at a bar is suddenly waxing eloquent about his new phone or offers to buy you a drink of a "really cool new vodka").[2] While these tactics may work in the short term, they are certainly no long-term strategy, and of course, they carry the potential to backfire when people learn they've been duped. Either culture will genuinely adopt a brand and promote it through word of mouth or not. Period. Think about it. We are living in a world where, after slipping away to the restroom to escape the creepy person at the bar who seems a little too eager to convince you that his or her chewing gum is the best he or she has ever tasted, you may find yourself in the seemingly blissful privacy of the toilet confronted with—yet another ad!

BATHROOM BRANDING: JUST HOW LOW CAN IT GO?

Yes, indeed, we are in the era of bathroom branding. Marketers, desperate to reach consumers, have discovered the space on the back of bathroom stall doors and, for men, in front of urinals, resulting in electronic ad displays called "viewurinals." This is interruption marketing at its most vulgar; it's hard to imagine a more undignified venue for our life's work. Most important, any real opportunity for a meaningful consumer relationship is diminished. Would you befriend or fall in love with someone who attempted to pick you up in a toilet? If you really wanted to do serious "bathroom branding," you might succeed if you offered the consumer something of true value and appropriate given the context of the situation, such as some type of branded disinfectant-coated seat cover.

REPARATION AND RECONSTRUCTION: A NEW ERA BEGINS—AND WE ARE ALL BEAUTIFUL

Consumer-created movements, such as *Adbusters,* are only an early signal of reactions to the dishonesty and overabundance of brand communications that attempt to usurp culture. *Adbusters,* perhaps one of the best symbols of this movement, is an organization using sophisticated marketing techniques to bring attention to the detrimental aspects of today's prevailing marketing practices, those considered exploitative and dangerous to culture and the advancement of humanity. In addition to addressing issues surrounding corporate corruption and globalization at large, the highly politicized, extremely smart and edgy publication takes and uses the best practices from our profession (such as expert art direction and copywriting) to explore themes of mental pollution and brand manipulation. A glance or two is sufficient to give us all a powerful impression of exactly what's wrong with advertising today. It remains in our power to put marketing back on the right, ultimately more profitable, sustainable path.

The lesson: Tell the truth—the whole brand truth, three-dimensional consumer truths, our own truth, and nothing but these truths. Make the truth a collaborative exercise—built on shared insight—and create brand realities that are fascinating and fun.

CHOICE: The Ultimate Point of Difference

Cultivate the consumers' right to choose. Compete ferociously against other brands to solicit consumer collaboration because, in the end, whatever the consumer says is true and what is true sells. Consumers always have been our best consultants. It's only now, however, that they have come to realize their power and level of control. Allow consumers to define what is best for them, and deliver on that expectation at a variety of price points and through a range of distribution channels. Why? Because you will open new markets and allow for broader opportunity for spontaneous cohort marketing, which is the evolution of what has been known previously as *affinity marketing.*

Cohort marketing will aggregate entire lifestyles and provide a two-way interchange resulting in the proliferation of branded artifacts conducive to enablement of three- versus two-dimensional consumer realities.

GRAVEN IMAGES: BRANDS AND CONSUMER SELF-ACTUALIZATION

At their best, brands and brand communication become the props and backgrounds within the context of self-actualized lives or at least markers in lives lived with some level of authenticity. The props, however, should never overshadow the real lives, becoming objectified, projected, artificial graven images that are worshiped as lifeless symbols for a presumably self-actualized living being. As in the previously cited documentary, *The Century of Self,* recent books such as *Commodify Your Dissent*[3] by Frank and Weiland have done a great job of vilifying business, particularly given its role in rewriting reality in marketing's chosen image. Yet they offer no solution—neither to consumers nor to marketing professionals. What's needed is a method through which brands can legitimately take on greater cultural meaning, improve lives, satisfy needs, allow for consumer expression, bring delight to daily existence, and make buckets upon buckets of money, fueling faltering economies—the same economies on which most persons depend for their livelihoods and which, in general, help to promote higher standards of living.

Thus, in keeping with the cultural writing on the wall, not to mention my own beliefs, each chapter of this book is intended to be one stepping stone on the path toward solution and, dare I say it, marketing redemption. The examples and ideas covered in this book were, above all, selected to address the intrinsic flaws of classical marketing and to demonstrate some historical and contemporary examples of alternate and ethical approaches. But beware: I would be misleading you, as many contemporary marketing books seem to do, were I to suggest that there is only one marketing template for culturally friendly, consumer-loving, commercial success. There is no single template for success. You, in fact, may be charged with creating such a template within the context of your work and your life.

Success is a dangerous word. What is success without self-respect? The following section shares key theories on this topic from Ivy Ross and her colleague Mukara Meredith.

HAKOMI PRINCIPLES OF MINDFULNESS

As referenced in Secret #2, since Ivy Ross worked on her brilliant Platypus project, she has gone on to Old Navy and works with Mukara Meredith to add an additional, even more groundbreaking element of visionary theory to her approach. Mukara, who has 25 years of experience teaching, consulting, and working with the healing arts, has created a new holistic model of leadership called MATRIXWORKS.

The practices of MATRIXWORKS draw from an understanding of chaos theory and quantum physics, a powerful model that supports a new understanding of group life and dynamics. Ivy and Mukara have jointly proposed a methodology geared at harnessing the interpersonal energy of employees in an effort to create a new model of collaborative internal creation.

The following Hakomi principles of mindfulness are based on Ivy and Mukara's system. They apply the importance of awareness of one's real self within the context of the reality of others, nonviolence, and the unity of mind and body to the topic of the true potential of brands and branding.

1. *Mindfulness.* To approach marketing with mindfulness is to challenge existing marketing teaching. Instead of attempting to create need, we should focus on understanding and satisfying existing needs/desires. The world has enough need—and, for that matter, enough brands. We have not only the right to look into consumers' hearts but also the obligation. In the end, a mindful business/creative approach must translate into consumer benefit and will remind us of our unique importance in satisfying human need.

2. *Nonviolence.* Marketers today need to challenge the language of marketing—which is almost always violent or adversarial. Consider such terms as *target market,* which sounds as though we are hunting for deer rather than discovering needs, *stealth marketing, guerrilla marketing,* and *viral marketing.* Beneath the radar. Marketing professionals refer to *arsenals* of competitive strategies. The future of competition between brands (a vision shared by everyone from the CEO of Procter & Gamble to the CEO of Burberry) will be one of corporate collaboration. Brands will fuse values to create hybrids—aggregations of like needs—promoted through mechanisms I have broadly coined as *cohort marketing.*

3. *Unity of body and spirit.* Marketers need to understand the notion of "brand soul," which is about creating authentic brands that provide a holistic reflection of consumer culture. In this sense, we can talk about *spirit* in the broader sense of *spirit of the time*—or *zeitgeist.* I propose that one aspect of product ethics is the degree to which a brand, a product, a retail experience, or an advertisement truly reflects culture—for better or for worse.

The rest of this chapter demonstrates how smart marketing, advertising, design, public relations, and product-development specialists have responded ethically to the drivers of this new consumer revolution.

If advertising and branding are reflections of culture, do we have any ethical obligations beyond that of being accurate mirrors? This was the question I posed to Matt Eastwood, and the following section contains his response. Matt Eastwood has been identified by London's *Campaign* magazine as "one of the industry's unicorns—a young, proven talent, capable of managing a large agency creative department." As national creative director and vice chairman of DDB Australia and formerly chief creative officer of Y&R North America, he oversees some of the most innovative and recognizable creative projects in advertising today. His ability to guide an integrated agency vision across all accounts and into multiple and surprising media outlets has established him as a modern visionary.

INFUSING OPTIMISM: WORDS FROM A WUNDERKIND

Matt Eastwood Provides His Take on the Future and the Responsibility of Advertising

The question has long existed that if advertising and branding are reflections of culture, do we as creators of advertising and branding have any ethical obligations beyond that of simply being an accurate mirror? The reality is that we as creators have incredible power. And with that power comes accountability. While advertising per se can't create culture, it can disseminate a point of view to an exceedingly large and diverse audience. This is where the responsibility is—and the opportunity. I like to view every piece of communication as an opportunity to inject optimism into the world. This is not to say that I'm looking to project a Pollyanna view of the world but rather that I'm looking for opportunities to display optimism through under-

standing, honesty, or diversity. Dove's recent "real women" campaign is a perfect example. For too long beauty has been defined by narrow, stifling stereotypes. Why not use this brand's voice as an opportunity to instill optimism into the minds of American women? Real women have curves. This advertising is a celebration of that. Therein rests the power and obligation of advertising.

Today's consumer demands that "goodness" be built in, not laid over brands. As cited in the January 24, 2005 edition of *Brandweek*'s consumer survey across multiple categories, "The consumer is wise to marketing's game of charades and expects more from a brand today than ever before." Product performance does not guarantee a successful brand but never should be discounted. A brand, however, also must regularly question the success and cultural relevancy of its "performance" and continuously expand, and, if necessary, even reinvent itself. In some respects, the theories of branding have become academic constructs. Why, for example, must the ingredient list of a product appear on the back of the package? Why can't a logo change every year? Why can't typographic fonts vary from product to product and year to year, like fashion, reflecting the emotional nuances between different products and times.

I am not suggesting branding anarchy. I am, however, stating that rules for rules' sake are not what marketing is about. Great marketers know this.

As new discoveries, changing cultural contexts, and implied consumer contracts render what was once true false, and visa versa, the days of earning a degree in marketing, finding a job, and then never refreshing your knowledge of marketing and society are over. Perhaps, like doctors, marketers actually should be recertified every five years, testing their knowledge of consumers and all the methods of consumer connection available to them via technology and other culturally created methods of direct dialogue.

Real brand-to-consumer bonding is not created by manipulation or subconscious messages. It happens when the consumer and the brand look each other squarely in the eye. Factoring in the phenomenon of the informed, empowered consumer, the fallacy of early marketing's premise, and the sharper sword of "technology-enabled consumer influence," I believe that the future meaning of business ethics will be defined, shaped, and measured by a fundamentally good consumer.

THE "GOOD" IMPERATIVE: THE "GOOD" IDEA, THE "GOOD" CONSUMER, AND THE "GOOD" BRAND

I propose that marketing, branding, public relations, product design, and advertising are commercial vehicles with two objectives: (1) fueling economies/businesses and (2) honestly contributing/enabling tangible and intangible, culturally authentic human satisfaction. To date, brands have focused almost exclusively on the first side of this duo of success measurements, giving short shrift to the second. I am not suggesting that we should abandon luxury industries or whimsical products or that we all should turn in our laptops and go work on sustainable collective farms. When I speak of the "good" consumer and the "good" marketer creating "good" brands, I am not even remotely suggesting that unrealistic expectations of consumer altruism will prevail and that avarice suddenly will disappear or should. It's not for me or you to judge. In fact, to paraphrase/modify a 1980s entertainment-derived notion, some greed is good as long as it includes a greed for honesty and genuine consumer satisfaction. These traits are genuinely human, and marketing is not responsible for making them disappear. In fact, we have no right to even try.

However, disregard for the natural environment, degradation of other human beings, and indifference to contemporary culture(s) are not going to be particularly effective points of difference that allow one to perpetuate brands and branding. Think about it. How could they be? We are not living in the naive, gullible culture of the 1930s—or, for that matter, even the culture of last year.

A CAUTIONARY TALE—NOT SUITABLE FOR IMMATURE AUDIENCES

When as marketers we find ourselves looking for opportunities to create desire rather than seeing and satisfying the desires that already exist, we invariably find ourselves veering off an ethical path. Much of the marketing and advertising directed toward children exemplifies this because in many of these cases the desire to possess the advertised object (toys) is so clearly fabricated and not at all a real need. Of course, children do need toys for healthy development, but do they need a mountain of toys? Do they really need all those sugar-laden munchies or addictive candy?

Children are an exceptionally easy target for inflicting fabricated need because they do not have the same ability to filter or be selective in their desires as adults do, which is why the question of ethics looms particularly large when marketing and advertising to children. The strategy behind "marketing to the cradle," as it's so aptly called, is startlingly clear: Seduce at the weakest point, win brand loyalty early, and hook them for life. The whole process sounds dirty and distasteful. Yet the strategy has worked and is working—for now. But what about tomorrow? What about your children's children? Will it work for them? Does it personally work for you?

There are exceptions to this practice. Look, for instance, at Lego. Look at some of public television's inspiring, wholesome dialogue with children and the parentally approved licensed products that

result. The lesson: You do not have to exploit any consumer's Achilles heel to appeal to his or her desire. Thank goodness for Big Bird and Cookie Monster.

Luckily there exist splendid examples of brands based on reflected realities that already have touched humans in very sensitive, ethical ways. The results can be incredibly strong, almost attaining mythic status, yet they always seem to remain grounded in human values and shared experience.

The rest of this chapter is devoted to further examples of what I consider to be truly ethical branding, branding designed with compassion, vision, and cultural sensitivity. Each example also reflects the reality, albeit sometimes stylized, of consumers' lives and legitimate human needs, thus vicariously placing the consumer where he or she should be—full front and center stage.

In the following case study, Bayada Nurses demonstrates how a real set of human needs, expressed in intimate, realistically conveyed human terms, resulted in a stronger brand and, for some, a more positive impression of marketing as a discipline. Bayada Nurses is what I consider to be a poster child for a new class of brands: good in the services it provides, the profit it returns, its internal policies and external policies, commitment to its employees, marketing practices, and genuine commitment to consumer. It is a truly living brand.

BAYADA NURSES: BRINGING HEROES TO THE HOME FRONT—A BRAND WORTH LOVING IS A BRAND THAT PUTS CONSUMERS FIRST

by Doug MacGibbon, President of IHA, Inc.

Founded in 1975, Bayada Nurses is now one of the largest home health care providers in the United States. However, the company's

rapid growth didn't start until over two decades later, in the fall of 1998. This was when IHA, Inc., was selected to develop and launch the corporation's first branding program.

Because of the national shortage of nurses that continues to this day, the company's growth was limited by not having enough nurses to fill the needs of its clients. The objective of the program was to enhance nurse recruitment without relying solely on monetary incentives, severely restricted by health maintenance organizations and Medicare cost-control measures.

The IHA created a "psychic income benefit" associated with being a Bayada nurse—the distinction of being treated like a hero. The full branding theme line that the advertising agency created for Bayada now has grown to take its place among the pantheon of famous branding themes in America—*Heroes on the Home Front.* Spot television was selected as the primary medium, even though conventional wisdom says that if your primary audience consists of only two million people, the total number of nurses in America, television isn't efficient. When the first commercial aired, nurses literally came in off the street (before the commercial, it was difficult even to get a few answers to a Bayada classified ad), asking if they could join this great company that would give them the recognition they always yearned for—to be treated as heroes.

Before the heroes' campaign, Bayada Nurses employed 4,000 nurses in 80 offices nationwide. The company now employs more than 8,000 nurses in more than 110 offices across America. Annual sales of the company have doubled. The original launch commercial—a "minimovie" 30 seconds long—now has been airing continuously for seven years and depicts a Bayada nurse battling a severe thunderstorm to reach the home of her quadriplegic patient. In nursing circles, the commercial has become a cult classic, a drama that nurses never seem to tire of.

The following is a behind-the-scenes account of how IHA, Inc., built the brand.

When I first met with CEO Mark Baiada, he held my rapt attention for a couple of hours as he explained how the rich tradition of nurses—originating on the battlefields of nineteenth-century Europe—was a critical component in his organization that brought medical care to people who were unable to leave their homes. Mark told me that he aspired to someday create a brand of nurses—a value-added identity that would give him a negotiating edge, particularly with his insurance-company clients and in his nurse recruitment efforts. The latter area was of critical importance because he could only grow his business as fast as he could hire the nurses to supply the services. And nurses aren't easy to recruit. For one, they are highly educated and feel greatly underappreciated by the health care industry. Second, there was—and still is—a severe shortage of nurses. So the competition for the good ones is fierce and expensive, requiring companies to pay nurses signing bonuses as though they were pro athletes.

After this meeting, I engaged the process we use to develop substantial, long-lasting branding ideas—what we refer to as the "killer creative process," or KCP. People always ask me how do you come up with advertising ideas. My own technique is to turn off the left side of my brain while absorbing what the client is telling me about his business with the right side of my brain. In other words, I don't want to hear the client's story in logical, left-brain terms but rather in emotional, right-brain feelings. I can fill in the logic later. But the emotional part is the seed for the big branding idea. Thus all I could think about as Mark was briefing me on a vision for a brand identity for his business was nurses bravely caring for the wounded on battlefields and even the nurses who caringly nursed me back to health when I was lying in a hospital at seven years of age, hooked up to an IV, with a 106°F temperature for two weeks because I had contracted encephalitis. I remember nurses looking at me from above my bed. I thought they were angels.

The purpose of the KCP is to identify the brand-building idea, free and clear of execution of that idea. A branding program that isn't based on a meaningful idea that consumers readily embrace won't have the substance to stand the test of time. Our KCP solves the problem of how to isolate the big branding idea. Once identified, the creative team has the roadmap, as it were, to expand on this idea with a powerful execution. The first two questions in our "creative work plan" set aside the strategy document for a moment. The first question is: What is the *key fact*—the key cultural reality and human impact of the product or service? It requires a single-minded statement that sorts out from all the information about the product, market, competition, and so on, the one insight that is most relevant to the brand and, as important, to the consumer.

The second question is: What is the *problem the advertising must solve?* This assumes that if there isn't a problem affecting the brand in the marketplace—or an opportunity in the case of a new brand introduction—there wouldn't be a need for a brand-building program or message evolution in the first place. The statement of the problem should grow out of and be directly related to the key fact and its relevance within the context of modern culture and consumer need.

We used a resulting core concept board to confirm that we were on the right track with our heroes idea and to become privy to the wants and dreams of nurses everywhere. In short, we strove to put ourselves in the consumer's shoes. Then, developing the TV, print, and all the other components of an integrated advertising program was a piece of cake. To use a term from baseball, when a creative team understands what to expect from a pitch before it is thrown, it can swing for the fences.

When we presented the core concept to nurses, we were able to correct a potential disconnect that would have derailed our finished execution. They loved the spirit of nursing history and tradition that was depicted in the core concept, but they missed seeing a patient featured on the board. Although we tied in the patient to the copy, the nurses wanted to see, front and center, a patient. Because, as we quickly understood, taking care of people is what draws men and women to nursing. Thus, when we were rolling out the finished execution in storyboard form, we had made the journey through a storm to the home of a quadriplegic patient the centerpiece of our 30-second movie. The Bayada Nurses heroes TV advertisement is now in its seventh straight year of capturing the imagination of nurses across the country and has been part of virtually doubling the size of Bayada's business.

Author's Note: I was so inspired by Doug's case study that I simply had to speak directly with Mark Baiada, president of Bayada Nurses, a successful businessman, supporter of consumer rights, and proponent of positive engagement both for the clients of Bayada Nurses and for its employees. Supporting the credo, "The Bayada Way," as it has been named, the motto "Our clients come first" is both simple and profound. Mr. Baiada and his wife, Ann, plan to visit each of the company's 124 service and support offices as part of a cross-country bus tour (see Figure 5-1).

FIGURE 5-1 ■ Heroes on the homefront. Mark and Ann Baiada are two of the ethically driven heroes of Bayada Nurses. Standing before the Bayada Nurses bus, they begin their trip down the Bayada way.

After reading the preceding case study, some of you may be thinking that although the advertising did serve an ethical purpose—reflecting cultural mores on altruism by creating a positive representation of nurses that provides a solution to a legitimate and underserved need—it still employed emotion and artifice to help make its point. You are right. Yet the approach and resulting advertising campaign are as clear a demonstration of ethical advertising as any. To support this position and delve a little deeper into this question of when artifice or emotional influencing becomes unethical emotional manipulation, I interviewed Elaina Zucker, Ph.D., the acclaimed author of the book *The Seven Secrets of Influence,*[4] which is a time-tested guide revealing the art and science of persuasion by teaching people "influence skills" for both their careers and their personal lives. The following section presents her views on influencing customers.

THE ETHICS OF INFLUENCE

an Interview with Elaina Zucker, Ph.D.

QUESTION: **Where does influence end and manipulation begin?**

ZUCKER: **Let me start with the definition of *influence.* Really, it's *my* definition. I define *influence* as the ability or capacity or power to change a person's (or people's) attitudes and/or behavior without the use of formal authority or physical power. Interestingly, an archaic definition of the word *influence* is "a mysterious fluid from the stars, said to have magical powers over people." What's cool about this is that just like magic, influence, when it's done really skillfully, seems like magic, but in fact, like magic, it requires a great deal of skill and practice behind the scenes before it can seem effortless. Comparing influence and manipulation, I use the following as an explanation. It depends on two dimensions: intent and effect. On the first one, intent, I have to ask myself, "Are my intentions honorable?" "Do I intend to add value, give benefit, enrich or enhance, or enlighten the other person?" And regarding effect,**

"What is the effect on the other person or persons?" "Does he or she feel enriched, or does he or she feel used, exploited, or 'had'?" If I can answer positively on both these counts, I would say that I have positive influence at work. If, on the other hand, the intent is not honorable and the resulting effect is one of feeling ripped off, then I would say it's been manipulation. The other component is that manipulation is kind of sneaky, underhanded, and not known to the recipient (kind of like subliminal advertising), whereas positive influence is up front and clear.

QUESTION: Is influence bad if it is used for a good cause or to advance a good person?

ZUCKER: It's a process, a skill that is a neutral, values-free, kind of like nuclear or electrical power, which can be used for good or ill. Whether it's "good" or "bad" depends on the intent and the effect I just described.

QUESTION: Do you consider marketing/advertising a form of influence, or is most of it manipulation?

ZUCKER: Of course advertising and marketing are a form of very powerful influence, which is why marketers have to behave responsibly when they are using these powerful tools to persuade people what to do. For example, if you are advertising cigarettes and saying that they're *not* harmful to your health, you have some serious reckoning to do with your ethics.

QUESTION: As technology between consumers and brands increases, do you foresee consumers influencing brands more or less? Why?

ZUCKER: I think if brands are smart, then of course they'll listen more and more to their consumers to learn what they want and need. And equally important, what they don't want and don't need!

QUESTION: When information about products becomes completely understood and old-fashioned smoke-and-mirrors marketing and brand creation evaporates, how will brands and companies differen-

tiate between brands—how might they employ some of the ideas you have advocated?

ZUCKER: **I do think if marketers themselves learned these few simple principles of the secrets of influence, they would have a much clearer strategy for differentiating between consumers and groups and therefore a much more focused, more authentic message. Authenticity is everything. Nothing persuades us more than the truth.**

If Elaina is right and one of the important first steps to creating a more authentic—and eventually ethical—brand message is through understanding how to influence different consumers based on their very individual, unique perspectives, then much can be accomplished by making honest cultural reflection our primary objective.

BRAND HEROES: THE LESSONS OF GREAT NONPROFIT BRANDS

No book referencing ethical brands would be complete without some discussion of nonprofit brands. But even the principles supporting a nonprofit brand or organization provide valuable insight into the for-profit arena, given that, as mentioned earlier, differences between the two often blur. This section provides an example of a nonprofit that has truly excelled at being ethical not only by virtue of its nature but also through the dignity, caring, and authenticity of its everyday operation. And coincidentally, it too has labeled its many volunteers and donors heroes. This is proof positive that marketing does have the potential to become something more than marketing. Marketing and your role in it also have the potential of heroism as well.

DKMS: WE ARE MANY, WE ARE ONE

DKMS Americas combines heart-felt humanitarianism with advanced technology and awareness generated via the generosity and contributions of world-class celebrities to address one of the world's many existing desperate human needs. DKMS is a global nonprofit organization dedicated to promoting awareness of leukemia and other blood-related diseases and to maintaining a database of potential bone marrow and stem cell donors for those in need. Through the use of the Internet and other advanced connective technologies, DKMS has grown from a small grassroots organization to one with 1.5 million donors. Truly a "consumer-created" brand, the genesis of DKMS was the very personal quest of one family to save a loved one. Today, despite its large numbers, it still operates in the most intimate one-to-one manner possible.

I am personally involved with DKMS Americas as a volunteer creative director for the organization and have endeavored to help establish its presence in North America with the hope of eventually expanding into South America. Starting small, the first step was to adapt the highly successful European charity's model to the U.S. market and then provide everything from ads, posters, brochures, and an "Americanized" Web site. DKMS had to invent itself based on the unique circumstances of each patient and enable each patient to personally mount, with our support, a heroic yet simultaneously intimate campaign. Uniquely, DKMS helps each individual seeking a donor to create his or her own Web site that links to the DKMS database and other related databases, and it even will provide centralized assistance in support of individual, independent drives—including advice on everything from awareness-generating public relations events to more sophisticated methods such as Web-based and/or direct-mail solicitation.

DKMS: THE HUMANITY OF ETHICS

an Interview with Katharina Harf, CEO of DKMS Americas

DKMS is dedicated to the proposition that no one of us is an island. No disease is as isolating as indifference. No gift is as great as the ability to give. In its fight against leukemia and other autoimmune blood disorders, it acknowledges that, indeed, we are many in our need, yet we are one in our power to provide solutions to often desperate, real, yet individual need.

QUESTION: How did DKMS come into being, and how is it that you came to be involved with the charity's expansion into the United States?

HARF: My mother was sick with acute leukemia, had relapsed already once, and was in dire need of a stem cell transplant. She found a donor but not a perfect match, and she did not make it. Her death empowered us to help other people who were in need of a stem cell transplant. My immediate family, friends, and sympathizers organized in my family's living room. We created what you refer to as a spontaneous brand. In the first year alone, DKMS recruited 68,000 donors. Today, DKMS is one of the largest bone marrow donor centers in the world, with over 1.5 million donors. I got involved in the expansion of DKMS to the United States because I was looking for a calling and have spent as much time living in the United States as I have living in Europe. I like to think I grasp both cultures, which will aid to bridge the gap between the European and American arms of DKMS. I had been working in management consulting and for luxury brands but never fully fit in. I never imagined I could have a calling, but there it was, just lying in front of me.

QUESTION: What is the mechanism through which the foundation enables its consumers (both donors and recipients) to forge strong emotional connections with the organization, "the brand," without, in most cases, donors and recipients actually meeting in person?

HARF: The brand is actually all about connections that go beyond the physical. There is tremendous satisfaction of both emotional (donor need) and physical needs (the recipient). The connection that is forged is the realization that we are *all* connected, and DKMS provides the link to these other human beings. At the end of the day, humans live in a world of interdependency. Becoming a donor gives one a chance to save the life of another human being. The two might not know each other, don't look alike, or never meet, but part of their genetic makeup is the same. We celebrate the heroic deeds of our donors as well as the many other volunteers, both corporate and private, who celebrate the transcendent notion of heroism. Some donors say that "saving a life" has been their greatest accomplishment. In my case, I would have to agree with them.

QUESTION: Darryl McDaniels, formerly of Run DMC, and Jennifer Lopez will join your first U.S. drive, focusing on saving the life of a young mother in Queens. Why is it that Darryl was approached and consented to endorsing the organization? Why is it that a European organization chose to target not only other Europeans and Americans of European descent but also communities that you saw as being underserved? Why the concern for North and South America?

HARF: Although existing organizations, many of which are supported by the government, address difficult-to-reach communities, we wanted to echo our concern for all persons. Because of his broad audience and positive message, Darryl was approached not because he is an African American and there is great need in that community; rather, he was chosen because he is a man who speaks to the fact that truly everybody counts, which is the credo of our organization. Compassion has nothing to do with borders and, least of all, nothing to do with race. We can never thank Darryl and all our "heroes" enough for the support and unselfish kindness they have and continue to show. And in very real, personal ways, we can never thank our clients enough for allowing us to become more than marketers; I thank them for allowing each of us involved in DKMS to become fully human.

QUESTION: **What are your next steps? How can people help?**

HARF: **We have begun donor recruitment in 2006. And you can bet that every new donor will count. Since insurance companies do not pay for the initial typing, we will have to fund a lot ourselves, but we also will rely on monetary donations. Unfortunately, we have to count cents because every penny can bring us closer to saving something priceless, a human life.**

For more information on DKMS Legion of Heroes, please check out the DKMS Web site at www.dkmsamericas.org (see also Figure 5-2).

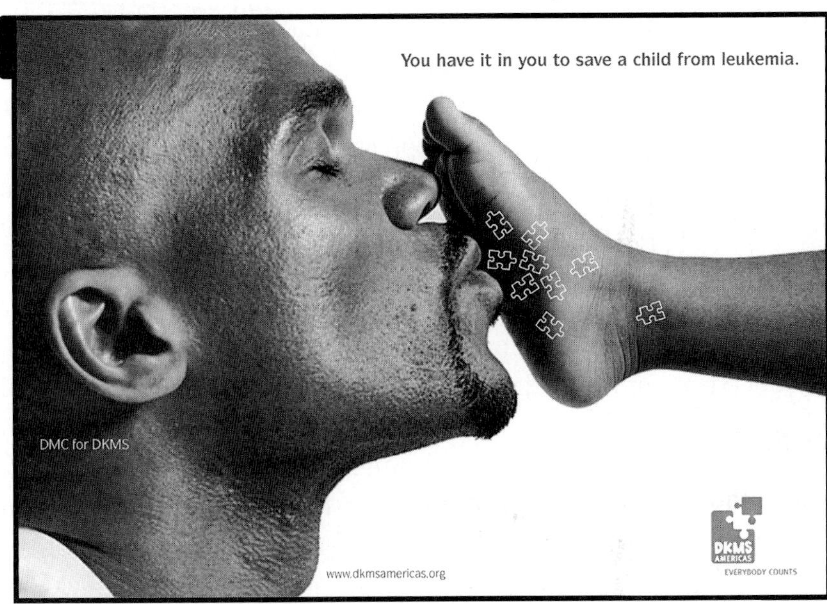

FIGURE 5-2 ■ **In a sublime gesture of humility and love, Darryl McDaniels, the veritable father of hip-hop and an ongoing contemporary artist and symbol of hope, captures the essence of DKMS.**

THE NOBLE BRAND:
COMMERCIAL BRANDS AS CATALYSTS FOR POSITIVE SOCIAL CHANGE

Just as we have discussed the obvious importance of nonprofit, noble brands such as DKMS, we need to also include a discussion of the potential for more utilitarian brands to effect tremendous positive social change. Many noble, wonderful brands are clearly striving for a high standard of ethics and are exemplary. However, you should note that it is not a requirement for a brand to be noble to be ethical.

As consumers increasingly express not only a strong desire for corporate/brand transparency and ethical practices and also a certain level of "brand activism," brands need to reflect the desire of consumers to make the world a better place. Since "cause branding" has become a veritable racket today, there are many examples of brands that would seek a noble image but remain shallow in their attempt to seduce consumers in their superficial, ultracalculated, highly publicized, pseudoethical gestures. The cases where brands are unselfishly offering value to consumers via their commitments to positive social change are not nearly as common as one might suppose, despite every social indicator suggesting that a new philanthropic cultural consciousness is leading many brands in that direction—at least from a superficial perspective. Fortunately, there have always been exceptions—which is why hope springs eternal. The following cases paint portraits of brands that have succeeded in hitting their noble mark.

HEWLETT-PACKARD

A recent Hewlett-Packard print ad that shows an old computer morphing into a tricycle and has the following copy:

By 2010, an estimated 350 million outdated computers will end up in landfills worldwide. HP began its first PC recycling program 11 years ago. Today we process 6.5 million pounds of product each month globally, turning old PCs into material that can be used to make new PCs, car parts, and even bright red tricycles. To recycle your unwanted computer hardware, visit www.hp.com/plus_recycling.

Here, the consumer is not only told how "good" the brand is in terms of its recycling efforts, but the consumer also is invited to join in the efforts and given information on how Hewlett-Packard will help him or her get rid of old computer hardware. Thus the consumer is given an accessible means to participate in the program—without having to buy a Hewlett-Packard product or make any monetary contribution whatsoever.

AMERICAN APPAREL

This American-made brand is manufactured in downtown LA through innovative, vertically integrated manufacturing processes that seek to prove that the sweatshop need not exist. Guilt-free (and brand-free) fashion is the idea here.

A recent American Apparel print ad announces:

The freedom is back. 4,000 people making it happen. Almost every stage of our manufacturing and marketing occurs in the same building in downtown Los Angeles.

ETHOS WATER BY STARBUCKS

This wonderful brand concept was created to help children around the world get clean water. The brand promise is simple: Buy bottled water, and some of the profits will go to funding various global efforts in third-world countries to provide clean, safe water for children and their families in partnership with organizations such as Unicef, CARE, and WaterAction in South America, Africa, India, and Asia. The tagline, "Every bottle makes a difference," says it all.

This brand is only the latest effort by Starbucks to build an ethical brand (and brand image, of course). The company's efforts in this area have been consistent, well-orchestrated, and seemingly sincere with projects such as the Commitment to Origins program, which supports fair-trade coffees that help to build small coffee growers' ability to compete in the global market and also protects the environment where coffee is grown. Starbucks honestly admits that its work in this area is also self-motivated—informed by the goal "To guarantee our long-term supply . . . and fulfill our responsibility as a leader in the global coffee community." Starbucks has long supported educational programs as well, such as literacy outreach programs in local communities.

Social responsibility, however, is not the only mark of a noble brand. A brand that reflects culture and collective dreams—and pushes those dreams to the forefront of changing social mores also can, in my opinion, qualify as noble. Think of the television show *All in the Family* and how it raised awareness of interracial harmony through satire and humor. Think of *Will and Grace* or *Queer Eye for the Straight Guy* and how they have diffused animosity against gay people. Think of hip-hop music and how it has, at least for some members of the African-American community, taken the sting out the word *nigger,* replacing it with an empowerment of sorts. Similarly, Playboy is a brand that has come full circle. During the era of its conception, women most often were objectified in the media. And in very real ways, women remain objectified even today.

However, as the Playboy brand has evolved to acknowledge women within the context of modern culture, this brand that some women historically have found objectionable has taken on the positive, dream-fulfilling aspects and translated these "good" and empowering qualities into products designed for the pleasure and self-esteem of women not merely for the gratification of men. In some ways, it has become a "white knight," ethical, perhaps even feminist brand within the context of our time—a time vastly different from the time surrounding the original magazine's 1953 inception. For women, the gesture of wearing the Playboy label or any of its related iconography could be viewed as a liberated pronouncement of choice. The celebration of femininity and the celebration of fun fashion are no longer diametrically opposing choices. Given the quality of the licensed products and the integrity of its staff (including many intelligent, accomplished females), I approached Playboy Enterprises with some questions. Take a look at the following section and share the company's intriguing responses.

THE EMPOWERED BUNNY

an Interview with Alex Vaickus, President of Global Licensing at Playboy Enterprises

QUESTION: **Your clothes are not costumes chosen by men for women to wear; they are clothes that women elect to wear because they enjoy them. What would you have to say about the phenomenon of various groups reclaiming the stereotypes that may have once surrounded them and taking ownership of their contemporary meaning?**

VAICKUS: **The society in which we live today is more relaxed, free, and open than it was when *Playboy* launched in 1953. *Playboy* has played an important role in liberating cultural shift, one that has enabled oppressed groups to attain empowerment. A way of attaining empowerment is through the reclamation of language and the embracing of stereotypes in order to control and redefine them. I think the postfeminist trend toward wearing sexy clothing to reclaim and redefine femininity is very empowering and a part of this sensibility.**

An important founding premise of the magazine is that good girls like sex, too, which was a radical idea in 1953. *Playboy* does not shirk from the more racy or difficult questions because of a false or any imposed dogma of propriety, and so we became the only mainstream media outlet that could deal frankly with sex, and many other issues, whether we're talking about civil rights, politics, or war. This attitude has benefited women, the real victims of sexual repression in the past.

QUESTION: While *Playboy*, the magazine, continues to appeal to a largely male audience, what is it about the Playboy brand that makes it so appealing to women?

VAICKUS: Playboy is a sexy brand, and many women want to be and/or feel sexy. We believe in satisfying their choice. Coupled with the fact that Playboy is a lifestyle brand that promotes independent thinking, we present a winning combination for women. It goes back to attaining empowerment. Women use Playboy to show their independence, ability to think freely, and that they are in control of their sexuality. When a woman adorns herself in Playboy fashion, whether sportswear or lingerie, she automatically feels empowered.

Another of Playboy's key elements is we've always been concerned with the female perspective. If the magazine can help men to understand the female mind, our readers can have a better time communicating with women, which leads to more artful seduction and better sex. In short, a better world. When a reader looks at the Playmate photos, what he's seeing is a beautiful woman presenting herself as she wants to be seen. The photo is the apotheosis of her desire, the thrill of her realizing a dream of sexual empowerment. It's the secret of our success. It's why our brand extensions work.

It's worth noting that 20 percent of our readers are women, as are 34 percent of our college reps and 85 percent of our licensed product consumers. Playboy also supports many woman-positive not-for-profits, including Planned Parenthood, the American Civil Liberties Union Reproductive Rights Project, the Center for Women Policy Studies, the National Women's Political Caucus, the Vietnam Veterans of America Women in the Military Project, Bosom Buddies, Dress for Success NY, and Women Make Movies.

Moreover, many women have written for and been interviewed in the magazine, plus, of course, many female celebrities have not only appeared in *Playboy* but also have worn Playboy products. Playboy's 50th Anniversary Designer Collection was driven by female products: a Versace gown and shoes, Wolford hosiery, MAC Cosmetics, a

Diane von Furstenberg wrap dress, Garrard Jewels, a Kathrine Baumann minaudiere, a D-Squared top, and Peter Golding denim.

QUESTION: The aesthetic quality of everything you are doing is extremely high. What insight led you to realize that the key to building a successful Playboy brand franchise would rely on the integrity of the products sold under the brand name?

VAICKUS: *Playboy* is a half-century old. Longevity, especially in the magazine business, is exceptionally rare. One of the many reasons *Playboy* continues to lead the world as the best-selling men's monthly magazine is its endless dedication to the highest-quality award-winning art and photography. This is reflected in our powerful archives, now with more than 15 million images. Our archives help to inform and inspire our product-development teams while keeping our products true to the brand, relevant, and on trend.

With one of the most recognizable icons in the world, we realize the power of aesthetics on a brand's success, and we incorporate quality and deliberate aesthetic judgment across every line of business, especially global licensing. Playboy strives to control not only the aesthetics of a given product but also the context and presentation of the product through lifestyle boutiques. We currently have three—in Tokyo, Las Vegas, and Melbourne—with more on the way. Our stores themselves are designed to reflect the essence of the Playboy lifestyle and deliver an experience. They are places to interact with the brand in a constructive environment.

QUESTION: Everyone today is talking about experiential marketing. To what extent have you leveraged the existing brand in order to stretch it into other categories and other levels of brand experience?

VAICKUS: Playboy is an extremely elastic brand with significant relevance across multiple media and product categories. In addition to opening freestanding stores that allow our customers to experience the brand across the globe, we plan to add location-based entertainment venues. Our first casino and club in over a decade will open next spring as the Playboy Tower at the Palms Resort and Casino in

Las Vegas, which will allow the consumer to fully experience the aspirational nature of the brand through a rooftop night club, the city's first high-rise "sky casino" overlooking Las Vegas, a Hef Sky Villa, a Playboy retail store, and much more. Plans for additional sites are in development. In addition, we continue to grow in the interactive category with video games and other multimedia products that also will allow consumers to further experience Playboy.

CONCLUSION: Love by Any Other Name Is . . . War!

In this chapter we have spoken about how the burgeoning era of consumer empowerment means the end of a certain kind of "brand worship" and harkens a new level of brand ethics and social responsibility. While I strongly believe that this change is beginning and will continue to grow, there are those of us who are resolutely stuck in an era of "brand love" (which is to say seduction of the consumer) versus consumer love.

Allow me to clarify: We should love consumers enough to see their needs. We then should satisfy *those* needs. Consumers will love the brands and products we create. Any other kind of induced brand love is pure seduction, which may feel good and work for a while. However, if you want a true marriage between your customer and your brand, one with enduring respect, you will have to choose between a relationship and an affair. An ethical marriage of equals may be intimidating at first. Meaningful commitments usually are. But the commitment will be worth it because it will completely redefine the notions of finite product life cycles while indefinitely energizing, creating, and evolving brands.

This chapter was meant to both uplift and challenge you. It serves to remind you of the reality of our age and what you may realistically encounter as you try to do your job and maintain your own sense of integrity and humanity within the context of that job. In won't be easy. You often may find yourself as a lone voice raging against an infrastructure based on last century's marketing models and morals. You may get fired a few times. But I implore you to have courage. Courage will propel your brand and your career and, in almost every way, shape every aspect of positive social and commercial change.

BE BEAUTIFUL

CELEBRATE AESTHETICS IN EVERYTHING YOU DO

We have made you a creature of neither Heaven nor of Earth, neither mortal nor immortal, in order that you may as the free and proud shaper of your own being fashion yourself in the form you may prefer.

—*Pico della Mirandola,* Oration on the Dignity of Man

INTRODUCTION:
The Changing Face of Beauty

Secret #5 introduced the notion that beauty and business ethics are, in fact, connected. Like ethics, the definition of beauty is so very personal. It is both concrete and abstract. It is visible and invisible. It is a concept that is applied to our self-perceptions, projected expectations, and the functional and experiential aspects of brands and brand messages. In this chapter we will discuss both (1) how commerce is only now beginning to allow culture to define who, what, and why something is beautiful and (2) how the democratization of great design has raised the stakes in terms of consumers' expectations of "brand beauty." This chapter will visibly bridge commerce and culture and provide insight into the future of beautiful branding. It will lead us to one conclusion: Beauty is what consumers find beautiful in themselves, in the products they consume, and in the experiences that define brands. And once again, the notion of consumer as creator, whether directly or indirectly, will be reinforced.

The business implication: Today's brands must be beautiful and well designed—both inside and out—and according to strict *cultural* specifications. While we are beginning to see some evidence of greater acceptance of the diversity of human beauty, it is still overwhelmingly clear that a conventionally beautiful man, woman, or child, when associated with a brand, typically is more commercially "valuable." And if the person happens to be a celebrity—with attributes, either real or manufactured, that support a lifestyle or idea that is relevant to a product category—then that "face" is still the best face of all—at least for now. A few years ago Coty Inc launched an Isabella Rossellini cosmetics line called Manifesto. Similar to the later and now iconic Dove campaign, the Manifesto campaign promoted the concept of diverse, inclusive feminine beauty. The initial results were disappointing. The campaign did not appear to be aspirational enough for women. Years of unconscious conditioning, the result of idealized images in entertainment and advertising, actually have, on an unconscious level, distorted our perception of beauty and, sadly, of ourselves. But now this finally seems to be changing. As marketers, we must remember this sad folly so as never to repeat it. Once was bad enough. Twice would be unforgivable.

The change in attitude (both by brands and by consumers) reflected by the Dove ads marks true progress and justifies our eating a bit of crow. How much can change in just a few short years? How much more will change in just a few more? How many more years will it take before marketers realize that they don't define beauty? And moreover, should not even try.

Collectively, we remain at the tip of the iceberg, with the liberation of real beauty standards just turning the bend. We can choose to actually become cultural partners in this exciting shift—while still selling brands and products. I am not just referring to cosmetics or fashion brands. I am referring to the projections of beauty all brands must reflect in their visual personifications as expressed through various forms of brand communication. Oddly, in the meantime, there still remains a vestige of consumer preference for seeing the faces of celebrities or of idealized models rather than reflections of ordinary or fascinatingly original faces—which, according to my "commerce-reflecting cultural" definition of ethics, means that we can only move at the rate that culture moves.

One need only consider the fact that in 2006 the Grammy Awards, which aired on the same night as *American Idol*, scored lower ratings than *American Idol*. With evidence so strong, we can no longer deny the phenomenon of consumer as creator and the "everyman star."

Today, a celebrity endorsement or licensed product is not sufficiently relevant to sustain a brand idea over time unless it measures its relevance relative to consumers and culture. Ultimately, celebrity-based brands should be little more than vehicles enabling consumers to choose their costars—to live their dreams in real time, to live their dreams *actually* versus vicariously. The business implication here is that when marketers see the existing beauty of all their consumers, brands, both old and new, automatically will enjoy an opportunity for expansion—with the notion of beauty and a beautiful life expanding, becoming more inclusive. This will enable new categories and new twists on brands at the same time as we become better able to explore new markets and customize existing ones—be they ethnic, gender, age, geographic, or lifestyle-based.

By now you must realize that I am a contradiction. I am an advocate of commerce, economic competition, and profit. I am also a consumer advocate with an abiding respect for culture and self-determination. How do I reconcile my double life? I don't have to. The fact is that when you (1) see beauty in everyone (as discussed earlier) and create ideas rooted in an appreciation of that beauty and (2) enable a consumer-defined beautiful life, the natural result always will be successful, both ethically and financially. The remainder of this chapter will explore the power of design in the enablement of beautiful lives led by beautiful consumers. The inherent beauty of the consumer is henceforth implied. The beauty of the product is the topic at hand and one of the leading measures of an ethical brand.

When talking about the aesthetics of brands, almost inevitably Target comes up as an example. I greatly admire Target, yet I believe that it's now time to look at some other, even further-evolved models. In the beginning, the quality of Target's advertising surpassed the reality of its consumers' retail experiences and brand offerings. Target is now obviously working on the reconciliation of both the promises and the truth of the brand. This is an important lesson. Brand experience consists of both ideas and images, brands and function. In this chapter we'll look at how other brands are succeeding at this and finally examine how some of the great designers—such as Karim Rashid and the students and faculty of the renowned Parsons The New School For Design—are successfully enabling beautiful lives through designs that build brand soul into even the most everyday products.

WHOSE BEAUTY:
WHAT IS GOOD DESIGN?

Product identity and beauty are often evaluated separately. This is a terrible mistake. Beauty, within the context of product and brand identity, is not at all about abstraction. In fact, the value of "image" actually can be quantified—or so claim some of the world's leading branding experts, such as Interbrand with its well-known brand-valuation model. If one concedes that beauty is a part of brand image, then a brand's being perceived as beautiful, as expressed in a culturally relevant context, is always the way to success. Regardless of whether brand identity and product designs are created for rat poison or haute couture, there are criteria by which design can be deemed elegant or coarse, vulgar or beautiful. I believe that all brand identity must be beautiful—which is not to say that it needs to reflect traditional, static standards of "good taste." Culture is changing constantly, and therefore, so too are definitions of good taste. Beauty is, after all, culturally defined, linked to functionality, and varies from place to place—there is no "one" flavor of beauty. Beauty can have an edge, and it certainly doesn't have to be "idealized." It just has to capture our hearts and our imaginations—and enhance or enable the lives consumers wish to live. Remember, many paintings depict squalor with exceptional honesty and beauty. Not all people want to have beautiful paintings of fruit surrounding them. Thus beauty remains open to cultural interpretation. Yet the necessity for beautiful brands is clearly no longer a choice but a consumer demand.

Strangely, but often enough in monetary terms, beautiful design costs the same as bad design to create, and in the long run it is a far better brand investment than almost any other element of the marketing mix. Unfortunately, however, it is an element that still gets short shrift—both in how seriously it is taken by marketers and in the monetary value they are willing to invest in this most intimate of marketing tools. Even the smallest company can afford a trip to a contemporary museum—often one of the best reflections of aesthetic *zeitgeist.*

Don't you think that most companies could sacrifice one day of so-called productivity to delve deeper into the question of good design, good taste, and the nature of modern beauty?

The importance of design even exceeds the value of the ingredients/materials of which a product consists. For example, take the following insight of Tracy Young, president of Sweerts and Vaas and formerly vice president of a division of Fabrikant, one of the world's leading jewelry manufacturers. Young helped launch a line of men's jewelry that fused unusual and/or diverse materials such as titanium, stainless steel, high-tech ceramics, gold, and diamonds to create really fantastic jewelry—much of which is intended for a broad audience and sold at an accessible price. These designs are extremely innovative and elegant and speak to consumer desire for personal expression and a progressive self-image.

According to Young, one of the new drivers of jewelry consumption has less to do with materials than it does with reflecting prevailing cultural acceptance of design "substance" as a key component of style/value. When asked about what percentage of a jewelry manufacturer's ability to differentiate itself relies on materials and what percentage is based on design, she said:

> *Jewelry falls into the category of luxury as it does not fulfill a life-sustaining need (Marilyn Monroe's diamonds are a girl's best friend reference aside). In jewelry, one cannot separate the materials from the design and the finished piece. Stainless steel is a material commonly found in appliances, and many would not consider it a luxury material. However, when Cartier uses stainless steel as the material for a men's watch band, the material takes on a new dimension and becomes a luxury item through association with the brand and the emotions that the consumer has when wearing the item. Young men today look beyond the traditional materials of gold and silver in their jewelry. Tungsten, rubber, stainless steel can all be used to create items that allow young men to adorn themselves and express their individuality. Additionally, new generations are looking for new materials that define their generation. ABS (plastic) is not considered a luxury material. However, when Motorola added diamonds to the Baby Phat telephone, all of a sudden the item became a luxury item.*

Great design is inextricably linked to product and package experience (and technology)—often constituting the most engaging element of brand experience. If one listens to the myriad marketing experts, all of them seem to place increasing emphasis on the importance of well-designed products and packaging, in addition to retail environments, as part of a more evolved consumer relationship. For example, in the past decade, many different categories of consumer products, from snacks to household cleaners, have begun to realize that the best "advertisement" they can buy is a fantastic package. From product design to architecture, marketing clearly has been experiencing a golden age of commercial design—applied to all aspects of brand experience, including retail environment, the Internet, advertising, graphic design, and perhaps most important, packaging and product design. This certainly has something to do with the culture's changing concept of luxury. It even has created a new class of designer rock stars, an interesting development for those overly cost-conscious marketing cynics previously convinced that beauty was dead. For an interesting perspective on this cultural shift toward beauty, see the following section from Massimo Redaelli, senior vice president of IMG Fashions, Paris, whose roster of style-setting celebrities, models, and actors ranks it as the world's number one international model management firm as well as a leading resource in the area of talent scouting. The agency oversees more than 70 clients, including superstars Gisele Bundchen, Tyra Banks, Heidi Klum, Erin Wasson, and Shalom Harlow.

THE FUTURE OF FASHION; THE FASHION OF LIFE

an Interview with Massimo Redaelli

QUESTION: **Style is becoming one of the most important methods of brand differentiation. Do you agree with this comment? Please explain.**

REDAELLI: **I totally agree. Product differentiation is going to be more about style, design packaging, image, perception, and so on than ever before. It is somehow already happening in mass consumer goods; for example, think about organic products in the 1980s (small underground hippies' stores) and now (stylish tofu packaging in fancy corner department stores). Fashion has been selling dreams since the very beginning, and that's why it is the perfect model to reference when evaluating brand design. Details, design, image, quality, consistency (what fashion does best) will be applied more and more to consumer goods in search of an emotional element that will drive "product differentiation," not to mention the purchase decisions of consumers across categories.**

QUESTION: **The border between luxury and mass imagery continues to blur, while style and design continue their rise in consumer importance. Are there any brands, celebrities, or designers that you feel are particularly culturally relevant and on the verge of brand explosion?**

REDAELLI: **It will be interesting to see where the fashion world will go, with consumer goods coming closer and closer to this evolution. I believe that true luxury fashion will go back to its roots, "couture." Fashion designer, celebrity, and luxury brands will seek originality, uniqueness, exclusivity, local flavor, and limited editions. We will see many elements that either extend a celebrity's personality into consumers' lives or heighten a brand's exclusivity, such as a return to fashion's roots with a movement toward tailoring, made to order, and couture. What will be interesting to watch is to what extent and in what form these same elements will be applied to other price segments of fashion, as well as other categories of products. In some ways I believe that the art of marketing is the art of fashion—whether most marketers know it or not.**

What the 1960s were to advertising (arguably known as its golden age), the 1990s and the beginning of the twenty-first century will be to design and all experiential media, making it all the more important for marketers to truly understand the power of great design. Only then will they be able to leverage this element of the marketing mix in order to maximize the value of brands in an era rapidly veering toward increasing commoditization. In response to this era, I've created a definition of beauty and great design within the context of business that hopefully will help you to better appreciate not only the value of your brand but also the bargain good design constitutes relative to all the other elements at your disposal. I have developed three easily understood criteria/measures of great product design, all of which remain consistent across categories and distribution channels and are closely linked to brand differentiation, profit, and sales. But this is not all. They are also related directly to the hands-on enablement of consumer culture.

According to my criteria, good design must reflect the elegance of functionality, the charm of culturally shared wit and contemporary relevance, and the ethics of uncompromising craftsmanship and sustainability.

CRITERIA 1: THE ELEGANCE OF FUNCTIONALITY

More and more, consumers expect 100 percent assurances of product functionality and style from products and services, including comfort, quality, and an aesthetically evocative mise-en-scène. They will pay a premium for these things and will want them from brands offered even at bargain price points. Examples of this are Kohler hardware, Mac computers, La-Z-Boy furniture, Bally shoes, Motorola telephones, and adidas athletic apparel.

CRITERIA 2: THE CHARM OF CULTURALLY SHARED WIT AND CONTEMPORARY RELEVANCE

Great design concepts acknowledge and embrace a shared cultural perception of symbolic meanings. Interestingly, after a long period of minimalism emphasizing "less is more," consumers have come to realize that design, like time, is a continuum and that nods to prior aesthetics are not necessarily a compromise of modernity. Some examples of this include iPod, FCUK, Virgin, Baby Phat and Phat Farm, Dell, and Ikea.

CRITERIA 3: THE ETHICS OF UNCOMPROMISING CRAFTSMANSHIP AND SUSTAINABILITY

Similar to the arts and crafts movement of the early twentieth century, we are in an age that celebrates both advances in technology and the timelessness of fine craftsmanship. While *synthetic* isn't a bad word, it must be balanced with organic integrity and a human touch. Mercedes-Benz, Dom Perignon, and Chanel illustrate this concept.

An example of these criteria can be found in Japanese culture, where packaging and product design have, indeed, become an art and one of the principal measures of brand quality. On a trip to Tokyo, Anne Mihara of brand consultancy Anne and Friends, took me to a very fancy supermarket to see "presentation quality" fruit. The fruit belonging to this exclusive category are cultivated, much like bonsai trees, deliberately, according to very precise, exacting aesthetic criteria (i.e., cantaloupe are considered most beautiful when

> *Outstanding commercial design plays an inherent role in the improved standards of living and range of choices available to consumers as they project meaning into products and brands.*

they have only three perfect leaves). Anne explained how in the early days of Japanese-Western business collaborations many non-Japanese would overlook the symbolism of having a basket of "perfect fruit" placed in their hotel rooms.

In the past, non-Japanese guests would take a bite of a strawberry and leave the rest of the $1,000 basket of fruit to rot. They had not been culturally conditioned to expect or appreciate the notion of perfect yet natural product design. And they did not understand the honor that the gift of this perfect design implied. Today, however, international executives now appreciate the gesture more, owing perhaps in part to heightened appreciation for product and packaging design. It is no secret that many of the world's finest packaging and product designers look more and more to Japan for inspiration, not unlike their predecessors in the arts and crafts movement prevailing after the turn of the last century. As a result of Western design raising its bar, Western consumers have followed suit in raising their collective expectations. The Japanese reverence for beauty is such that the entire notion of form versus function is virtually nonexistent. Both are assumed. There is a great lesson here for brand designers.

As the rest of this chapter will explain, the three dimensions of design evaluation I have outlined are the keys to taking any product and increasing its perceived value through the unwritten language of great design (as per the example of the value of one brand of cantaloupe over another). But remember, value does not necessarily mean an expensive price; it also can be translated as the silent yet competitive aesthetic advantage that one brand has over another—regardless of category or price point.

What does this mean for marketing? How will the evolution of design and the redefinition of beauty affect brand creation and product design? The answer is fairly straightforward. Just as the casting of "living brand productions" ultimately will reduce down to two very different options—epic sagas with casts of thousands or monologues or one-man shows—design is moving in a similar direction. In other words, there always will be a strong and legitimate market for Maseratis, custom-tailored suits, and fine leather goods—and there also will be a market for inexpensive, fantastically designed trash baskets. However, there will be no tolerance for bad brand design no matter what the price point. As a result, increasingly we will need to defer to what I refer to as *aesthetic oracles,* designers and design agencies with an affinity for and commitment to cultural reflection.

Some of these designers, or aesthetic oracles, are better than others. And some aren't oracles at all. There is no one sure measure to immediately distinguish the two unless a track record of consumer-relevant design history exists. This is not to say that you should never give new designers or design agencies a chance—quite the contrary is true. However, as a rule, whether established or not, the more in sync the designer is with the way real people live real lives, the more likely it is that he or she is the real thing and will treat your brand with the aesthetic respect it deserves.

Understanding whether or not you are in sync with the consumer is only the first step. In business, as in most things, the next step is application. Let's look at how some great designers are applying these standards to some of today's hottest products.

DEMOCRATIC BEAUTY: DEMOCRATIC DESIGN

The celebrated product designer Karim Rashid has come to represent the epitome of democratic design and has an unparalleled facility for both visual and verbal expression that allows his attitudes regarding design and all its social ramifications to be easily understood despite their complexity. Among his multitude of talents, he is also a brilliant businessman. His designs make money for his clients. And he provides consumers with a unique option to live in a unique way—surrounded by democratic beauty.

Karim's work makes people look beyond themselves. He insists that everything be designed with a human being in mind. He combines this notion with insistence that the objects also be perfectly designed. Yet, in the end, of course, no human and no design are perfect. He is trying to push us where we seem to want to go (yet, because of the nature of our humanity, it is merely an aspirational *place* so distant that we will not see its shore). This explains the simultaneously ephemeral yet contradictory timelessness of his designs. The following ideas about design and its relevance to commerce and culture, extracted from his book, *Evolution,*[1] express some of the most profound insight into the relationship between aesthetics and brands that I have ever read. Renowned for inventing new words for new ideas, Karim Rashid manages to coalesce what seem to be a series of divergent cultural and design questions.

THE BIRTH OF SENSUALISM

> *I have described my work as Sensualism (sensual minimalism). It is a broad term I use to explain that minimalism is dead—it is too austere for the average person. It is not about real living; in fact, it is uncomfortable and challenging. Sensualism is about contraindicating minimalism; it is about having only what is essential, but with a friendlier, engaging, and organic relationship.*

The preceding mirrors only one of Karim's sensibilities and fiercely defended aesthetic philosophies. As I have already mentioned, he is also a great commercial advocate, offering the following systematic strategies for successful product development.

> *There are several strategies to "deproductize" and develop successful products:*
>
> 1. *Design objects that meet all the criteria, not just one: beauty, performamce, meaning, cost, seamless production, no manual labor, ease of assembly, smart material, recyclable, spatial, human, behavioral, democratic, and simple.*
>
> 2. *Make companies aware of the humanism of our products—the human connection and condition are key to successful objects.*

3. *Show companies that quality creates higher margins and greater brand loyalty.*

4. *Subtract SKUs [stock-keeping units] that are complex, confusing, noncommunicative, labor-intensive, made from too many parts, high-maintenance, and culturally irrelevant.*

5. *Design flexible, extensive, relaxed, modular, interchangeable, reconfigurable, multifunctional products.*

6. *Remove collateral, streamline distribution, manufacture on demand, drop-ship, manufacture locally, use global positioning, and so on.*

7. *Promote, teach, and disseminate a direct, simple philosophy—design experiences versus objects. Form follows subject.*

8. *Design creates its own market.*

9. *The object is the brand.*

The following section, "Beyond Design: The Architecture of Meaning," contains a Coty interview with Karim, in which he provides a behind-the-scenes snapshot of his collaboration on the Davidoff brand's Echo fragrance for the Lancaster Group (now known as Coty Prestige).

BEYOND DESIGN: THE ARCHITECTURE OF MEANING

an Interview with Karim Rashid on Echo by Davidoff

QUESTION: **What does Davidoff represent to you? Could you describe in your own words the Davidoff universe?**

RASHID: **A sort of a cool, refreshing liberal sense of freedom, or space, or spiritual infinity.**

QUESTION: **What were your sources of inspiration?**

RASHID: **I was inspired by trying to create a bottle that is masculine and feminine at the same time, something that is comfortable, engaging, experiential, and human. I was interested in creating an object that is flexible or appears to be like liquid, as if the bottle did not need to exist, but there is a new innovative top on an abstracted undulated piece of glass.**

QUESTION: **How did you work to create the bottle? How did you start?**

RASHID: **I started with developing very radical ideas of a nonserialized bottle—the idea of a production bottle, which via an intentionally variable production process, would result in each bottle being randomly unique. Therefore, each bottle would be one-of-a kind, no two the same. In the process, I developed a glass that has the appearance of diversity and that in its material tends to divert the eye and change its feeling.**

QUESTION: **How long did it take to achieve the final design?**

RASHID: **I worked quite rigorously at about 10 concepts for about one year.**

QUESTION: **Could you describe the bottle in your own words? What does it represent to you?**

RASHID: **Even though the object is basically minimal and rectangular, the glass is compound and undulated, so that the glass speaks about liquid beauty. I love the idea that the experience of the perfume is immaterial, and the bottle is the material catalyst—undulated, wrinkled, like a bottle that has been squeezed.**

QUESTION: **What about the name Echo and the design of the bottle?**

RASHID: **The name works really well; the bottle is like a stream in the woods, and I can hear the echo!**

QUESTION: **How did you work with the marketing team?**

RASHID: **I listened closely but tried to not compromise too much—in order to retain the character of the bottle (it was originally going to be a gel material in a frame and not glass).**

QUESTION: **What are the trends you see in the area of design? How is Echo by Davidoff part of it?**

RASHID: **A new global casualness is taking place—a relaxed technological world where tactility and things are pleasurable and engaging (see Figure 6-1).**

FIGURE 6-1 ■ Karim Rashid's Davidoff Echo bottle—design that captures our common desire to be heard, touched, and satisfied.

TOMORROW IS TODAY: ENLISTING TOMORROW'S VISION NOW

Parsons The New School For Design has been acknowledged as one of the world's finest institutions of its kind. Founded in 1896, the school educates design leaders who contribute significantly to the quality of life through expertly designed and responsible products, built environments, and visual communications. The school cultivates an outstanding and diverse student body and faculty, develops innovative curricula, fosters partnerships that support education and research objectives, and teaches design in the broader context of society (www.parsons.edu).

The following case study gives us an exciting model of the future of culturally inspired design and introduces several of tomorrow's aesthetic oracles (the "real thing" as previously described). In addition to the following examples of real-world collaboration between students and faculty and both commercial and nonprofit corporations, you will be provided with information regarding how *you and your organization* can tap into the talent of Parsons now, using the vision of the future to connect your brands to a new generation of design-driven consumers.

PARSONS DESIGN LAB

Parsons Design Lab provides students in the school's design departments with opportunities to apply their skills, ideas, and knowledge outside the academic environment. In some cases, the sponsors of projects are pillars of commercial industry who have chosen to explore a problem, concept, material, or technology with student designers.

In some instances, students are asked to be the problem setter, defining an opportunity for design to effect a change in the world. In particular, the Parsons Product Design Department is committed to rethinking the role design plays in the world and encouraging an entrepreneurial spirit. Toward that end, the Product Design Department actively engages the not-for-profit community and international businesses to challenge students in collaborative real-world projects. Corporate and nonprofit partners in Parsons Design Lab have included companies such as DaimlerChrysler, Piaggio, Siemens, Fossil, Microsoft, Samsung, and Coty Inc, to name a few (http://productdesign.parsons.edu).

DRIVING TOMORROW'S STYLE

The Piaggio relationship began in 2005. Piaggio USA, Inc., the manufacturer of the renowned Vespa scooter, partnered with Parsons The New School For Design to reimagine this incomparable icon of Italian style within the context of twenty-first-century American culture. Students were charged with developing new fashions, accessories, and product ideas and concepts to integrate Vespa into the values and lifestyles of the U.S. teenage and 20- to 30-year-old markets and to broaden and "futurize" the Vespa in the context of modern urban living, the economy, and ecosustainability in light of increasing traffic congestion.

Restricted only by the limits of their imaginations, students in the fashion design, product design, and design and technology programs at Parsons created concepts for a lifestyle collection ranging from clothing to wearable technologies, accessories, and even new features for the scooter itself. "Vespa challenged students from Parsons to come up with creative ideas for attracting young people to adopt scooter culture and change how people think about transportation," said Paolo Timoni, CEO of Piaggio USA, Inc. "The resulting designs impressively combine the long heritage and tradi-

tion of Italian design and manufacturing with the progressive ideas fostered by this quintessential New York design school."

Inspired by the on-the-go Vespa lifestyle, the fashion collection melds sophisticated urban style with highly active designs for men, women, and children. The product collection includes:

- *Beat Pods.* The antithesis of the iPod, Beat Pods are designed for sharing music with others while walking down the street or riding through the city. The speakers, shaped like oversized ear buds, are connected by a sleek cord that wraps easily around the wearer's neck or the handles of the Vespa scooter (see Figure 6-2).

FIGURE 6-2 ■ Vespa Beat Pods: entertainment anytime anywhere.

- *Vespa chain lock.* Taking a lead from street and bike messenger cultures, the Vespa chain lock transforms the locking device for the Vespa into the ultimate fashion accessory. An ironic twist on securing one's valuables, the object used to protect the Vespa is now a treasure itself. Made from titanium with a Vespa-engraved lock plate, the chain lock not only secures the parked Vespa but can be worn on the body in multiple fashions (see Figure 6-3).

FIGURE 6-3 ■ Vespa chain lock: turning function into a fashion accessory.

- *Vespet.* Locking securely onto the back of the Vespa, the Vespet is designed for transporting Vespa pets in style. Its aerodynamic shape emulates the sleek curves and lines of the Vespa, and it is available in a matching color palette. The top of the case is a transparent window that enables pets to enjoy the passing scenery (see Figure 6-4).

FIGURE 6-4 ■ The Vespet: a sleek ride for your beloved pet.

The design team includes David Hamilton, Joe Hwang, Patti Tower, Soner Onen, and Thomas Scholz. For more information, visit www.vespausa.com/parsons.

SIERRA CLUB MISSION

Students from Parsons The New School For Design also recently created concepts for new glassware and dinnerware collections for the Sierra Club, inspired by the organization's mission of preserving and protecting the environment. Founded in 1892, the Sierra Club (www.sierraclub.org) is a nonprofit organization dedicated to exploring, enjoying, and protecting the planet. Currently, the Sierra Club is licensing various product lines, yet the collaboration with Parsons is the organization's first foray into home design. "We wanted a fresh new design approach for tableware, one that would convey the spirit of the Sierra Club brand," said Johanna O'Kelley, director of the Sierra Club's licensing program. "In that spirit, we embarked on a glassware and dinnerware collection that would allow consumers to integrate environmental protection into their everyday lives. Realizing the talent and fresh perspective that students can provide, we chose to work with Parsons to develop the collection, and the results are outstanding. We have been extremely impressed by the innovative spirit and design caliber of the students at Parsons."

The project was developed by two teams of undergraduate students, with each team designing two glassware and two dinnerware collection concepts. The Embrace dinnerware and glassware collection and the Roots dinnerware and Cheers glassware collections by the team of Lindsey Clark, Jennifer Divello, Hideaki Matsui, and Laura Schalchli create a dialogue between the manmade and natural worlds through form, patterns, and textures.

The team of Racha Bahsoun and Kimberly Price designed glassware and dinnerware collections that draw on the themes of nature and sustainability. The Flip Me glassware collection is a set of stackable, two-in-one glasses that are a simple and space-efficient alternative to ordinary glassware. The Family glassware collection is a set of nesting glasses—wine, cocktail, and water glasses that share similar contours that create a sense of unity when they are placed together in an elegant embrace. The Growth dinnerware collection is inspired by one of the tenets of the Sierra Club's mission—growth and progress. This is expressed through abstract geometric shapes that come together to form an organic pattern. The Heritage dinnerware collection draws from another central element of the Sierra Club's mission—recycling. Here, traditional English-style china patterns are deconstructed and recomposed using modern design language. The Sierra Club now is exploring partnerships with manufacturers to produce and sell these glassware and dinnerware collections (see Figure 6-5).

FIGURE 6-5 ■ **Heritage dinnerware collection from the Sierra Club.**

I also worked with Tony Whitfield and Hugh Phear at Parsons on a Coty "Fragrance of the Future" project. We challenged students to explore the future of fragrance, bottle design, and their impact on current and future human existence. The two winners of this design scholarship were Elizabeth Lindstom, who created a fragrance bottle containing a flower seed that could be planted after use, and Wilhelm Liden, whose vision of future packaging fused the notions of glamour and vulnerability, elegance and truth. His innovative design magnified the print of the list of ingredients on the reverse label of a disk-shaped bottle and was the epitome of rational elegance. Thus, in the end, Elizabeth's sustainable truth and Wilhelm's consumer respect won the competition. When it comes to commercial design, the type of consumer respect and social responsibility depicted by Elizabeth combined with the elegant expression of consumer understanding depicted by Wilhelm point the way to equally important design considerations.

It amazed me that although it was not included as a requirement, every single student's submission included an element of social responsibility. Perhaps as a partial result but more likely because of the school's own commitment to design as a source for the betterment of the human condition, Tony drove a new program called "A Good Life," which focuses on providing solutions to global issues. You will see some extraordinary examples of these solutions in the next section.

PARSONS: "A GOOD LIFE"

by Tony Whitfield, Chair, Product Design and Development

Dedicated to providing an expansive professional education for its students, the Product Design Department has been encouraging faculty and students to inquire broadly into issues and problems that go beyond the constructs of the commercial marketplace. These efforts have been remarkably fruitful.

In 2003, by introducing the theme of "A Good Life" as a point of departure for the whole department, we extended the scope and demands of these nontraditional product inquiries, especially for our seniors in their thesis work. Each of the 38 seniors was required to collaborate with a nonprofit organization as a resource and inspiration for the thesis effort. Students had broad choices of topic, cause, or area of need. They had to get familiar with the mission statements and goals of organizations that were not familiar to them. They had to get interested in something that mattered. It was a big gamble, but it paid off remarkably well. Pedagogically, it shifted the learning dynamic. We largely avoided the common one-on-one tension between student and instructor/advisor over what kind of design expression was most compelling and timely. With the per-

spectives of the staff and clientele of the nonprofit organizations—and their insights and needs—the advising sessions and critiques centered on questions of effective solutions to real problems. Students were opened up to new dimensions of research and were challenged to represent themselves as emerging professionals with usable skills. We began to realize that the nonprofits provided a unique and privileged access to research and development settings. Students were able to design need-driven responses to real-world problems. The influence of the nonprofit organizations raised the level of department conversations by putting a focus on creative problem solving. Although the concerns of the commercial marketplace were subordinated, students and faculty realized that successful solutions in the nonprofit arena often can spawn new markets with the opportunity for substantial commercial impact.

As an additional bonus, student portfolios were enriched in new ways based on demonstrable accomplishments outside the academic halls and the usual boundaries of design disciplines. Reports from last year's graduates indicate that their thesis work was appreciated and applauded by prospective employers. Today we continue to collaborate with nonprofits and expand our horizons for teaching product design.

Through the theme "A Good Life," the Product Design Department demonstrates its dedication to improving the prospects of student success by providing innovative teaching and learning resources in a challenging context, one that contributes to personal professional development and broader social betterment.

Here are a couple of examples from the "A Good Life" program:

- *Aqualoop.* Aqualoop is a secure water container that reduces the risk of contamination in populations affected by the HIV/AIDS epidemic in sub-Saharan Africa. The ergonomic and adaptable container allows water to be filled only from certified sources provided by humanitarian organizations. Aqualoop consists of a specifically designed valve and a unique and flexible water bladder that can be carried easily in a variety of ways (see Figure 6-6).

FIGURE 6-6 ■ Aqualoop, combining function with cultural sensitivity.

- *Tactile subway map*. This project is a tactile floor map for the NYC subway system, which has limited access for the sight impaired. The goal of this thesis project is to make it easy for the sight impaired to navigate and use the subway. Inspiration was derived by the textured walls used for indoor rock climbing. The tactile floor map uses the textures of "tactile colors," a simple system of 12 standardized textures that correspond to 12 colors. The textures are added to the tactile floor map, but their scale is enlarged so that people can feel the texture through their shoes or by cane, guiding them along an airspace path (see Figure 6-7).

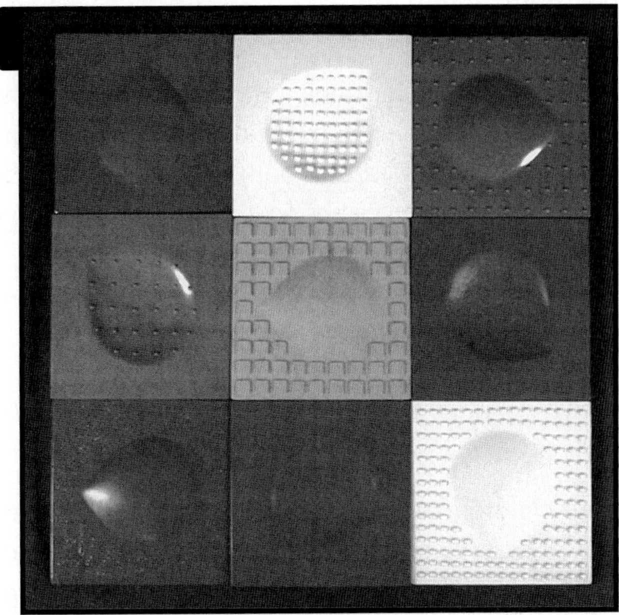

FIGURE 6-7 ■ Tactile subway map: the design of what can't be seen.

For more information on how your for-profit or nonprofit organization can link or might collaborate with Parsons on similar projects, please contact whitfiea@newschool.edu.

THE HEART OF BEAUTY: TWO ESSAYS

As the preceding examples confirm, at the heart of most great design is, you guessed it, heart. Following are two essays about the relationship between beauty and brands written by two women from different disciplines, one in advertising and the other in marketing and licensing. First is Theodora Borsen, partner and creative director at Della

Femina Rothschild Jeary and Partners advertising, and second is Denise Sakuma Wertz, brand director and director of global licensing at Invista Apparel. Traversing their different disciplines, however, is one common thread. Each recognizes the need for beauty in branding, no matter what the product is, and both of them have been responsible for many commercial successes as a result of that recognition.

A BEAUTIFUL WORLD

by Theodora (Teddy) Borsen of Della Femina Rothschild Jeary and Partners

Since we were children, we have grown up with the concept of beauty. From an early age, we not only want to grow up to be beautiful, but children as young as three understand the concept of beauty and how it affects their lives.

Beauty and design play a big part in our lives not only in terms of advertising images but also in our choices in everyday living. Manolo Blaniks, iPods, plasma TVs, and Kohler Whisper Toilets, as well as hundreds of other products we surround ourselves with, are better designed, aesthetically pleasing, or empowering in some way. Not only do we select products to adorn our bodies that make us feel good, such as makeup, fashion, and jewelry, but we also feel more beautiful by choosing accessories that complement our new sense of aesthetics. The design of a cell phone and the new Pentax Optio Digital camera that is the size of a credit card—these beautifully designed objects are selected not only for their functionality but for their looks. Today, everything has the potential of becoming a fashion accessory for our art-directed lives.

Marketers have become aware of this trend and are depending on aesthetics as a major attraction and the brand evangelists to spread the word in order to create a need for better design—be it in cars, electronics, or home design. Martha Stewart—the guru of home design—has created a world of beauty and a multimillion-dollar

operation, Martha Stewart Living Omnimedia, based on this assumption and has brought it to the masses. Hers is a world of manicured lawns, beautiful gardens, and homes adorned with tastefully designed products. Cooking is an art that is desired not only for its taste, but also for its artful presentation. She has created a new generation of lifestylers who have enhanced their lives with design and have become obsessed with creating their own beautiful worlds.

Pentax is one of our clients, and the main marketing feature for this small, beautiful camera is the fact that it is so small—revolutionary for a 4-megapixal digital camera. In fact, my own personal criterion for selecting a camera and cell phone is that they be small enough to fit in my Fendi Croissant evening bag.

The fact that we create our own beautiful worlds and are able to make magic in the midst of calamity now takes on a new meaning on a global scale. Beauty always has played a role throughout the ages—cultures have been influenced by notions of beauty from the times of Cleopatra to Marie Antoinette to Jackie Kennedy, but never have so many people been so obsessed on such a huge scale. Trend analysts look to the need for escape as one reason. A raging war, a bad economy, and longer life spans foster the need to look good, and a multitude of other reasons all contribute to the importance of beauty in our lives. People want to live longer and look good. For example, plastic surgery has become available to the masses because of reality TV shows and celebrities openly revealing "they've had a little work done." The stigma is removed, and the ordinary person wants an "extreme makeover," or like MTV, he or she wants a famous face in order to look like a favorite star.

Advertisers are catching on, marketing products that will make us look more beautiful or feel more beautiful or that simply are beautiful in themselves. The huge explosion in skin care follows this trend—with the promise of younger-looking skin, reduced wrinkles, or plastic surgery in a bottle. And the products themselves are creams that shimmer and shine and are decadently delicious, made from precious minerals or caviar or other rare ingredients. Every drugstore is also filled with cheaper versions of the luxury products, from Dove to L'Oréal, that promise the same thing.

As William Somerset Maugham said: "Beauty is an ecstasy; it is as simple as hunger. There is nothing really to be said about it. It is like the perfume of a rose—you can smell it and that is all!"

And that is all. Some brand platforms are created on the single strategy—the aesthetic of beauty—and the public has bought into the myth. When it comes to culture and the consumer, there are only truths. Truths we either accept, dispute, or glorify. The trick is making the beautiful choice, the informed act of differentiation. To illustrate, consider the following questions:

- Is the iPod really better than the other MP3 players?
- Does drinking lots of water really make your skin feel more beautiful?
- Are diamonds really a girl's best friend?
- Do people really look better when they're tan?
- Do designer labels really impress?

Consumers are asking these questions, and we must be prepared to answer them. We must reassure consumers that in their personal quests for beauty, we are providers of the tools necessary for the quest—we will enable construction of their individually assembled beautiful worlds.

TOUCHING THE DIVINE

by Denise Sakuma Wertz of Invista Apparel

I believe that all of us are born with a touch of divine, which when awakened allows us to radiate and produce beauty. It is a "loving" energy that literally overflows into everything and everyone around us: transforms our work, our communications, our relationships. When this divine talent is in use, the best in us engages and communicates with consumers and the world at large. You and the output of your talent will automatically evolve your brand into something divine, of a higher level—seductive, aspiring, appealing, just beautiful.

Marketing has been a journey for me. However, that journey requires my reaching out to observe the journeys of my consumers, and also reaching in, to authentically respond to what I see based upon my authentic, inner self. When consumers experience this divine power communicated via the senses (taste, smell, texture, touch, sight, and sound) and intertwined with personal emotions and intellect, they suddenly experience "IT." A book, a food, a drink, an outfit, an accessory, a play/movie, a car . . . or even a special someone . . . "IT" awakens the best in them. They feel, quite simply—alive! And, what's the key to a brand attaining "IT"? "IT" is love.

This love transforms marketing's final output. It is the element fueling the power of a brand. The saying that "beauty is in the eye of the beholder" is also true for love. "Love is in the air" and makes the world around you more beautiful. Love is the essence to beautify the world. If true beauty comes from within . . . , believe me, the same happens with love. Design and aesthetics will constantly evolve to trigger consumer desire and love for your brand. "Brand-Beauty" should be visible at all consumer interfaces and touch points. I would say that "marketing at its best is like a beautiful love affair."

The LYCRA brand has built and nurtured a natural love affair with consumers and has transcended its status from an ingredient fiber into a brand that is emotionally connected to consumers. The brand not only represents the "look better, feel better" factor of comfort, quality, and functionality, but it also connects to the emotions and needs of human beings. The LYCRA brand is loved by us because IT "HAS IT." It is a brand with a soul and touch of divine. You can't actually see it, but more importantly it is there . . . inside . . . coming from within.

CONCLUSION: What Lies Ahead? The Two Sides of Tomorrow

Ultimately, without beauty, there would be no brands. Every product, service, and experience would be reduced to commodity status. Without brands, there would be no need for what we do. There would be far less pleasure and expression in consumers' lives. So what does the future for branding hold? Every indication is that both (1) advances in technology that allow for the fusion of performance and great beauty and (2) culturally inspired, responsible design will differentiate the beautiful brands from the not-so-beautiful ones. It will become the distinguishing factor separating commodities from brands. It may be what transforms marketing as we have known it to an agent of social change, economic stability, and increased social tolerance and cross-cultural appreciation. It may become the thing that matters most.

By no means will the expressions and manifestations of the beauty of brands have a single face or project one value. I will leave you with two designs that I believe reflect two different, equally fascinating expressions of the influence of technology and culture on design. One celebrates total immersion in our digital world from an intensely sensual aspect, whereas the other uses new technological expertise to explore and recreate the beauty of the past. Both represent benchmarks of *meaningful* commercial design. They manage to fuse commerce with culture. They marry advances in technology with the sensitivity only possible via a human hand.

001COTY

Sensitive to these ideals, in 2001, Coty Inc launched 001Coty—a concept fragrance, an idea very much akin to the notion of a concept car. The objective was not to create a permanent brand. 001Coty was created as a reflection of culture, cementing Coty as a modern company, as comfortable with its history as it is within the context of today and even the prospects of tomorrow. To create this limited-edition fragrance, advertising, and packaging, Coty Inc sought to reflect the convergence of biology and technology. The flask, modeled after a simple, modern design from 1917, is enclosed within a flexible skin made from the same type of plastic used to cover prosthetic limbs, simulating and symbolizing that technology need not live in the absence of human touch. The unisex fragrance was intended to evoke the smell of electricity, the scent of digital information, and a complex marriage of naturally inspired olfactory notes (see Figure 6-8).

FIGURE 6-8 ■ To execute a simple retro-themed bottle, Coty Inc embraced exciting new technology.

The fragrance was featured and exhibited at the Cooper-Hewitt National Design Museum of the Smithsonian Institution and is also part of the Munich Museum of Modern Art and the Royal Danish Museum. The Web design, created by the renowned team of Brown and Ryan, was nominated for a Chrysler Award. In addition, the concept won honorable mention in *I.D.* magazine's annual design review in August 2002.

FRAGILE

The cult of modernism has, until very recently, been driving twenty-first-century commercial design. The following design provided by centdegrés, one of Europe's most highly acclaimed design agencies and one that I am proud to help launch in North America, demonstrates that vision is not always seeing the future while totally ignoring the past. In fact, the future actually may consist of technology that allows us to reinvent a "better" past—no less sentimental, no less real than the images and associated emotion preciously locked within the context of our own most beloved memories.

The bottle created for Gaultier's fragrance Fragile employs the latest technology to recreate a perfect snow globe, complete with golden snowflakes showering a single, elegant femme fatale in flickering light. Futuristic technology allows centdegrés to defy time and deliver a magical glimpse into a golden world, a golden time, caught forever in something as simple as a bottle, as fragile as a memory captured in mid air (see Figure 6-9).

FIGURE 6-9 ■ **Reflections of a golden world captured by a bottle that capitalized on our continued fascination with memories of a more beautiful time.**

It is fitting that this chapter, with its emphasis on design and the commercial value of beauty, leads us to the conclusion in which we will apply not one but all the ideas and methodologies suggested throughout this book. Why is it so fitting? Because what we are about to do is beautiful, deliberately so. Designed to be useful. Designed to bring joy. Designed to fascinate.

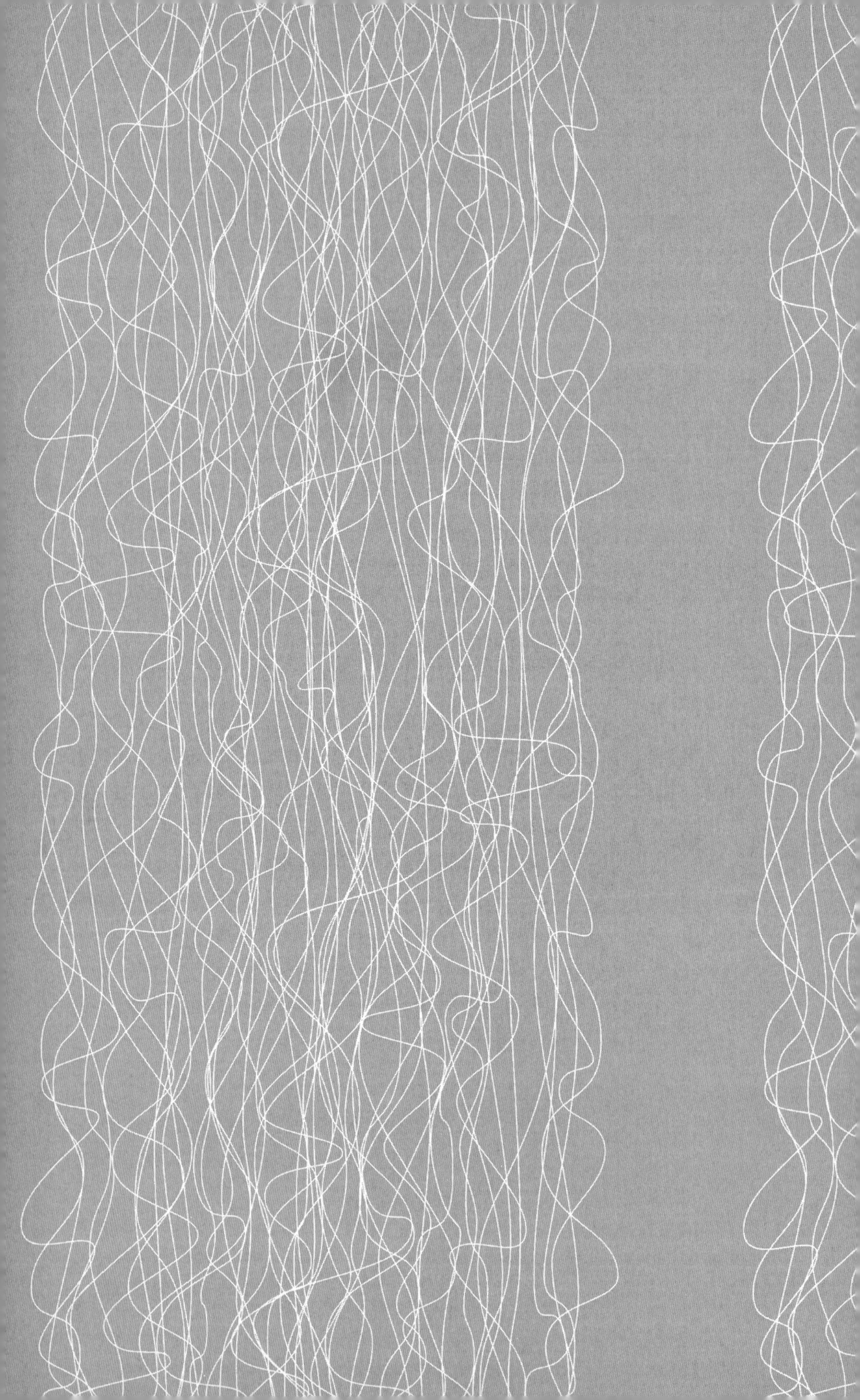

CONCLUSION

BUILD A BRAND-NEW WORLD—A MODEL FOR VISION

PUTTING IT ALL TOGETHER AND BUILDING YOUR OWN LIVING BRANDS MARKETING PLAN

> **What was any art but a mold in which to imprison for a moment the shining elusive element which is life itself—life hurrying past us and running away, too strong to stop, too sweet to lose.**
>
> —*Willa Cather,* The Song of the Lark

FREEDOM OF CUSTOMER:

EMANCIPATED BRANDING IN THE AGE OF CONSUMER COCREATION

Marketing is not a science, a collection of theories, or an art. Although I believe that while art and creativity, in all their varied forms, are increasingly garnering the respect they deserve in business, the fact remains that even the best-laid plans or beautifully executed campaigns do fail; consumer connection either happens or it does not. Predicting the success of brands is an act of intimacy, a brand-new element of the marketing mix, and one that still struggles to emerge in a business world built on a model of alleged objectivity designed to create an illusion of cause and effect.

Virtually the only way to provide people with what they want anymore is to allow them to take part in the process of creation. Another word for consumer-created branding is *consumer-business collaboration.* The future of brands will be entirely dependent on whether they reflect something real, a true consumer need and/or desire, or whether the brand is merely a self-absorbed reflection of itself and the marketers who would rather attempt to recreate culture than to embrace it.

Almost every creative brief I have ever received or written has, in one form or another, cited the absurd notion of brand values. While brands have both tangible and intangible value, they cannot, indeed should not, be confused with the human beings whose values they reflect; *they should not assume the role of graven images. Brands have values only because humans have values.* It sounds simple, doesn't it? Yet virtually every marketing textbook or recent book targeting professionals already working in the field refers to "brand values." This is a mistake.

One should never forget that the word *marketing,* when used as a noun, is a philosophy. Marketing in fact ultimately may influence culture. If and when culture chooses to make the invitation to improve the likelihood of this adoption, all one need do is respect and reflect culture as it exists, as it naturally evolves.

In this concluding chapter, the focus will be on modern marketing. *Marketing* as a verb, not a noun. This final chapter is about action, for your actions have the profound ability to satisfy both physical and psychological needs on a grand scale. It will be your actions that enable real lives to be lived with greater fulfillment and, to a certain extent, for the dreams of real human beings to come true.

In this chapter we will apply the principles established throughout this book to several existing or potential brands. This chapter will show you a step-by-step process for the application of the ideas we've been discussing. My goal is to provide you with the mechanics to enable you to create the type of marketing that you long to create. In this spirit, I am going to demonstrate how to differentiate a real brand from a false one and recommend that unless a brand is rooted in some sort of reality, even if it is a selected, simulated reality, it's not really worth the time to create or perpetuate.

I hope to demonstrate how, once you know you have the ingredients of a real brand, each of the concepts, trends, and insights shared in this book may help you to further your career, evolve your profession, and make the world and its people more satisfied. The case studies in this chapter are provided to take you through real-world examples of diverse brands in varying stages of evolution. They unfurl to represent the *living brands* process, which can be used on any brand to pinpoint cultural relevance, that is, business viability and opportunity. I will apply the principles of this book methodically and provide a skeleton of what I would call a truly consumer-cocreated brand and its potential brand extensions.

As you know by now, it is not a question of if the consumer will assume a role in brand cocreation; it's a matter of when. Consumers will have their say—in terms of both brand and product creation. This is an undeniable cultural transition that we, as existing or new marketing professionals, must acknowledge or, figuratively speaking, die. Not only is this power shift good for consumers, but it also will be a good yet admittedly challenging time for us.

Both culturally and technologically, today's consumers have both the will and the means to change the world. As with the missed opportunity resulting from marketing's inability to recognize the significance of karaoke 20 years ago—a sign of the beginning shift from a voyeuristic to a participatory culture and the advent of reality entertainment—we don't have time to waste. We simply don't have the luxury of 20 years to wake up slowly to the reality of today's real world and still remain a legitimate, relevant part of it. This next step toward consumer cocreation does not require our approval—or even the consumer's permission. It's way beyond that. Cultural evolution does not seek or grant permission. It is spontaneous, much in the way that many of tomorrow's brands will emerge spontaneously. And rather than evolving over time, technology will accelerate the phenomenon. When it happens, it will happen with a vengeance. Be prepared. This marks the beginning of no less than a cultural and business revolution.

Culture is literally moving faster than we are—or can. But try. Please try. We must race to catch up with culture, anticipating its real needs and satisfying them—all before the needs change once more. The simple secret to creating and maintaining brand relevancy is your commitment to hear and respond to the ever-changing voice of the consumer. The living brands approach I have suggested asserts that no marketing plan should be without a 10-year vision—anything less suggests a lack of confidence and fatalistic anticipation of obsolescence.

The connecting factor in each of the case studies presented in the rest of this chapter is their potential for ongoing cultural relevance and their abilities to evolve over time. As long as a brand continues to (1) enable the consumer's performance of self, (2) remains true to its promise, and (3) is adapted to the realities of human life and human expectations, it is capable of remaining in growth mode until such time that it no longer supports culture in the broader sense. You will note that not all these brands are chronologically new. Those that already exist and prosper do so because they are rooted in culture, enjoy a high emotional quotient, and remain perpetually relevant to their consumers.

I will overlay the trends advocated in this book to demonstrate that no brand need ever die as long as it continues to support the reality of its time and the lives of the persons living in that time. I believe in each of these brands and classify them as prototypes for the consumer-centric, collaborative brand creation and promotion model that I predict will necessitate the complete reevaluation of marketing as we have known it. During the course of the case studies, my suggestions are provided as a sort of guided line of questioning, advocating the role of the consumer and relating back to the principles promoted in this book. Regardless of your specific product, your specific role in the marketing process, your brand's stage of development, or the sector of consumers to whom you hope to appeal and empower, the lessons to be learned from these following "living" case studies cover a deliberately broad spectrum of challenges and opportunities meant both to inspire you and provide you with a place to start.

I invite you to experience the following three brands—each of which could be said to fall into one of the three immortal emotional categories of "sex, drugs (herbal, of course), and rock and roll"! I hope that you will have fun diving into these diverse brand biospheres and imagining yourselves to be the person(s) responsible for their architecture. Each of these brands is, in my opinion, a potentially great living brand. Otherwise, I would not have included them. But please decide for yourselves. Evaluate them, dissect them, and even disagree with me, but at least consider the lessons to be learned as each brand story leads you to your own conclusions.

CASE 1: SEX

PL>Y PLAYING WITH CULTURE

PL>Y is a new brand, brilliant in its consumer observation and inspiring in its attempt to breathe life into a saturated category. Conceived and developed by Jeff Danzer, Intimo's executive vice president of marketing and creative director (formerly the mastermind behind what was at the time an equally groundbreaking take on fabulous undies, 2(x)ist underwear), PL>Y was brought to life by Danzer and the company's talented design team.

In a sea of sameness, Danzer's 2(x)ist underwear certainly stood out because of his uncanny ability to make everyone, including his consumer, feel important and valued—even sexy. The hugely successful 2(x)ist brand was a brand that simply took comfortable men's underwear and reshaped the cup to provide a contour enhancement that women have long expected of their undergarments. In other words, some men (actually most men) would love to make as strong and attractive impression in their Levi's as they would in their best Armani suit.

This is not anything any focus group would dare reveal. Few men, with perhaps the exception of me, would admit they'd love to have a shapelier backside. But because Jeff studied behavior, putting third-hand accounts of behavior aside, he realized that his proposed brand really addressed a "desire" most men had but were afraid to admit. Jeff had to see beneath the emperor's new clothes and fit him and all of us with the underwear of our dreams.

He also addressed the fragile, sometimes insecure male psyche by making it okay to wear 2(x)ist by enlisting the endorsement of the straight and incredibly hunky Jason Sehorn as the spokesperson. This made the brand 2(x)ist okay for straight men because Jason is, after all, a macho straight athlete married to the lovely Angie Harmon (of *Law and Order* fame). He gave men (men across every demographic and psychographic profile) what they wanted and concurrently diffused any embarrassment they may have felt by virtue of wanting it.

While 2(x)ist was a breakthrough, an intimate wear line celebrating male beauty and sensuality, his latest venture takes us a step further, incorporating the fun of music. He has evolved the original 2(x)ist platform of overt sexuality to make something entirely new; he has now created a sensual *and* playful brand intended for both men and women. Danzer has created a new line of youth-focused underwear called PL>Y. The fashion line is, as its name would suggest, openly playful, celebrating both male and female beauty and sensuality (addressing the senses on a multisensorial level) in a very fresh, completely original, fun way.

BRAND FOUNDATION

Determine if the brand foundation has all the elements necessary to legitimately be a brand. Evaluate the brand concept for its contemporary relevance. Consider the potential connections—brand expansion into other categories, application of an alternative branding architecture, and cobranding and licensing potential. Consider the following.

To create the PL>Y line, Jeff and his colleagues spent months hanging out with young people, watching how they live and how they play. Hosting both planned and impromptu focus groups that were more like parties than traditional clinical interrogations, Jeff observed that just as certain clothes are deemed daywear and others are reserved for partying, underwear that is functional and relevant to today's youthful lifestyle would be a logical next step.

In keeping with the universal appeal of music and technology's enablement of entertainment anytime, anywhere, Danzer developed the iBoxer™, a breakthrough line of underwear that provides a pocket for the wearer's iPod so that people everywhere can dance with ease and style in their underwear! Then he signed a deal with iTunes and purchased songs that he gave away as a gift with purchase, which added legitimacy to the product and gave the iBoxer iTunes' implied endorsement.

Each of the brand's three lines has its own "patent pending" point of differentiation. The first item to hit the market is the iBoxer, the world's first and only boxer specifically designed with a pocket engineered to hold an MP3 player or cell phone. iBoxer recently launched at specialty stores and at select department stores such as Dillard's and Macy's West. As part of the launch of the iBoxer, PL>Y offered free downloads from iTunes. The line is a hit among high school and college students who like to hang around the house or in their dorms in their underwear listening to their iPods or carrying their cell phones. It also has become a big hit at the gym.

Because today's youth is always on the move, the underwear is also designed with a special built-in pouch to allow the underwear to be rolled up and in on itself to minimize size for suitcases or storage. Wherever you go and wherever you play, PL>Y has got you covered.

For the launch of PL>Y in July 2005, instead of arranging the usual intensely boring, completely scripted press event, Jeff Danzer created a totally unique interactive event. He enlisted a number of other brands, such as House of Groove, Smartwater, Cafe Mozart, David Barton Gym, Floot, Coors Light, GIANT, and Sony and BMG Entertainment to actually collaborate on a launch event that modeled itself more after reality television than after traditional, stale public relations events. Famed photographer Randee St. Nicholas shot the brand's first advertising campaign live, during the actual press event. The photo shoot featured several of New York's hottest new underwear models, along with the invitees—young hipsters and the press—reveling together at a party. It was a great example of what I've described in this book as a concentrated brand biosphere. The whole group became involved in the actual advertising photo shoot. In this way, news of the creation of the brand began to spread before a single official word about the brand was uttered in the media.

BRAND ANALYSIS: HYPOTHETICAL CONSTRUCT

Now that you have the background, let's spend some time examining hypothetical branding considerations to determine if PL>Y is a living brand by asking key questions in nine different areas and examining the answers.

QUESTION SET 1
Authentic Cultural Foundation for the Brand

Do you feel that the preceding idea/culturally driven phenomenon is an authentic foundation for a brand or brands based on authentic needs—physical or emotional?

Answer: People (particularly young people) have a need to express their sexuality and youthful irreverence in a playful manner. For many, the quest for a beautiful (aka perfect) life would not be complete without the joy that only music brings.

Question Set 2
Category Compatibility

Is the brand idea compatible with the categories in which it has chosen to manifest itself?

Answer: Entertainment + intimate wear? Sounds like a match to me!

Question Set 3
Brand Concept Category Compatibility

Determine whether the brand idea is applicable (meaning linked to key purchase drivers) across one or more categories.

Answer: Current categories include fashion-intimate wear

Question Set 4
Real Underlying Existing Need the Brand Satisfies

Determine if this brand and its future extensions are capable of satisfying a real, existing human need or desire in a way no other existing brand could/can. For now, you should disregard product function and focus on the underlying idea. Determine if the brand or its extensions will create artificial demand or unrealistic and potentially destructive demand. You must confirm that the brand supports an existing human need and desire. Be careful to differentiate between trends and fads.

Answer: You could argue that there certainly will be a "next" iPod, in which case the PL>Y underwear line as it exists today would become obsolete. However, the revolutionary concept of celebrating the "entertainment everything" era with fashion in terms of designs that cater to portable electronics is certainly an idea with, well, lots of "play" left in it to say the least! Perhaps even more important, the need for people to express sexuality and unapologetic joy in a more open, playful manner seems to be a concept that could continue to offer an ever-enlarging "brandscape" for those with the vision to see it.

Question Set 5
Competitive Review of Existing Brands in a Similar Category

This is where your subjectivity and integrity come into play. Based on the category or categories you have selected, and based on the nature of your business, conduct a competitive review of existing brands. Will this brand deliver a significantly differentiated brand experience to consumers versus other similar products? If you can honestly answer yes to this question, then proceed to the next question. If you can't, then abandon this brand. The future of true brands cannot be based on lies or wishful thinking. Also, determine if you are dealing with a brand or a product. In either case, determine if there is a proprietary technology, product attribute, shared consumer/brand philosophy, production method, doctrine of social responsibility, or exceptional consumer experience to propel or support the premise of the brand. So, I repeat. Will this brand versus other similar products deliver a significantly differentiated brand experience to consumers?

Answer: Apart from vibrating hotel beds, the answer is a resounding yes.

Question Set 6
Brand Evolution and Continuing Cocreation Potential

Does this existing or proposed brand have the potential for continued evolution and consumer cocreation, delivering both functional and emotional benefits on an ongoing basis? If not, then know you are beginning an affair—not forging a consumer relationship. Any success will come as a result of being in the right place at the right time—which is a phenomenon that will probably not stand the test of time. In today's world of seemingly endless brand extensions—a brand that only seems appropriate in one category and is incapable of relevant evolution is rarely worth the time and investment to create.

Answer: The PL>Y brand has strong potential for ongoing consumer collaboration and delivery of emotional benefit. The brand allows consumers an opportunity to experience and express their sexuality in a fun, playful manner and connects with the accelerated desire for an entertained life—24/7, 365 days a year.

Question Set 7
Brand Relevance

Determine if the brand is relevant.

Answer: The proliferation of iPods everywhere and the trend toward personal expression/performance as signified by reality TV tell us that the time is right for this brand. Refer back to my earlier comments on the shift from a voyeuristic to a participatory culture for even further confirmation.

Question Set 8
Brand Biosphere Capabilities

Are there technologies, social structures, or other resources that would allow for ongoing consumer dialogue and consumer or business-to-business collaboration? How can this brand remain personally connected with your consumer? Is this a brand capable of eventually creating a "brand biosphere"—an immersive, complementary brand reality enabling a consumer's performance of self?

Answer: The PL>Y Web site (currently under construction) obviously could be an important element of creating a brand biosphere for this techno-youth-culture–centered brand. Free downloads of music are a given. Opportunities for social interaction among consumers would be great, allowing people to share music files and recommendations and perhaps even streaming video clips of themselves dancing in their favorite pair of PL>Y underwear. Also, an online "zine" featuring CD reviews and articles about music would be an excellent idea.

Question Set 9
Contemporary Culture Checklist/Relevance Gauge

Requirement: PL>Y must reflect at least one prevailing trend. If it does not connect with three or more, chances are that it will not succeed.

PL>Y Report Card

☐ 1. Mood and experience enhancement

GRADE: 5 STARS: ★★★★★

The PL > Y brand is clearly in sync with the mood and experience enhancement trend. The creation of a fully evolved brand biosphere for a brand such as PL > Y could mean the creation of experiences such as branded D.J. lounges, record stores, and nightclubs. A record label and satellite radio channel are a given.

☐ 2. Humanized technology

GRADE: 5 STARS: ★★★★★

What can lend a more human touch to technology than fashion that enables people to groove in their underwear? As this brand expands beyond its current offering, keeping this trend in sight will be crucial as a means of ensuring success. As technology evolves into more possibilities for "wearable technology" to merge with fashion, the potential for a brand such as PL>Y is exciting and manifold. What will nanotechnology and intelligent fabrics bring to the table for techno-fashion brands such as this? Your guess is as good and potentially as fascinating as mine.

☐ 3. Everyman empowerment

GRADE: 5 STARS: ★★★★★

This brand is a perfect match for everyman empowerment. The brand touches on the democratic aesthetics movement and drive for personal expression. It is all about clever, cool, and accessible high design—reinforced by the legendary association with the universally recognized admiration for the iconic democratic high style of the iPod.

☐ 4. The luxury of ethics

GRADE: 2 STARS: ★★

If PL > Y were to hypothetically download safe-sex messages or somehow reinforce improved self-images across the general population via a broader reflection of body types, the brand would have the potential of taking on a greater altruistic meaning. However, perhaps another approach would be to promote rising stars, thus facilitating consumers to directly influence the future of musical evolution.

If the brand in question ranks highly in one or more of the preceding four trend categories, you can safely assume that it is culturally relevant—at least in those countries generating the highest percentages of GNP.

CONCLUSION

PL>Y touches on so many culturally relevant markers and—in a rare move—does so with charm (see Figure C-1). Its future will be linked to technology and the broadest possible definition of its category. It has the potential of becoming an icon for a master brand signifying the party that you wear, the party you become, the party you self-select. In addition, it has several additional potential category applications, including:

- *Fashion.* A wide variety of men's and women's fashions that combine the concept of technology with fashion accessories (stylish bags and strap-on carriers for portable devices in particular)
- *Fragrance and beauty.* Fragrance, cosmetics, sensuous bath/body and other personal care products
- *Entertainment.* Cable TV, radio, record label, PL>Y dance in your underwear contest reality show, nightclubs, bars, restaurants
- *Electronics.* MP3 players, stereo equipment, cell phones, digital cameras, camcorders
- *Food and beverage.* PL>Y all-day energy drinks, energy bars, other portable snacks for the on-the-go consumer

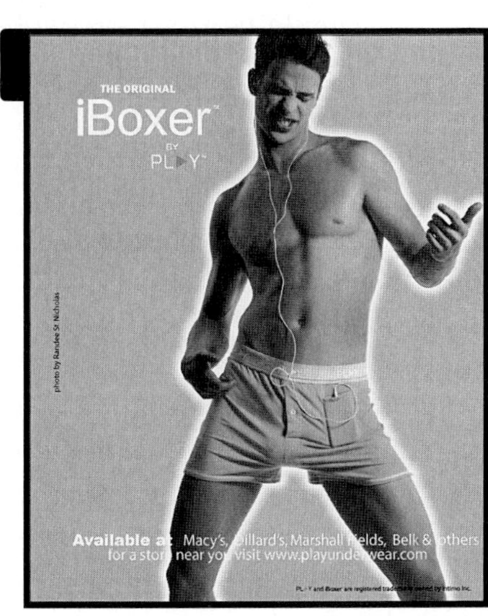

FIGURE C-1 ■ **Dancing in your underpants. When two brands satisfying the same general need unite, the fusion can be explosive. Both girls (and boys) just want to have fun.**

CASE 2:

DRUGS (THE HERBAL KIND)

THE ACCIDENTAL BRAND: BENEDICTINE HERITAGE™—A 1500-YEAR-OLD NEWCOMER

Products created by the Benedictines have been viewed as extensions of deep religious conviction and a dedication to the commitment of bringing beauty to the world. Dom Perignon, Benedictine liqueur, Grammy-winning music, holistic remedies, Benedictine-inspired rug and textile patterns, fine soaps, and personal-care products are only a few of the many products that have resulted from this commitment to quality and beauty. The Benedictines encourage participation in the intellectual, visual, and performing arts as human crafts that are of vital importance to a full life.

Curiously, to this very day, the Benedictine Heritage brand has yet to be fully leveraged or acknowledged as the brand powerhouse it already is. It all gets back to the notion that a lot of individuals in marketing reject something out of fear of failure before they actually give consumers a chance to reject things themselves. And traditional marketing has viewed religion as too risky.

Despite the many supporting explanations of why Benedictine Heritage should be considered a brand, a contemporary and relevant one at that, to my knowledge, the Benedictine Heritage brand has never made it into an MBA marketing textbook. Hopefully, this may change. Benedictine Heritage—the brand—is and continues to be a brand based on an abiding love of the consumer and attentiveness to his or her needs.

BRAND FOUNDATION

St. Benedict founded his sanctuary, his monastery, and his tribute to the Lord's service in AD 529. Although Benedict likely had no intention that the preservation of culture would become an important contribution of his monks, the monastery actually provided the beginning of a new effort to preserve the treasures of human culture in the centuries to come.

First in importance in the Benedictines' dealings with all whom they meet, regardless of religion, race, or nationality, is recognition of the unique worth and importance of each individual. Respectful interaction is one of the foundations of Benedictine doctrine and is reflected tangibly in a variety of some of the world's best-loved products—many of which are not necessarily associated by consumers with the Benedictines.

Instead, many may appear to some as merely products, loosely connected with an implied limited brand endorsement. One well-loved Benedictine motto is *Ora et Labora* ("Pray and Work"), and it has led to a number of genuine products that span multiple categories, at least a few of which are now household words. The connection between categories is the degree of excellence the consumer has come to expect from any product created by the Benedictines for secular consumption. Although diverse, with a broad range of tastes and expectations, the consumers of Benedictine or Benedictine-inspired products share at least one belief—an understanding of and appreciation for the differences between a product created with integrity and one that is not.

Consumer respect, honesty, quality, purity of ingredients, and ethics permeate any product touched by the Benedictines. In fact, the Benedictines deserve credit for introducing Western culture to the notion of a balanced life, a life where work is inherently dignified, needs are deliberately simple, and the body is a temple, a gift to be cherished and maintained. In short, they indirectly invented the tagline of "mind, body, and soul" a thousand years or so before Madison Avenue started putting it on everything.

The Benedictines always have been authentic and have survived for 15 centuries (as a religious order and as an unofficial brand) despite the changing needs of the world around them. By listening attentively to the voices of people and responding generously to their needs, they have unknowingly elevated branding, setting a standard to which very few of today's giant brands dare aspire.

The Benedictines' commitment to hospitality is not an option. It's a mandate. Much like the mandate of collaborative branding most of us will face, these values are built on a way of life. And like tomorrow's brand, a spirit of hospitality extends to an interest in and acceptance of other cultures, reaching beyond the spiritual world and having a positive impact on the creation of goods and services infused not only with cultural appreciation but also with the quality only love and the pride of enriching the lives of others can bring.

The brand is best described by Abbot Primate Dr. Notker Wolf, the highest representative of the Benedictine Order. According to him:

> *Fifteen hundred years ago, Benedict of Nursia, the founder of the oldest monastic order in the Western Church, instructed his monks to live by the work of their own hands. This injunction led to an appreciation of the value of manual labor greater than in any other civilization. Monks cultivated whole regions of Western Europe. In doing so, they always paid particular attention to natural ecological conditions. They regarded nature as God's creation and as his gift from which their food and medicines could be drawn. Over the centuries they developed a sophisticated system of medicinal herbs, essences, oils, and ointments, which made it possible to cure many illnesses. Today we are growing in a renewed appreciation of these benefits, applying them once more in the care of body and soul. The human person is seen as a whole and shines with a new beauty. A vision from the past is becoming a new vision for the future of mankind.*

BRAND ANALYSIS: HYPOTHETICAL CONSTRUCT

Again, let's see how this brand stands up to the key questions about what makes a true living brand.

QUESTION SET 1
Authentic Cultural Foundation for the Brand

Do you feel that the preceding idea/culturally driven phenomenon is an authentic foundation for a brand or brands based on authentic needs—physical or emotional?

Answer: People today have a tremendous desire for trusted, ethically produced quality products that reflect a holistic "mind, body, soul" philosophy.

Question Set 2
Category Compatibility

Does the brand fit legitimately in the categories in which it has chosen for itself?

Answer: Personal-care products, holistic herbal remedies, music, alcoholic beverages, and home furnishings/carpets—all these existing categories reflect areas where the Benedictines have amassed an unsurpassed expertise and reputation for dependable craftsmanship. And even these ventures are far from being fully developed.

Question Set 3
Brand Concept Category Compatibility

Does the brand idea have applications across one or more categories?

Answer: Yes, the current product categories are as follows:

- Publishing, retail gift, hospitality
- Beer, spirits, bread
- Nurseries
- Music
- Crafts, paint, furniture, rugs
- Cosmetic and homeopathic products

Question Set 4
Real Underlying Existing Need the Brand Satisfies

Can this brand—and future aspects of this brand—fulfill a legitimate human need in a way no other existing brand could/can? Or does the brand or its extensions actually create artificial demand?

Answer: The Benedictines are a real, existing creative force behind these products—not a fabricated, ultimately empty "brand story" concocted by an advertising agency or a manufacturer somewhere. People today are hungry for this kind of authenticity and the opportunity to explore and connect with a fascinating tradition and rich culture through well-crafted, truly unique product offerings. The depth of brand promise and the potential level of delivery are extraordinary.

Question Set 5
Competitive Review of Existing Brands in a Similar Category

What can this brand deliver that is significantly different versus what can be delivered by other brands?

Answer: The many books published by the Dalai Lama or those created by L. Ron Hubbard might be considered brands with similar potential. However, Benedictine Heritage represents the values of a far broader cross section of consumers around the world and has the largest ability for expanded brand stretch.

Question Set 6
Brand Evolution and Continuing Cocreation Potential

Does this brand have the potential for continued evolution and consumer cocreation, delivering both functional and emotional benefits on an ongoing basis?

Answer: The Benedictines were the first to develop products based on need. Their continued dedication to nondenominational free education for children around the world guarantees that the brand, like the order, will remain intimately involved in the observation and natural evolution and betterment of societies everywhere.

Question Set 7
Brand Relevance

Is this brand truly relevant?

Answer: One has only to look at the enormous proliferation of herbal supplements and remedies, nature-based skin-care solutions, and organic foods to see that, if authentically executed, this brand could be successful beyond anyone's wildest dreams, with hypothetical products living on virtually every aisle of stores as diverse as Whole Foods, Collette, Target, Boots, and even Home Depot.

Question Set 8
Brand Biosphere Capabilities

Will this brand be able to remain personally connected with the consumer? Can it establish a brand biosphere?

Answer: In the creation of a true brand biosphere, the Benedictine Heritage brand could have a profound ongoing impact on people's lives. Think of a yearly retreat at a Benedictine spa or hostel. Think of trusted herbal remedies for every health problem with an information-rich Web site. The potential here is great also for ongoing consumer dialogue. Imagine, for example, establishing a Benedictine Herbal Institute that could allow people to come and study the ancient art of herbal medicine with the Benedictines themselves.

Question Set 9
Contemporary Culture Checklist/Relevance Gauge

Requirement: Benedictine Heritage must reflect at least one prevailing trend. If it does not connect with three or more, chances are that it will not succeed.

Benedictine Heritage Report Card

☐ **1. Mood and experience enhancement**

GRADE: 4 STARS ★★★★

The Benedictine Heritage brand fits surprisingly well with this trend, given the entertainment-oriented products such as specialty alcoholic beverages, hospitality, and music. And the calming effects of its music provide serenity to scores of consumers, transcending religious affiliations. Of course, the herbal-based brands and skin-care products also relate to this trend in terms of the importance of sensory experience. This is an area where the brand should look to grow—food, spas, and branded venues such as restaurants and retreats.

☐ **2. Humanized technology**

GRADE: 3 STARS ★★★

The Benedictines are certainly in sync with this trend in terms of their respect for the need for humans to be more deeply in touch with their own true nature. It's the technology part of the brand that is difficult to reconcile with its foremost premise. Perhaps entering categories such as stereo speakers and/or scientifically confirming the benefits of its homeopathic remedies might address this challenge. The Benedictines are obviously a very intimate, human-touch brand, and the way to go with this trend might be to focus on the "countertrend" to twenty-first-century technological wizardry, which would be to focus on how the Benedictines offer a salve for the coldness of the modern world through the intimacy of a more personal touch. Perhaps Benedictine heritage products should have labeling with photographs of the monks who created them with quotes about what the process was like and their own personal feelings about the Benedictine work credo.

☐ 3. Everyman empowerment

GRADE: 5 STARS ★★★★★

The work ethic, craftsmanship, creativity, and quality of design of Benedictine Heritage products speak to this trend. Although it may not be immediately apparent, the Benedictines reflect the concept of "everyman empowerment" in terms of the ultimate respect for the individual and the expression of and reverence for the unique creative spark in all of us.

☐ 4. The luxury of ethics

GRADE: 5 STARS ★★★★★

The Benedictines, of course, are the very definition of the ethics-of-luxury trend. They look on the world not as something to be ruthlessly exploited to their own ends but as sacred ground entrusted to all for care and safekeeping. They manifest this in a concern for the physical aspects of life as well as the spiritual. Philosophy bound by unshakable ethics and a code of shared commitment, the Benedictines live the tradition of proper, sustainable, and moderate use of material goods. How much more modern and relevant could a brand be? On the broadest scale, the Benedictines strive to inculcate a consciousness and concern for the quality of the natural environment.

CONCLUSION

Curiously, although herbology was invented by the Benedictines and herbal gardens are an integral part of monastic life, the Benedictines have not yet fully explored the business opportunities clearly demonstrated by the success of "heritage" brands such as the Santa Maria Novella brand of personal-care products, which clearly has differentiated the idea, the spirit, and the quality behind the products from specific religious associations.

The Benedictine Heritage brand also has some interesting potential new category applications such as:

- *Food and beverage.* Benedictine philosophy provides a perfect foundation (see Figure C-2).

FIGURE C-2 ■ **The Benedictine Heritage brand seamlessly stretches between categories and moves effortlessly through time. For example, Andechs beer has been produced since 1455. The Benedictine collection of rugs is a more recent success.**

- *Tourism.* Again, a perfect match for everything from restaurants and hotels to resorts and spas.
- *Personal care.* Products could be explored under the concept of timeless purity and natural cure.
- *Holistic medicine.* Ancient herbal expertise and the tradition of healing and integrity.
- *Music and entertainment.* Various areas of these categories could be approached by the brand under the concept of "labor of love." The Benedictines own music that has not been played for more than a thousand years. Imagine limited-release ring tones or CDs. Disney watch out.
- *Fashion.* Benedictine quality of fabric and design and craftsmanship.

For more information about the Benedictine Heritage brand, please e-mail heinke.martens@alphagroup.com.

CASE 3: ROCK AND ROLL

ROCK SCENE BRANDS LLC: FROM INSIDER MAGAZINE TO BRAND

Rock Scene clothing? Who else could dare fuse rock's sacred scroll with today's cutting-edge fashion and the desire for self-expression than Andy Hilfiger? Who better to stamp authenticity and an artist's vision on that brand than Mark Weiss, renowned photographer, best known for his ongoing photo essay on the authentic soul of rock and roll? The newly launched fashion brand, Rock Scene, is perfectly poised to become a cultural icon—much like the magazine from which its inspiration is derived. Imagine an underground magazine being resurrected and reinfused with meaning for a whole new generation.

Andy Hilfiger is the brother of Tommy Hilfiger and owner of Sweetface Fashions, manufacturer of Jennifer Lopez's fashion line of the same name. He is also an acclaimed rock musician, who, in collaboration with Mark Weiss, a famous rock photographer, has purchased the rights of the now-defunct magazine *Rock Scene,* which was the rock bible of the 1970s and early 1980s. It was responsible for generating some of the greatest rock and roll legends of all time. Mark owns photos of everyone from Blondie to Marky Ramone and continues to "recruit" contemporary celebrities in their support of this rock bible.

From the premise of that magazine, Andy, Mark, and creative entrepreneur Tara Barrett have created a clothing line reflective of the philosophy once espoused by the magazine. And to heighten the authenticity, stars such as Blondie, Joan Jett, the New York Dolls, and the Ramones actually have played a direct role or influenced the brand's clothing designs. Imagine the significance of that. Stars on the music scene, both classic and new, are sporting early prototypes of the fashion in a groundswell of spontaneous support.

From CBGB to retail outlets—the message is the message. It is a message that people still want to hear. Half the authenticity of the brand comes from the type of direct cultural immersion both Andy and Mark have experienced first hand and are now sharing based on the methods I have advocated throughout this book. Both Andy and Mark were and are cultural participants, not spectators; they instinctively and collaboratively came to the same conclusion at the same time—that the vibe that fostered the creation of the original *Rock Scene* magazine has returned. And Tara, representing a younger eye, has functioned to adapt the idea, making it relevant to a new audience while ensuring continuation of its cultural integrity.

What is that integrity? It is integrity based on challenging the status quo. You see it everywhere. Irreverent commercials making fun of other commercials, such as the Snuggle ad that mocks the famous Chanel No. 5 ad of the 1980s. And if rebellion were not in the air, why would the word *antibrand* ever have entered both the cultural and professional vernacular? Having lived it once before, both Andy and Mark can smell the change. The result: Rock Scene, the new fashion incarnation of an idea as relevant today as it was almost 30 years ago. Rock Scene has managed to change form successfully yet retain its original, timeless meaning.

BRAND FOUNDATION

Let's start with a brief history of *Rock Scene* magazine. Established in 1973, this irreverent cult music magazine covered the music scene in New York, London, and elsewhere around the world from the mid-1970s through the 1980s. Its pages were populated with well-known rock writers such as Lenny Kaye (rock critic/producer and guitarist for the Patti Smith Band) and Lisa Robinson (renowned rock author and critic) and photo spreads by famed rock photographer Mark Weiss. The magazine documented—and celebrated—the rise of glam rock and punk in New York City, covering such bands as Patti Smith, David Bowie, the Ramones, the Dictators, and the Sex Pistols, with a brief reemergence and focus on heavy metal in the late 1980s.

Part tabloid, part "fanzine," *Rock Scene* was where you could get an insider's view of what happened before or after the show, the social world beyond the stage—backstage, parties, the street, and so on—and became part of the "scene." For some, *Rock Scene,* the out-of-print publication, was the underground link between the artists of an era. It was like a wireless device that shared a communal value for members of a club. It enabled—you guessed it—the performance of self. It was a step-by-step instructional guide to living in a rock and roll brand biosphere. It also provided the perfect foundation for building a powerful, culturally connected brand.

Today, the culture of rock and roll has come full circle. Rock always has conveyed the notion of rebellion, righteous indignation, and overt sexuality and is, to many, the ultimate symbol of uninhibited, free self-expression. Even though in some ways the world (particularly the United States) seems to be getting more conservative, a new undercurrent of cultural revolution and rebellion seems to be swelling, as evidenced by youth activism and counterculture movements such as Russell Simmons's Get Out the Vote Campaign and the antiwar activism reminiscent of the outrage of earlier generations. This time not only will the revolution be televised, but there will also be some senior citizens represented in the ranks. In other words, take disenchanted youth who love clothes and combine them with nostalgic mature rebels who love clothes plus discretionary income, and I can already hear the amplified bass sound of money flying into cash registers.

Interestingly, Rock Scene is also actually a powerful example of the legitimacy of a countertrend such as we have been discussing (conservative/rebel—the more one pulls in either direction, the stronger the counter pull will become). The result is that today's rock culture has never been more revered as a powerful and glamorous symbol of freedom, while, interestingly enough, retaining the cachet of a noble icon representing the very spirit of perseverance and continued dedication to fighting of the good fight.

BRAND ANALYSIS: HYPOTHETICAL CONSTRUCT

QUESTION SET 1
Authentic Cultural Foundation for the Brand

How authentic is this brand?

Answer: Very. The profound human need for rebellion, righteous indignation, and self-expression will never disappear.

QUESTION SET 2
Category Compatibility

How compatible is this brand's ideas with the categories it has chosen for itself?

Answer: Rebellion, rock and roll, and fashion are a perfect match.

QUESTION SET 3
Brand Concept Category Compatibility

Does this brand have applications across more than one category?

Answer: Several, including these current product categories:

- *Fashion.* Jeans, knit tops
- *Fragrance.* Under consideration

Question Set 4
Real Underlying Existing Need the Brand Satisfies

Does this brand satisfy a real human need, or is it ultimately creating an inauthentic demand for itself?

Answer: Because of its inherent authenticity, rock and roll is not easily "branded." Therefore, what could be better than an insiders' rock brand created by both up-and-coming and established rockers?

Question Set 5
Competitive Review of Existing Brands in a Similar Category

Can this brand deliver a unique experience in comparison with others like it?

Answer: Sean John, Phat Farm and Baby Phat, Beyoncé's new line, House of Dereon, Sweetface by Jennifer Lopez—these brands all are examples of fashion brands merging with music. Yet none fully addresses the need for expressing raw disregard for convention the way Rock Scene can. Each has its own unique features—yet none touches the consumer's heart in exactly the sweet spot of Rock Scene. That's because Rock Scene is a brand like Harley-Davidson, and it's a breed apart. Rock Scene also has an authentic link to behind-the-scenes rock and roll nostalgia that none of these other brands is able to leverage.

Question Set 6
Brand Evolution and Continuing Cocreation Potential

What is the potential for this brand to continue to evolve and continue to be a legitimate cocreation with its consumer?

Answer: The Rock Scene brand has tremendous potential for ongoing consumer collaboration and delivery of emotional benefit. Through the brand, consumers can stay connected to newly emerging music culture—particularly via the Web site and any other entertainment-focused subbrands.

Question Set 7
Brand Relevance

How relevant is this brand?

Answer: The existence of the previously mentioned burgeoning category of music stars' clothing lines (Stefani, Beyoncé, etc.) and the prevalence of glam rock/retro rocker styles everywhere (even on children's playgrounds) signify a ripe environment for this brand.

Question Set 8
Brand Biosphere Capabilities

What is the full potential for this brand to remain connected with the consumer and ultimately create a brand biosphere?

Answer: Just like the original magazine, Rock Scene online could be both a product and a place where rock aficionados can connect and experience the scene. The Web site could provide backstage photos and concert video clips galore, with classic rockers interviewing new rock artists as well as new artists interviewing classic icons. Simulcasts, á la the Victoria's Secret model, could recreate New York's now sadly closed, or closing, CBGB on a global scale.

The site could provide a place where fans could find out where bands are performing around the world and post reviews of live concerts—fans speaking to other fans speak directly to the brand. Also, the site could have a series of ongoing contests:

- *Unsigned bands contest.* Bands submit demos to be reviewed by established musicians and voted on by actual consumers—an antidote to the sometimes insipid, staged classic reality show *American Idol.* At the end of the year, the winner could get a photo shoot with Mark Weiss.
- *Rock Scene photo contest.* Consumers submit rock photos. People whose photos are posted on the site will win a week with Mark Weiss, accompanying him on a live rock shoot.
- *Rock Scene "girl or boy next door" contest.* Consumers submit sexy photos in which they are wearing Rock Scene T-shirts. The

winner might get his or her photo posted on the Web site and receive a classic photo signed by Mark Weiss.

Question Set 9

Contemporary Culture Checklist/Relevance Gauge

Requirement: Rock Scene must reflect at least one prevailing trend. What are its chances for success?

Rock Scene Report Card

☐ **1. Mood and experience enhancement**

GRADE: 5 STARS ★★★★★

Positioned as an entertainment-based brand, Rock Scene is all about mood and experience enhancement. The Rock Scene name says it all, really. It is about creating and being part of a scene. There is no limit to what this can mean for the brand. The brand can become about concerts, nightclubs, cars, fashion, or electronics—as long as the focus remains on creating an authentic and powerful brand experience that reflects the adrenaline and self-expressive freedom of a rock and roll lifestyle.

☐ **2. Humanized technology**

GRADE: 5 STARS ★★★★★

As a nostalgia-based 1970s brand that harkens back to a simpler era, more innocent, yet undeniably decadent and overtly filled with both innocent and lascivious "human touch," Rock Scene responds beautifully to the humanized technology trend. It is life amplified. Rock Scene's Web site, for example, is very much in sync with this trend because it encourages very human direct connections between people—postings of band reviews by average consumers, a chance for unsigned bands to become recognized, a chance for anybody to see behind-the-scenes footage of their favorite band and find out where they are playing. As the brand grows, the focus on responding to this trend could move more to the forefront as the brand moves more into portable music devices and other means of music delivery. And truly, can you think of a better use for Les Neumann's holographic experience pods we discussed in Secret #3?

☐ **3. Everyman empowerment**

GRADE: 5 STARS ★★★★★

The entire concept of uninhibited self-expression inherent in the brand personality will tap into this trend in the most profound way. In addition, the brand will provide consumers with a means to realize dreams by providing up-and-coming undiscovered rock musicians a vehicle for discovery, as well as providing fans with a means of hooking into emerging rock culture and a venue for expressing their hidden dream of being a rock star.

☐ **4. The luxury of ethics**

GRADE: 4 STARS ★★★★

The Rock Scene brand will reflect people's growing need to express their righteous indignation. Rock and roll lyrics today provide a new generation with an anthem to protest everything wrong with the world. But, as we have seen with this trend, it is indeed a luxury to do so, and as an accessibly chic fashion brand, Rock Scene will provide both the substance and style that this trend demands.

CONCLUSION

Provided that the initial conceptualization and execution of Rock Scene's platform remain solid, it has tremendous potential for expansion into a wide variety of categories. Because it is an entertainment-focused brand based on the bigger ideas revolving around rebellion, community, expression, and sexuality, it could become a megabrand, like Virgin, that touches consumers via a myriad of cohesive branded touch points—everything from beverages to travel to communications (see Figure C-3).

Its potential for expanding into other categories is huge and includes:

- *Fashion.* Men's, women's, children's, lingerie, accessories, jewelry.
- *Fragrance and beauty.* Fragrance, cosmetics, bath and body products.
- *Entertainment.* Cable TV, radio, record labels, Rock Scene reality TV show for striving bands, concert halls, nightclubs, bars, restaurants.

- *Electronics.* MP3 players, stereo equipment, cell phones, digital cameras.
- *Food and beverage.* Why not beer, for example, Rock Scene brew? Or a caffeinated beverage à la Red Bull that will help rockers to party all night?

For additional information on Rock Scene licensing, go to www.rockscenefashion.com.

FIGURE C-3 ■ Perhaps no other group represents the underground passion of Rock Scene better than the Ramones. Marky Ramone does honor to the brand's new fashion incarnation by donning a branded Rock Scene T-shirt.

THE IMMORTAL BRAND:

The Brand Is Dead, Long Live the Brand

The Living Brands Living Media marketing approach refutes the notion of inevitable brand death. Brand death is a preposterous concept, given that a full 80 percent of all products that are leaders in their categories today were leaders in their categories 60 years ago. Brand immortality is possible. For any brand, at any age, the secret to survival and success is merely a function of technological or cultural obsolescence—and of course, the culturally derived accuracy on which a brand is built. Rather than the monolithic, almost sacred rigidity of brands created as recently as yesterday afternoon, today's brands must be content with and celebrate the fact that a vibrant, vital brand is never really completely built.

Once something is finished, the natural progression is death. The answer: Refuse to ever finish.

It is only after a brand has explored every cultural application and potential category stretch or cobranding option that is has been fully and exhaustively constructed. Thus, to all of you: Keep on building!

Building and change are the basis of growth and life itself. Whether it is a brand or yourself, you must be forever poised to reinvent while simultaneously retaining the conviction of what you are. You must never loose sight of your impact on others and the promise of a bright future filled with continued value and unique contribution.

This outlook requires a strong long-term yet flexible brand vision. None of us can truly envision what tomorrow's markets may bring or where consumers' (let alone our own) dreams may wander. Yet we owe it to our brands and to ourselves to remain vigilant and to see what begs to be seen.

Brands live only to the extent that they accurately reflect the values and needs of human beings. The up side of this revelation is that because brands are not human beings, the prevailing business notion suggesting that brands, as part of their business life cycle, eventually should be milked and ultimately be left for dead is a ridiculous hoax. An idea is incapable of dying; it is only capable of becoming obsolete and/or abandoned.

To impose a death sentence on a relevant brand is merely one of a number of suicide strategies predicated on yesterday's marketing models. The myth has been perpetuated by archaic marketing theory and taken as reality by even some of the smartest companies. These theories concentrate on such things as the present value of cash and maximizing earnings in the short term to finance corporate expansion into other emerging categories and other brands—a furious attempt to create even more unnecessary brands, inventing bigger and better "need" in a world filled to overflowing with too much authentic, unfulfilled desperate need. Enough already!

If a brand is maintained, fed with technological innovation, and constantly remodeled with a relevant, cultural veneer, then this whole "inevitable brand death" concept has been one, big, wasteful brand hoax. The solutions are simple: (1) See and feed the need that is, (2) address new needs as they arise, (3) enjoy higher margins through expanded investment in existing-brand *life support* rather than cloning or mutating new needs to justify new brands, and (4) create new brands only when the consumer demands it.

CLOSING THOUGHTS: THE IMPORTANCE OF YOU

I hope that the ideas and case studies included in this book have convinced you that you do indeed have superpowers. And you have the option of using them for good or evil, for profit or loss, for self-promotion or to change the world. It is my hope that this book helps to bring you some new insight that just might change your life and enhance your professional joy. Yes, the words *business, work,* and *joy* can be used in the same sentence without contradiction. More than anything, I want all of us to know joy and create joy. Without joy, we are betraying ourselves and everyone else, the consumers of our brands included. If you remember nothing else from this book, remember this: You can do what's right by consumers, create stellar brands, advance your career, and make both money and history.

As a marketing professional, you finally have the permission and the mandate to make your and others' dreams come true—to make your mark on history—to better the human condition. Your chosen profession has taken on a profound new dimension. You are creating not only products; you are enabling the fulfillment of desire. Until now, you may have only had two options—to do well or to do good. And for some of you, you may not have even had this choice. Everything now has changed. You have the never-before-possible ability to actually achieve both, and you will have the support of a brand-new invincible force: the consumer and the culture he or she—and you—share. Shared meaning is, after all, both the ultimate act of intimacy in a lonely world and the best hope for redemption as it relates to our profession and ourselves. I wish you meaning in your lives. I wish that for you and the consumer. I wish that for us all.

POSTSCRIPT

It has been my privilege in this book to enter into your consciousness and plead my passion. I hope that even if you think I'm crazy and totally disagree with every word you have just read, you feel at least some joy knowing that a percentage of my royalties will be donated to Children of Nowhere, the spontaneously created not-for-profit organization dedicated to caring for Romanian children living with AIDS in a Bucharest orphanage.

And another portion will be donated to Parsons The New School For Design in its ongoing effort to reconcile product design and creation with the design and creation of a better world.

And while we are on the subject of creating a better world, please allow me also to encourage you to consider registering with DKMS. I have a strong feeling that somewhere, in the noblest part of your DNA, you contain something mighty, something unique, something both good and larger than yourself.

Because they are such an important group, please allow me to share a brief description of Children of Nowhere, written by Theodora Borsen and illustrated with photographs provided by famed photographer Richard Phibbs.

THEODORA BORSEN: CHILDREN OF NOWHERE

The desire for beauty sometimes forces us to search for other goals—to better our lives and the lives of others. We search within ourselves to find the true meaning of beauty in our lives. This quest led five friends and myself—all working in the fashion/image business to reach out, get involved, and make a difference in peoples' lives, for beauty's reach extends far beyond just the physical self. We experienced this when we adopted the cause of helping the forgotten children of Romania who are all HIV-positive, some abandoned by the stigma of AIDS, some orphans, all in desperate need of medicine, supplies, love, and attention.

We set out for Bucharest in May 2001—myself, creative director in advertising; Richard Phibbs, known fashion and celebrity photographer; Richard Jonas, copywriter and yoga teacher; Mark Chandler, set designer and prop stylist; Michael Capoposto, producer; and Gail Fisher, photographer assistant. Once in the city we went to the Victor Babes Hospital to meet Mary Veal, an American woman who runs the Calm Care program for the infected kids. We had been corresponding with her, and at first she was very reluctant to let us come because of the many sensational stories, TV reports, and pictures that had highlighted, in a very negative way, the political situation and exploitation of the Romanian children suffering from AIDS.

Our hope was to go to Romania and, of course, to bring money, supplies, and gifts, but more important, to photograph these children in a different way—to capture their spirit, showing them laughing, drawing, playing—just depicting their everyday lives and their everyday beauty—a beauty that transcends affliction and what to many of us would be despair. We went there and did something revolutionary—not only did we celebrate their beauty but we also celebrated their humanity and their courage. We found children filled with hope and gave them a great time. They gave us something more—a cause. We have dedicated our efforts to this cause and have created a nonprofit organization called Children of Nowhere whose goal is to effect change that will enhance these children's lives—to allow them to live with dignity.

Dignity is a beautiful thing. These children have taught us about the wonder of dignity, about how it empowers people by making them feel good about themselves, often discovering beauty that was previously unseen, sometimes even by themselves. This should be a broadly applied, recurring theme in marketing brands in today's age of what Raymond terms *living media.* Both personally and professionally, our responsibility is to give back and to try to make the world a better place and ourselves better players within a context bigger than ourselves. This is strong motivation for reflecting the beautiful and ethical, though branded, world Raymond would have us see. For he sees beauty as I see beauty, in the faces of our fellow human beings.

This then is our ultimate challenge—to reach a point when we can really see beyond the physical self and focus on the beauty of the human soul. For in the end, the soul is priceless. And brands reflecting soul transcend mere commerce. They, too, have the ability to become immortal, living extensions of compassion, abundance, and, most important, love.

For more information regarding how you can assist Children of Nowhere, you will soon be able to access info@childrenofnowhere.org or contact Theodora Borsen directly at tborsen@dfjp.com.

Mother in print dress with child.

Father and son.

NOTES

Secret #1

1. Karen Olsen, *Synergy: Transforming America's High Schools Through Thematic Instruction* (New York: Susan Kovalik, 1995).
2. Martin Lindstrom, *Brand Sense* (New York: Free Press, 2005).
3. Karl Greenberg, "Green Is Good: From Hybrid Cars to Hydrogen Fuel Cells, Automakers Are Using New Technologies for a Greener Market. Yet Some Are Still Hedging Their Bets," *Brandweek*, January 3, 2003, p. 16.

Secret #2

1. Jonathan Bond and Richard Kirshenbaum, *Under the Radar: Talking to Today's Cynical Consumer* (New York: Wiley, 1998).
2. Gerry Kermouch, "Consumer in the Mist," *BusinessWeek*, February 26, 2001.
3. Ibid.
4. Sarah Ellison, "P&G Chief's Turnaround Recipe: Find Out What Women Want," *Wall Street Journal*, June 1, 2005.
5. Stephanie Smith, "MediaVest—Media Plan of the Year—Best Use of Magazines," *Adweek* 45(25), June 20, 2005.
6. Richard W. Lewis, *Absolut Sequel: The Absolut Advertising Story Continues* (Hong Kong: Periplus Editions, October 2005), pp. 84–85.
7. Pamela Danziger, *Why People Buy Things They Don't Need* (New York: Kaplan Business, 2004).
8. Neal Gabler, *Life: The Movie—How Entertainment Conquered Reality* (New York: Alfred A. Knopf, 1998).

Secret #3

1. James Surowiecki, *The Wisdom of Crowds* (New York: Doubleday, 2004).
2. Ray Kurzweil, *The Age of Spiritual Machines: When Computers Exceed Human Intelligence* (New York: Penguin Books, 1999).

3. Steve Stecklow, "Virtual Battle: How a Global Web of Activists Gives Coke Problems in India," *Wall Street Journal*, June 7, 2005.

4. Howard Rheingold, *Smart Mobs: The Next Social Revolution—Transforming Cultures and Communities in the Age of Instant Access* (New York: Basic Books, 2003).

5. Thomas Frank and Matt Weiland, *Commodify Your Dissent: Salvos from The Baffler* (New York: W. W. Norton, 1997).

6. Adam Sohmer, "Technology: Showcasing Advertising's Tech Side," *Brandweek*, April 8, 2005.

Secret #4

1. "A Brand New World: Rose Marie Bravo, Chief Executive of Burberry, Foresees Exciting Times for Consumers and Challenging Ones for Brands," *The Economist*, March 31, 2005, p. 105.

2. Joe Flint and Brian Steinberg, "Ad Icon P&G Cuts Commitment to TV Commercials," *Wall Street Journal*, Monday, June 13, 2005.

3. Sergio Zyman, *The End of Marketing as We Know It* (New York: HarperCollins, 1999).

4. Rem Koolhaas, Miucca Prada, and Patrizio Bertelli, *2001 Projects for Prada, Part 1*. Fondazione Prada, 2002.

5. Ramin Setoodeh, "A Slippery Slope for Marketing," *Newsweek*, December 5, 2005, p. 45.

Secret #5

1. Naomi Klein, *No Logo* (New York: Picador, 2000).

2. Rob Walker, "The Hidden (in Plain Sight) Persuaders," *New York Times Magazine*, December 5, 2004.

3. Thomas Frank and Matt Weiland, *Commodify Your Dissent: Salvos from The Baffler* (New York: W. W. Norton, 1997).

4. Elaina Zucker, *The Seven Secrets of Influence* (New York: McGraw-Hill, 1991).

Secret #6

1. Karim Rashid, *Evolution* (New York: Universe, 2000).

PHOTO AND ART CREDITS

COVER AND PART AND CHAPTER OPENERS

Art courtesy of Karim Rashid

SECRET #1

Figure 1-1. Little Red Riding Hood

Photograph courtesy of Corneille Uedingslohmann

www.cue-architekten.de

Figure 1-2. Selfridges

Photograph and photography courtesy of Kitchen Rogers Design

www.krd-uk.com

Figure 1-3. Peroni Beer

Photograph and photography courtesy of The Bank

www.thebank.co.uk

Figure 1-4. Gaultier—Packaging

Photograph courtesy of centdegrés

Figure 1-5. Lift Off

Photograph and photography courtesy of Herbalife and Maddocks

Copywriter: Jen Caughey, Herbalife

Creative Director: Jen Caughey

Designer: Annmarie Siciliano

Design/Production Firm: Maddocks

Client: Herbalife

Figure 1-6. Rosiblu

Photographer: Michael Thompson

Photograph courtesy of Badger and Partners

Figure 1-7. Holographic Shirt

Photograph and photography courtesy of FWD (Storeage, LUST and T-A-P-E)

www.store-age.nl

Figure 1-8. Casa Camper Interior

Photographer: Marti Guixé

Photograph courtesy of Casa Camper

www.guixe.com

Figure 1-9. Progreso

Photograph and photography courtesy of Graven Images Ltd.

www.graven.co.uk

Figure 1-10. Emarat Reverse Vending Machine

Photograph and photography courtesy of Circle

www.circle-design.co.uk

SECRET #2

Figure 2-1. Me and my Scaasi

Photographer: Norman Parkinson

Photograph courtesy of Arnold Scassi

Figure 2-2. PUBLIC Mailbox

Photographer: Yuki Kuwana

Photograph courtesy of AvroKO

Figure 2-3. MTV logo

Photograph and photography courtesy of George Lois

Figure 2-4. Blonde Becomes Her

Photographer: Steve Vaccariello

Photograph courtesy of Jim Feldman Creative Direction

Figure 2-5. Brune

Photograph and photography courtesy of Brune Advertising—Paris

Figure 2-6. Ketel One

Advertisement courtesy of Ketel One and M&C Saatchi

Figure 2-7. Celine Dion—Belong

Photographer: Peter Lindbergh

Photograph courtesy of Coty Inc and Badger and Partners

SECRET #3

Figure 3-1. The Future of Fashion

Photograph and photography courtesy of Jeffrey Grübb

New Skool Studio

327 St. Nicholas Avenue, #5E

New York, NY 10027

Figure 3-2. Davis Shoe

Photograph and photography courtesy of Victor Chu, MIL. Digital Labeling

www.digitallabeling.com

SECRET #4

Figure 4-1. LYCRA Has It

Photographer: Brian Lovely

Model: Alicia Hall

Photograph courtesy of Invista

Agency: McCann Erickson

Figure 4-2. Rimmel Bus

Photograph and photography courtesy of Rimmel London, Coty Inc

Figure 4-3. Lloyd Hotel Library

Photograph and photography courtesy of MVRDV

www.mvrdv.nl and www.lloydhotel.com

Figure 4-4. Red Bull Interactive Bar

Photograph and photography courtesy of Checkpoint Media

www.checkpointmedia.com

Figure 4-5. Tholos

Photograph and photography courtesy of Tholos Systems

www.tholos-systems.com

SECRET #5

Figure 5-1. Bayada Nurses Bus

Photography and photography courtesy of Bayada Nurses

Figure 5-2. Foot Kiss—DKMS

Photographer: Omar Cruz

Photograph courtesy of DKMS Americas and Darryl McDaniels

Volunteer Creative Director: Raymond Nadeau

Agency: Hungry Ad Guys

Creative Directors: Rich Sprano and Jack Palencio

SECRET #6

Figure 6-1. Davidoff Echo Bottle

Photograph and photography courtesy of Coty Inc

Figure 6-2. Beat Pods Design

Photograph and photography courtesy of Parsons The New School For Design

Design Team: Risa Ishikawa, Hyo-Ryung Kim, Melissa Macquarrie, Moselle Spiller, Dong-Ho Yun

Figure 6-3. Vespa Chain Lock Design Team

Photograph and photography courtesy of Parsons The New School For Design

Design Team: Risa Ishikawa, Hyo-Ryung Kim, Melissa Macquarrie, Moselle Spiller, Dong-Ho Yun

Figure 6-4. Vespet

Photograph and photography courtesy of Parsons The New School For Design

Design Team: David Hamilton, Joe Hwang, Patti Tower, Soner Onen, Thomas Scholz

Figure 6-5. Heritage Dinnerware Collection

Photographer : Bryan Warakomski

Photography courtesy of Parsons The New School For Design

Surface design by Racha Bahsoun and Kimberly Price; dishes courtesy of Pottery Barn

Figure 6-6. Aqualoop

Photographer: Lucas Knipsher

Photograph courtesy of Parsons The New School For Design and designer Romi Hefertz

Materials: thermoplastic polyurethane elastomer (TPE), nylon

Figure 6-7. Tactile Subway Map

Photographer: Ronald Wright

Photograph courtesy of Parsons The New School For Design and designer Eunice Kim.

Materials: PVC plastic and rubber

Figure 6-8. 001Coty, A Fragrance for Now

Photograph and photography courtesy of Coty Inc

Figure 6-9. Fragile by Gaultier

Photograph and photography courtesy of centdegrés

CONCLUSION

Figure C-1. PL>Y

Photographer: Randee St. Nicholas

Model: Bryan Hawn

Photograph courtesy of PL>Y Underwear, a division of Intimo, Inc.

Figure C-2. Benedictine Heritage

Photograph and photography courtesy of Benedictine Heritage

Figure C-3. Marky Ramone of The Ramones

Photographer: Mark Weiss

Model: Marky Ramone of the Ramones

Photograph courtesy of Rock Scene

POSTSCRIPT

Mother in Print Dress with Child

Father and Son

All rights to reproduction of both photographs are owned by the photographer.

Photographer: Richard Phibbs

Photos courtesy of Children of Nowhere

AUTHOR PHOTOGRAPH

Photographer: Steve Vaccariello

INDEX

C

J

K

L

M

N

O

P

R

S

ABOUT THE AUTHOR

With a career that has spanned marketing, product development, advertising, and design, Raymond Nadeau has a global background that encompasses every element of today's marketing mix.

As the recipient of many prestigious design and cosmetics industry awards, such as the FIFI, the AIGA Award, the 2003 Cosmetics Industry Award for Best Executed Launch, the ID Award for excellence in design and advertising, and as a nominee for the Chrysler Award, Nadeau has lectured at Parsons The New School For Design in New York. In addition, he has been a frequent speaker and panel participant at prestigious institutions and industry events worldwide, including the Fashion Institute of Technology (FIT), *Advertising Age* conferences, the HBA Show, The Institute for International Research's Future Focus Seminars, and the Packaging and Design Summit.

Nadeau has been quoted in publications such as *Brandweek, Adweek, Global Cosmetics Industry, WWD,* and *W* magazines and has been profiled on Interbrand's Brand Channel. Under the LBLM (Living Brands Living Media) umbrella, he continues to work as a copywriter for numerous advertising agencies in the United States and Europe. Brune Advertising in Paris, one of his collaborating partners, was voted as the best up-and-coming French advertising agency in 1995.

Nadeau is also the executive creative consultant for Turner Media and the managing and creative director for centdegrés New York. He is a contributing editor to the London-based Global Design Registry and sits on the board of directors of the nonprofit Sputnik Observatory. He also collaborates with The Kind Group, a creative venture capital and brand development agency based in New York, whose clients include Target, Boots, and Virgin.

Nadeau graduated from the University of Kansas with a bachelor's degree in liberal arts; he later received his MBA from Pepperdine University's Graziadio School of Business in Malibu, California. He also attended New York's School of Visual Arts. A member of the World Future Society, the Fashion Institute of Technology Mentor Program, and the board of directors of the Sputnik Observatory, Nadeau also serves as a creative consultant for DKMS, a nonprofit global organization dedicated not only to promoting awareness of leukemia and related blood diseases but also to soliciting and identifying bone marrow donors. He resides both in Manhattan and Stillwater, Pennsylvania, with his partner, Jim.